The
Reference Shelf®

U.S. National Debate Topic: 2020-2021
Criminal Justice Reform

The Reference Shelf
Volume 92 • Number 3
H.W. Wilson
A Division of EBSCO Information Services, Inc.

Published by
GREY HOUSE PUBLISHING
Amenia, New York
2020

The Reference Shelf

The books in this series contain reprints of articles, excerpts from books, addresses on current issues, and studies of social trends in the United States and other countries. There are six separately bound numbers in each volume, all of which are usually published in the same calendar year. Numbers one through five are each devoted to a single subject, providing background information and discussion from various points of view and concluding with an index and comprehensive bibliography that lists books, pamphlets, and articles on the subject. The final number of each volume is a collection of recent speeches. Books in the series may be purchased individually or on subscription.

Publisher's Cataloging-In-Publication Data
(Prepared by The Donohue Group, Inc.)

Names: Grey House Publishing, Inc., compiler.
Title: U.S. national debate topic, 2020-2021. Criminal justice reform / [compiled by Grey House Publishing].
Other Titles: US national debate topic, 2020-2021. Criminal justice reform | United States national debate topic, 2020-2021. Criminal justice reform | Criminal justice reform | Reference shelf ; v. 92, no. 3.
Description: Amenia, New York : Grey House Publishing, 2020. | Includes bibliographical references and index.
Identifiers: ISBN 9781642656022 (v. 92, no. 3) | ISBN 9781642655995 (volume set)
Subjects: LCSH: Criminal justice, Administration of--United States--History--21st century. | Corrections--United States--History--21st century. | Prisons--United States--History--21st century. | Racial profiling in law enforcement--United States--History--21st century. | Criminal justice, Administration of--Technological innovations.
Classification: LCC HV9950 U8 2019 | DDC 364.973--dc23

Printed in Canada

Contents

3

Privatization and Mass Incarceration

4

The Scientific and Technological Dimensions

5

What the States Are Doing

Preface

Searching for Justice

In a 2019 article for George Washington University's *History News Network*, historian Tony Platt wrote "*Reform* is one of the most overused, misused, and Orwellian terms in the English language." Platt explains that over the long history of American reform movements there has been a combination of "benevolent rhetoric and punitive measures" promoting reform that increased suffering and served no rehabilitative purpose. As Platt explains:

> Historically, the overwhelming majority of reforms are top-down, state engineering initiatives that are never intended or designed to expand the rights or improve the well being of their recipients. One of the earliest examples was the Progressive Era's child-saving movement that formally did away with due process for juvenile delinquents. It recruited social workers, public health personnel, police, and urban reformers to send thousands of European immigrant youth to punitive reformatories, and Native American youth to boarding schools where they were punished for "speaking Indian." In the 1940s, the Preston School of Industry in California was 'organized like the military,' a former prisoner recalled. "We marched everywhere, and were always on Silence."[1]

Of course, not all reforms follow this pattern. There are democratic grass-roots reform movements that have also played an important role in shaping America's criminal justice system. The bail reform movement and the effort to establish a public defense system for the legal representation of all defendants are examples of movements that emerged out of populist activism. Too often, however, criminal justice reform has led to poor outcomes and deepened the oppression of already marginalized Americans.

Starting at the Beginning

It is necessary, within any human society, for leaders to develop laws that govern behavior. Laws serve many functions in society: they govern access to shared resources, codify the responsibility of government to the citizenry, and are intended to protect citizens from injury. A society also needs a system to manage individuals who violate, or who are accused of violating, these laws. This is where a society's criminal justice system comes into play—a system of governmental organizations and agents responsible for handling citizens who fail to adhere to the law.

An egalitarian justice system can provide protection for the citizenry, but criminal justice systems can also become tools of an oppressive state, furthering the ideological goals of the state or an authoritarian agenda. Prior to the American Revolution, the United States had no unified criminal justice system. Each colony adopted its own laws and policies, often incompatible with those adopted in other states. In most of the colonies, the laws and policies were handed down from England's monarchic system of law, which furthered the interest of the elite class. The earliest attempts at forming a criminal justice system in the wake of the American Revolution reflect the mindset of Americans emerging from this difficult victory. This new system placed emphasis on the liberties and rights of citizens, and the most important of those rights wee explicitly listed in the Bill of Rights. The adoption of the Bill of Rights was essentially a form of criminal justice reform in itself, largely because of the Eighth Amendment, which protects American citizens from "cruel and unusual" punishment. The interpretation of this amendment has been highly contentious, but its adoption signified a movement away from corporal punishment, whippings, brandings, and other forms of torture, and one toward incarceration.[2]

The shift from torture to incarceration was one stage of the age-old debate over the purpose of the criminal justice system. Some believe that criminal justice should punish criminals for their violations, arguing that harsh punishment deters crime among both repeat offenders and the general populace. Others believe that criminal justice should focus more on rehabilitating and reforming individuals convicted of crimes so that they can re-enter society. The shift to incarceration was promoted, in part, by individuals who objected to the way that criminals were often subjected to public humiliation and torture, but the incarceration system did not necessarily lead to wholesale improvements in the treatment of prisoners. In 1842, British author Charles Dickens visited the Eastern State Penitentiary, a Quaker prison in Pennsylvania. The prison was intended to be more humane than the practices used in states where corporal punishment was common. The conditions that Dickens describes, however, indicate that the system was not as humane as Quaker reformers claimed. Prisoners were kept in solitary confinement, forced to be silent, barred from any interaction, and given a bible in hopes that they would consider the moral implications of their actions. Dickens wrote:

> In its intention, I am well convinced that it is kind, humane, and meant for reformation; but I am persuaded that those who devised this system of Prison Discipline, and those benevolent gentlemen who carry it into execution, do not know what it is that they are doing. I believe that very few men are capable of estimating the immense amount of torture and agony which this dreadful punishment, prolonged for years, inflicts upon the sufferers; and in guessing at it myself, and in reasoning from what I have seen written upon their faces, and what to my certain knowledge they feel within, I am only the more convinced that there is a depth of terrible endurance in it which none but the sufferers themselves can fathom, and which no man has a right to inflict upon his fellow-creature. I hold this slow and daily tampering with the mysteries of the brain, to be immeasurably worse than any torture of the body: and because its ghastly signs and tokens are not so palpable to the eye and sense of touch as scars upon the flesh; because its wounds are not upon the surface, and it extorts few cries that human ears can hear;

therefore I the more denounce it, as a secret punishment which slumbering humanity is not roused up to stay. I hesitated once, debating with myself, whether, if I had the power of saying "Yes" or "No," I would allow it to be tried in certain cases, where the terms of imprisonment were short; but now, I solemnly declare, that with no rewards or honours could I walk a happy man beneath the open sky by day, or lie me down upon my bed at night, with the consciousness that one human creature, for any length of time, no matter what, lay suffering this unknown punishment in his silent cell, and I the cause, or I consenting to it in the least degree.[3]

Dickens's critique of Eastern State Penitentiary is an example of what Platt refers to as "benevolent rhetoric and punitive measures," in which trying to make an institution more humane resulted in detrimental results. The use of solitary confinement as an approach to criminial justice is still being debated today. Critics claim that such measures should be prohibited, perhaps even constitutionally banned as "cruel and unusual," while defenders argue that solitary confinement is an effective punishment for certain categories of criminals.

An Ideological Divide

For most of American history, the criminal justice system has been shaped primarily by those who feel that criminal justice should be more punitive than rehabilitative. Many Americans continue to believe that the stronger the policy, the more effective at deterring crime. Research has demonstrated, however, that harsher punishments do not lead to reductions in crime rates and in some cases even exacerbate criminal activity, as those accused of crimes commit additional crimes in an effort to avoid facing steep penalties. The lobby to make criminal justice more punitive is met with resistance from the lobby to make criminal justice more rehabilitative. The United States has seen progressive political periods alternate with periods of conservative control that focus on the punitive approach.

Most of the time in American culture, the conservative approach to criminal justice dominates, allowing the proliferation of increasingly severe punishments and sentencing guidelines. The so-called "three-strikes" laws, extreme penalties for drug crimes, and "truth in sentencing" laws are designed to ensure that those who break laws are subjected to maximum punishments. This has resulted in a rapid increase in the number of Americans imprisoned, so that, today, the United States is the global leader in incarceration. According to 2015 statistics, Americans made up around 4 percent of the world's population but housed 22 percent of the world's prison population.[4] The extreme growth of the incarceration industry has created numerous problems in the United States, straining the resources of states and cities and reducing the efficiency of courts. Since the late 1990s, many states have attempted to alter criminal justice policies in an effort to reduce incarceration rates, but such efforts have met with resistance from those who feel that existing policies are necessary to address the threat of crime and violence.

The mass incarceration problem is only one of the ideological debates that continue to shape criminal justice policy. There is also a contentious debate over whether criminal justice should be funded by taxpayers and organized as a public service or whether it should be shaped by free-market forces, enabling companies to profit from and contribute to the system. Another long-standing debate concerns the degree to which the system serves, or fails to serve, various facets of the population. Studies have shown that persons of color and the poor fare significantly worse when accused of crimes, and many have lobbied for changes to address how racial or class bias impacts the functioning of the criminal justice system. Others argue that bias is not a sufficient reason to risk changes that might limit the effectiveness of crime prevention.

Criminal Justice in the Twenty-First Century

The debate over criminal justice reform has been key in the 2010s. Since the election of Donald Trump in 2016, it has been overshadowed by immigration reform—the Trump administration's leading priority. Trump's controversial immigration policies, such as separating immigrant children from their parents, have however intensified the debate over criminal justice reform. Changes to immigration law have dramatically increased the number of individuals incarcerated for immigration violations, creating a new dimension in the debate over reform.

Funding priorities have also altered the pace and progress of criminal justice reform. For instance, Trump's decision to disband an Obama-era commission aimed at improving forensic science standards has led to a lack of federal effort in forensic science reform, an issue that many criminologists identify as one of the most important subtopics within the broader debate. The administration's skepticism regarding the existence of racial bias has also intensified debate and activism pushing for civil rights reforms of the police and court systems.

Outside of the specific policies put in place under the Trump administration, the criminal justice debate of the twenty-first century revolves around issues that were also much debated at the end of the last century and earlier: proposals for addressing racial and class bias in policing and the courts; efforts to reduce incarceration rates, bail and sentencing reform; and privatization of the incarceration industry and the influence of for-profit lobbyists on the politics of criminal justice reform.

One of the most significant changes to the current criminal justice debate has been in the field of technology. A host of new digital advances have provided police and federal agencies with controversial new technologies that raise questions about personal privacy and the ownership of digital data. In this arena, the criminal justice debate intersects with the ongoing debate over the balance between national security, public safety, and personal privacy. Emerging technologies, such as facial recognition algorithms that allow computers to rapidly identify individuals from visual recordings, have become one of the newest topics in this debate.

Overall, the Trump era has seen a decline in federal interest in criminal justice, but this does not mean that the debate has abated or that the effort to reform existing systems has ended. Many of the most prominent developments in criminal justice policy have always occurred first in the states, where smaller and more focused governmental organizations are better able to respond to public demands and changing conditions. From 2010 to 2020 a number of transformative laws passed in the states ranging from sentencing reform to capital punishment. These more focused legal and policy debates constitute the most active forefront of criminal justice reform as politicians, citizens, and criminal justice experts struggle to adjust state laws and policies to changing social and societal norms. Adjusting the laws on marijuana use in keeping with recent statewide legalization provides one example of how the states are enacting pioneering reforms that may later be echoed at the federal level. Even more recent is the debate over how criminal justice can function in the midst of a public health crisis like that caused by the spread of the Covid-19 disease.

Whether discussing bail policy reform or managing prison populations during a pandemic, debates on criminal justice are an important part of American political activism and development. These debates not only ask Americans to consider the costs and benefits of policies, but also examine the ideologies that underlie criminal justice. In the end, a nation's criminal justice system is not only a practical effort to address crime and punishment but also a reflection of its commitment to its citizens. This broader dimension to criminal justice, the moral and cultural dimension, is part of what makes criminal justice reform a perennially contentious topic.

Works Used

Dickens, Charles. "Philadelphia, and its Solitary Prison." 1842. *The Victorian Web*. Retrieved from http://www.victorianweb.org/authors/dickens/pva/pva344.html.

Oliver, Willard M., and James F. Hilgenberg. *A History of Crime and Criminal Justice in America*. New York: Pearson, 2006.

Platt, Tony. "The Perils of Criminal Justice Reform." *History News Network*. George Washington University. Mar 31, 2019. Retrieved from https://historynewsnetwork.org/article/171611.

Ye Hee Hee, Michelle. "Does the United States Really Have 5 Percent of the World's Population and One Quarter of the World's Prisoners?" *Washington Post*. Retrieved from https://www.washingtonpost.com/news/fact-checker/wp/2015/04/30/does-the-united-states-really-have-five-percent-of-worlds-population-and-one-quarter-of-the-worlds-prisoners/.

Notes

1. Platt, "The Perils of Criminal Justice Reform."
2. Oliver and Hilgenberg, *A History of Crime and Criminal Justice in America*.
3. Dickens, "Philadelphia, and its Solitary Prison."
4. Ye Hee Lee, "Does the United States Really Have 5 Percent of the World's Population and One Quarter of the World's Prisoners?"

1
Race, Human Rights, and Justice

By Fibonacci Blue, via Wikimedia.

Several organizations have formed to address racial bias in the criminal justice system. Above, a Minneapolis Black Lives Matter march for Jamar Clark, who was shot by police officers in 2015.

Human Rights and the Law

The Declaration of Independence and the U.S. Constitution explicitly forbid discrimination based on race and require that all Americans be treated equal under the law. This is a goal that remains difficult for America to achieve.

Hundreds of studies over several decades prove that racial and class disparities exist in the American justice system and that individuals are treated within the system based on their racial and social backgrounds. There is little disagreement among criminal justice scholars that racial and class disparities exist, but there is much disagreement on how best to address this issue and to what degree the issue affects how the system functions.

The End of Jim Crow?

The Atlantic slave trade in the United States began in 1619 when the Portuguese slave vessel *São João Bautista* sailed near the coast of the United States en route to Mexico. The Spanish were already developing an empire based on slave labor, but U.S. entrepreneurs had not yet seized on this tool of economic advancement. The *São João Bautista* never made it to Mexico, however, as it was taken over by two English pirate vessels. The twenty slaves who survived the ordeal were brought to the Virginia Colony and sold to tobacco plantation owners, marking the beginning of one of the most horrific periods of industrial growth in the history of the world.[1] White colonists exploited millions of African Americans, and while many objected to this system, the majority of white Americans ignored the higher-order moral questions because the exploitation of slave laborers provided substantial economic benefits. The slave trade is the reason that America became a world power and slave labor built American society.

The criminal justice system was shaped by slavery. The first laws governing non-white individuals codified their status as legal property, without legal rights and protections. It wasn't until the Civil War (1861–1865) that slavery was abolished across the United States and that African Americans were afforded access to citizenship. However, though granted their freedom on the constitutional level, African Americans living in the post–Civil War United States were not equal under the law. Racist legislators then enacted a series of laws, known as "Jim Crow" laws, which created a system of racial apartheid that remained in place until the middle of the twentieth century and still impacts outcomes for African Americans living in America.[2]

To understand the struggles of non-white individuals in the modern criminal justice system, it is instructive to look at how the Jim Crow system used the police and the courts to oppress former slaves and their descendants. The core of the American apartheid system was "segregation," a systematic effort to keep African American and white populations separate. Communities often invested only in services for whites, who were prevented from becoming familiar with African American people, which might lead to sympathetic efforts to undermine the continued exploitation of African Americans. Various state examples from the Smithsonian Institution illustrate the Jim Crow system:

> "It shall be unlawful for a negro and white person to play together or in company with each other in any game of cards or dice, dominoes or checkers."—Birmingham, Alabama, 1930

> "Marriages are void when one party is a white person and the other is possessed of one-eighth or more negro, Japanese, or Chinese blood."—Nebraska, 1911

> "Separate free schools shall be established for the education of children of African descent; and it shall be unlawful for any colored child to attend any white school, or any white child to attend a colored school."—Missouri, 1929

> "All railroads carrying passengers in the state (other than street railroads) shall provide equal but separate accommodations for the white and colored races, by providing two or more passenger cars for each passenger train, or by dividing the cars by a partition, so as to secure separate accommodations."—Tennessee, 1891[3]

Based on these examples, African Americans were not the only nonwhite group targeted for discrimination under the Jim Crow system, which was based on the belief that white individuals are superior to other races and should therefore dominate society. Not only was racism codified in the laws, but police, judges, and lawyers also demonstrated racism in the way that they treated individuals of different races. Though white supremacy no longer has the power and influence that it had in the late 1800s, white supremacist thought still plays a role in American politics in 2020.

The Jim Crow system was abolished through the collective struggle of millions of Americans who took part in the Civil Rights movement of the 1950s and 1960s. Though this movement saw the end of legal segregation, white supremacy endured. Over the decades, the legal system has evolved to a system in which racism had become "institutionalized" within America's criminal justice system. Institutionalized racism occurs when racist ideas shape the way that an institution's policies or practices perpetuate or deepen racial discrimination. Studies have shown that both unconscious and explicit racial prejudice and bias have an impact on the way that the American justice system functions.

Researcher Robert Entman conducted a series of studies in the 1990s demonstrating that popular culture, from news media to popular entertainment, tends to portray African Americans as having a greater tendency towards criminality than white individuals. In his 1996 book *The Black Image in the White Mind*, Entman discusses how African Americans are more likely to be depicted as criminals both in the news media and in popular entertainment.[4] This impacts the way that white citizens view African American citizens in relation to criminal justice. In a 2003 study published in the *Journal of African American Studies*, researcher Mary Beth

Oliver reported on an experiment in which mock juries were more likely to convict black defendants than white defendants. Further, studies indicate that white jury members in mock trial situations are more likely to recommend longer/harsher prison sentences for black defendants.[5]

In September 2018, *Washington Post* writer Radley Balko listed more than 120 studies stretching back to the 1990s which found evidence of racial bias and prejudice in the criminal justice system. The studies collected by Balko demonstrate that police prejudicially profile nonwhite suspects and are more likely to investigate, stop, search, and arrest nonwhite offenders; that nonwhites are more likely to be convicted for petty crimes and misdemeanors than white offenders arrested for the same crimes; that nonwhite individuals are more likely than white individuals to be arrested or investigated for drug crimes and then to be convicted; that nonwhite individuals are less likely to be selected for jury service and more likely to be convicted and given longer sentences by white-dominated juries; that nonwhite individuals are more likely to received death sentences; and that prosecutors and courts are less likely to recommend or accept plea bargains and alternatives to incarceration for nonwhite defendants.[6]

There is no longer a legitimate debate about whether or not racism impacts the criminal justice system. The debate centers around how this issue should be addressed. In the *New York Times* best-selling book, *The New Jim Crow*, researcher Michelle Alexander argues that the "Jim Crow" era never really ended and that the mass incarceration of African Americans is the modern echo of the impact of white supremacist thinking on American society and institutions. Those who disagree argue that America has already made many of the changes needed to further racial equality, and more prevalent in conservative white communities or in white communities that are racially isolated.

Public Safety and Public Welfare

The debate over race and criminal justice is just one facet of a larger debate over human rights and the justice system. Racial prejudice within the system is an example of one way in which the current criminal justice system fails to uphold international standards of human rights, which state that all citizens should be treated equally under the law. The debate over human rights and criminal justice also includes the perception of immoral or potentially abusive treatment.

One of the most notable manifestations of this debate concerns capital punishment. While some Americans believe strongly that capital punishment is to discourage criminal activity, others argue that the threat of death has proven an ineffective deterrent against crime, and that it violates standards of human decency. Other criminal justice practices that have come into question as they relate to human rights include solitary confinement incarcerating young offenders with adult populations, and the influence of politics in determining a person's sentence.

Debates over human rights and criminal justice often come down to a punitive approach to criminal justice, in which laws are designed to incapacitate and punish individuals for committing crimes vs a rehabilitative approach, in which the goal is to reform or rehabilitate individuals to rejoin and contribute to society. The death penalty and solitary convincement are part of a more punitive approach vs. therapeutic or welfare-oriented strategies.

When considering human rights and race within the context of U.S. criminal justice, it is informative to recognize that each nation's criminal justice system is a product of that nation's unique past and cultural evolution. Perceptions of race, justice, and human rights are all impacted by this history and thus, given the dramatic struggles with racial prejudice that the United States has endured, it is unsurprising that racial equality has yet to be achieved. Debates surrounding other human rights issues reflect an evolving effort to ensure that the American system of justice does not lag behind changing global standards.

Works Used

Balko, Radley. "There's Overwhelming Evidence That the Criminal-Justice System Is Racist: Here's the Proof." *Washington Post*. Sep 18, 2018. Retrieved from https://www.washingtonpost.com/news/opinions/wp/2018/09/18/theres-overwhelming-evidence-that-the-criminal-justice-system-is-racist-heres-the-proof/.

Dailey, Jane Elizabeth. *The Age of Jim Crow: A Norton Casebook in History*. New York: W. W. Norton & Company, 2009.

Elliot, Mary. "Four Hundred Years after Enslaved Africans Were First Brought to Virginia, Most Americans Still Don't Know the Full Story of Slavery." *New York Times Magazine*. Aug 19, 2019. Retrieved from https://www.nytimes.com/interactive/2019/08/19/magazine/history-slavery-smithsonian.html.

"The Entman-Rojecki Index of Race and the Media." *University of Chicago*. 1996. Retrieved from https://www.press.uchicago.edu/Misc/Chicago/210758.html.

"Jim Crow Laws." *American History*. Smithsonian Institution. Retrieved from https://americanhistory.si.edu/brown/history/1-segregated/jim-crow.html.

Oliver, Mary Beth. "African American Men as 'Criminal and Dangerous': Implications of Media Portrayals of Crime on the 'Criminalization' of African American Men. *Journal of African American Studies* 7, no. 2 (September 2003): 3–18.

Notes

1. Elliot, "Four Hundred Years after Enslaved Africans Were First Brought to Virginia."
2. Dailey, *The Age of Jim Crow*.
3. "Jim Crow Laws," *American History*.
4. "The Endman-Rojecki Index of Race and the Media," University of Chicago.
5. Oliver, "African American Men as 'Criminal and Dangerous': Implications of Media Portrayals of Crime on the 'Criminalization' of African American Men."
6. Balko, "There's Overwhelming Evidence That the Criminal-Justice System Is Racist: Here's the Proof."

The Growing Racial Disparity in Prison Time

By Weihua Li

The Marshall Project, **December 3, 2019**

The racial disparity between black and white people sent to state prisons is declining, and it has been for some time.

But criminal justice researchers say people of all races still aren't treated equally when it comes to one important measure: time served behind bars. While arrest and prison admission rates are dropping for black people—in 2016, black people went to state prison at five times the rate of white people, down from eight times in 2000—they are spending longer in prison than their white peers. This trend, noted in a report published by the nonpartisan think tank the Council on Criminal Justice today, potentially offsets broader efforts to make the system more equitable, the researchers say.

When it comes to drug and property crimes, black people are serving increasingly more time, growing at a rate of 1 percent or more on average every year, as the time served in prison by white offenders dropped. For violent crimes, although both groups served longer from 2000 to 2016, the prison time for black people grew at a rate almost twice as fast, according to the report.

The question is why.

Experts note that actors at several stages of the criminal justice system can influence how long someone ends up spending in prison. For example, prosecutors decide what charges to bring and what sentences to recommend. Judges have the discretion to hand down sentences. Correction officers can discipline people in prison, which then becomes an important factor when parole boards consider if they will release someone.

Criminal history also plays an important role, said William Sabol, a professor at Georgia State University who authored the report. During the decades of rising incarceration in the United States, a lot of people—especially black men—were arrested and pulled into the criminal justice system, leaving them with long criminal histories, Sabol said. Those records are often considered at sentencing and may contribute to today's disparity in time spent in prison.

Prosecutors rely heavily on someone's prior criminal history when they are deciding what to charge and what sentence to recommend, said Daniel Nagin, a criminology professor at Carnegie Mellon University's Heinz College of Information

In 2015, black people went to state prison at five times the rate of white people.

Systems and Public Policy. In Pennsylvania, for example, prosecutors determine what sentences to recommend by considering the severity of the crime and the defendant's past arrest history. A longer criminal history can lead to a longer sentence.

Many states, Nagin said, adopted similar guidelines in the 1980s. The initial intent was to make prosecutors' decision-making process more transparent and less prone to personal bias. The unintended consequence, however, was that communities that are heavily policed and prosecuted would now often be subject to longer prison terms.

Another potential explanation may come from the adoption of risk assessment tools, school zone enhancements or gang sentencing enhancements—initiatives that ended up disproportionately affecting people of color and how long they stay in prison, said Leigh Courtney, a policy associate at the Urban Institute.

Using school zone enhancement as an example, Courtney said if drugs are sold near a school the penalty can be much higher. The policy may sound logical, but it's much more likely to affect people who live in urban areas with a dense population.

The increase in prison terms among black people may also be associated with the movement away from aggressive prosecution of low-level crimes, said Lucy Lang, executive director at the Institute for Innovation in Prosecution at John Jay College of Criminal Justice.

In order to avoid appearing "soft on crime," prosecutors who decline to prosecute minor offenses and quality of life cases may double-down on violent and serious drug crimes, Lang said, prosecuting them more aggressively, which can lead to longer sentences.

"We need to rethink our responses to serious and violent crimes because lengthy prison sentences not only don't seem to be working," Lang said, "but they are part of what is perpetuating the unconscionable racial disparities in the system, despite efforts to eliminate disparities on the front end."

Print Citations

CMS: Weihua, Li. "The Growing Racial Disparity in Prison Time." In *The Reference Shelf: U.S. National Debate Topic: 2020–2021 Criminal Justice Reform,* edited by Micah L. Issitt, 7-8. Amenia, NY: Grey House Publishing, 2020.

MLA: Weihua, Li. "The Growing Racial Disparity in Prison Time." *The Reference Shelf: U.S. National Debate Topic: 2020–2021 Criminal Justice Reform,* edited by Micah L. Issitt, Grey House Publishing, 2020, pp. 7-8.

APA: Li, W. (2020). The growing racial disparity in prison time. In Micah L. Issitt (Ed.), *The reference shelf: U.S. national debate topic: 2020–2021 criminal justice reform* (pp. 7-8). Amenia, NY: Grey House Publishing.

Why Support for the Death Penalty Is Much Higher among White Americans

By Kevin O'Neal Cokley
The Conversation, November 27, 2019

Sentencing a person to die is the ultimate punishment. There is no coming back from the permanence of the death penalty.

In the U.S., the death penalty is currently authorized by the federal government, the military and 29 states. The primary rationale for using the death penalty is deterrence.

As public policy, I believe that capital punishment has largely not proved to be an effective deterrent.

Nevertheless, for decades the death penalty has been popular. However, support for the death penalty has been declining over the past 25 years and is near historic lows. Critics point to issues such as inhumane killing procedures, a plunge in crime rates and the death penalty's high cost.

I study the impact that public policies like the death penalty have on African Americans, and I see a problem that isn't often discussed in the media: the significant racial disparity in public opinion about the death penalty.

Racial Inequality

The racially inequitable application of the death penalty was highlighted on Nov. 15, 2019, when, in an unexpected turn of events, the Texas Court of Criminal Appeals halted the execution of Rodney Reed less than one week before he was scheduled to be executed for the 1996 murder of Stacey Stites.

> **Prosecutors, in spite of the illegality of excluding prospective jurors based on race, still use tactics to strike potential black jurors form the jury.**

The case was racially charged. Reed, a black man, is accused of killing Stites, a white woman, and was found guilty by an all-white jury.

The Reed case is one of many capital murder cases that present an opportunity to critically examine the application of the death penalty. As director of the Institute for Urban Policy Research and Analysis at the University of Texas at Austin, I lead an organization that is committed to the elimination of racial bias and disparities through promoting equitable public policies.

Since 1976, people of color have accounted for 43% of total executions and make up over half of inmates who are currently scheduled to be executed. In Texas, African Americans make up less than 13% of the population yet represent 44.2% of death row inmates. Nationally, African Americans make up 42% of death row inmates.

When both race and gender are considered, disparities in sentencing become even more pronounced. Homicides involving white female victims are significantly more likely to result in a death sentence than homicides with any other victim characteristics.

Disparity in Beliefs

However, beyond the explicit examples of racial bias in the criminal justice system that typically get the most attention, there remains another, more subtle bias related to the beliefs held by jurors.

People who oppose the death penalty cannot serve on a murder case jury where the death penalty is a possibility. Only individuals who say they would consider the death penalty can serve.

When you examine the numbers behind support of the death penalty, a trend emerges.

White people make up the core of support for the death penalty in the United States. Studies indicate that white people show significantly higher support for the death penalty than do black people.

This is consistent with a 2018 poll by the Pew Research Center, which found that 59% of white people favor the death penalty, compared with 47% of Latino and 36% of black people. Among white people, evangelical Protestants show the strongest support for the death penalty, with 73% favoring it.

Prejudice and Juries

Why do white people support the death penalty at much higher levels than black people?

According to research, one answer is racial prejudice. White Americans tend to associate criminality with racial minorities. In one study, researchers found that, after controlling for factors including education, family income, religion and political ideology, white people with stronger anti-black attitudes were more likely to support the death penalty.

It should come as no surprise that views about the criminal justice system diverge widely between black and white Americans, with black Americans being much more likely to see the system as racially biased.

Perhaps this explains why prosecutors, in spite of the illegality of excluding prospective jurors based on race, still use tactics to strike potential black jurors from the jury.

When juries are more racially diverse, that increases the likelihood that potential racism is discussed. What's more, social science research indicates that all-white juries convict black defendants significantly more often than white defendants.

In my view, in capital murder cases, an all-white jury combined with white support for the death penalty stacks the odds against black male defendants like Rodney Reed.

Print Citations

CMS: O'Neil Cokley, Kevin. "Why Support for the Death Penalty Is Much Higher among White Americans." In *The Reference Shelf: U.S. National Debate Topic: 2020–2021 Criminal Justice Reform,* edited by Micah L. Issitt, 9-11. Amenia, NY: Grey House Publishing, 2020.

MLA: O'Neil Cokley, Kevin. "Why Support for the Death Penalty Is Much Higher among White Americans." *The Reference Shelf: U.S. National Debate Topic: 2020–2021 Criminal Justice Reform,* edited by Micah L. Issitt, Grey House Publishing, 2020, pp. 9-11.

APA: O'Neil Cokley, K. (2020). Why support for the death penalty is much higher among white Americans. In Micah L. Issitt (Ed.), *The reference shelf: U.S. national debate topic: 2020–2021 criminal justice reform* (pp. 9-11). Amenia, NY: Grey House Publishing

LAPD Searches Blacks and Latinos More Often

By Ben Poston and Cindy Chang
Los Angeles Times, October 8, 2019

Los Angeles police officers search blacks and Latinos far more often than whites during traffic stops, even though whites are more likely to be found with illegal items, a *Times* analysis has found.

The analysis, the first in a decade to calculate racial breakdowns of searches and other actions by LAPD officers after they pull over vehicles, comes amid growing nationwide scrutiny over racial disparities in policing.

The *Times* obtained the data used in its analysis under a new California law targeting racial profiling that requires the LAPD and other agencies to record detailed information about every traffic stop.

The *Times* analysis found that across the city, 24% of black drivers and passengers were searched, compared with 16% of Latinos and 5% of whites, during a recent 10-month period.

That means a black person in a vehicle was more than four times as likely to be searched by police as a white person, and a Latino was three times as likely.

Yet whites were found with drugs, weapons or other contraband in 20% of searches, compared with 17% for blacks and 16% for Latinos. The totals include both searches of the vehicles and pat-down searches of the occupants.

Racial disparities in search rates do not necessarily indicate bias. They could reflect differences in driving behavior, neighborhood crime rates and other factors.

But the lower contraband hit rates for blacks and Latinos raise serious questions about the law enforcement justification for searching them more often than whites, criminologists said.

Stop-and-search statistics are commonly used by law enforcement agencies to gauge the disparate racial impacts of policing. The U.S. Department of Justice sometimes requires agencies with civil rights issues to collect and analyze the data.

But the LAPD's constitutional policing advisor said this type of analysis does not account for the complexities of a police officer's decisions in sizing up a situation and deciding how to deal with the people in a vehicle. Officers receive training on their own implicit biases and have a lawful basis for every stop and search they perform, said the advisor, Arif Alikhan, who recently left the LAPD.

Alikhan noted that the analysis includes stops where officers exercise little discretion and racial bias is less likely to be a factor, such as a search during an arrest.

"We don't pull people over based on race. We're not supposed to do that," Alikhan said. "It's illegal. It's unconstitutional. And that's not the basis [on which] we do it."

To some community activists and academics, the numbers heighten concerns that the LAPD could be singling out blacks and Latinos for invasive searches, damaging relationships with minority residents that the department has worked to strengthen since the dark days after the 1992 riots.

"Even if you have reasonable suspicion or probable cause, if you're not producing arrests that go directly to the highest levels of public safety, all you're doing is dragnetting, with a very high cost in trust," said civil rights attorney Connie Rice, a longtime LAPD critic who in recent years has worked with the department on reforms.

Mayor Eric Garcetti called the *Times* analysis "both important and timely" and said he is committed to "helping the LAPD make forward progress on issues of race and community relations."

"I look forward to our Police Commission and department leaders using this information to improve best practices, and I expect the department to work consciously and even-handedly to earn the trust of every Angeleno, every day, with every interaction," Garcetti said in a written statement.

LAPD Chief Michel Moore declined requests for an interview. He said in a written statement that the *Times* analysis does not tell the complete story because it does "not define or describe the circumstances of each stop or search."

The statement noted that the LAPD does not tolerate racial profiling and will discipline officers if necessary.

"We strive to ensure our stops and searches are lawful and done in a manner that builds community trust," Moore said in the statement.

The new findings follow a *Times* article published in January showing that the LAPD, including its elite Metropolitan Division, stopped black drivers at much higher rates than their share of the population.

According to the *Times* analysis of the new state data, black and Latino drivers and passengers were searched more often than whites in almost every part of the city.

Blacks and Latinos were more than three times as likely as whites to be removed from the vehicle and twice as likely to either be handcuffed or detained at the curb, the *Times* analysis found.

About 3% of blacks and Latinos stopped by the LAPD were arrested, compared with 2% of whites.

Overall, LAPD officers found contraband in 17% of the searches they performed. Most of the contraband was drugs or alcohol, while 9% was firearms.

The racial disparities begin when LAPD officers decide which cars to pull over. The *Times* analysis found that black and Latino drivers were stopped at higher rates than whites.

Of the more than 385,000 drivers and passengers pulled over by the LAPD from July 1, 2018, through the end of April, 27% were black, in a city that is about 9%

black. About 47% of those pulled over were Latino, which is roughly equivalent to their share of the population. About 18% of those stopped were white, when 28% of the city is white.

Asians, not including those of South Asian descent, made up about 4% of those stopped and 11% of the population. The LAPD searched 2% of Asian drivers and passengers who were pulled over.

An equipment violation, such as a broken taillight or tinted windows, was listed as the reason for more than 20% of vehicle stops involving blacks and Latinos, compared with 11% of stops involving whites, according to the *Times* analysis.

Such violations can serve as a pretext for officers to look for more serious wrongdoing. Pretextual stops are legal but have been criticized by scholars and civil rights advocates as giving too much license to law enforcement to operate on instinct rather than evidence.

In response to the earlier *Times* report showing similar racial disparities, Garcetti ordered the department to scale back vehicle stops. Through August, the number of stops performed by the LAPD was down 11% compared with the same period last year, while stops by Metropolitan Division were down by 45%.

For people who have been stopped and searched by the LAPD, the experience can be humiliating.

At a Police Commission meeting on Tuesday, Moore highlighted the overall decrease in vehicle stops, saying it was a response to residents' concerns about the disparate impact of traffic stops, particularly in South Los Angeles.

He said he will soon announce changes to Metro's crime suppression units, which community groups have demanded be withdrawn from South L.A.

Moore declined to elaborate on the changes, but he has previously spoken about possibly switching Metro officers from unmarked cars to black-and-whites as well as further reducing the reliance on vehicle investigative stops.

As night fell on South L.A. on a recent evening, two LAPD officers stopped a white Buick Regal.

They told the people in the car to get out. Then they spotted a handgun on the floor of the front passenger side.

"I know there's a gun in the car. Do you mind if we search the car?" Officer Charles Kumlander asked the two young black men and two young Latina women who stood facing a fence in handcuffs as a *Times* reporter and photographer watched. One of the men nodded.

Kumlander put the gun, along with a blue bandanna, on the hood of the car. Bullets spilled out. He fumbled through the women's purses.

The officers concluded that the gun belonged to the male passenger and let the others go.

"You shouldn't be driving around South L.A. with a gun wrapped in Crip colors," Officer Colt Haney admonished the women, who were from San Bernardino. "That's how people get shot."

LAPD officials did not allow a *Times* reporter to speak to the officers, who were with the 77th Street Division's gang unit. They briefed their supervisor, Sgt. Mario Cardona, on why they stopped the car at West 54th Street and South Vermont Avenue.

According to the officers, the front passenger was not wearing his seat belt and bent down to put something between his legs. The car's registration tags were also expired.

The car had tinted windows and was in a known gang area, and there were multiple people inside. The officers believed there was a safety risk and ordered the driver and three passengers to exit the vehicle. The gun was in plain view, so they could legally confiscate it and search the rest of the vehicle.

Demographically, the LAPD closely mirrors the city: 49% of officers are Latino, 10% are black, 31% are white and 10% are Asian, according to department figures.

As they cruise the streets of L.A., officers should be curious about what they see, Cardona told a *Times* reporter, likening the process to casting a line without knowing if you'll hook a small or big fish.

If a person seems out of place—for example, if he is wearing a hat associated with one gang but is on another gang's turf—an officer should find out who that person is, he said. But racial profiling is never involved, he added.

"Are we stopping you just because you're black? No," Cardona said. "You ran the light, so we'll do a traffic stop and figure out who you are."

LAPD officers found guns in less than 2% of searches they conducted, according to the *Times* analysis. More than 4 times out of 5, they came up empty-handed—no drugs or weapons.

Citywide in 2018, 43% of violent crime suspects were black and 40% were Latino, according to LAPD statistics. Experts say this does not justify the disparate search rates, because contraband is found less often on the groups that are searched more often.

"At its simplest level, it appears that blacks and Latinos are being subjected to a lower threshold of suspicion in order to be searched," said Jack Glaser, a professor of public policy at UC Berkeley who has studied traffic stop data.

Glaser said the 24% search rate for African Americans raises questions about whether LAPD officers are targeting them because of their race.

"If you are searching a quarter of the people you're stopping, you're looking to search people," he said. "You're not just pulling people over for running stop signs and then happening to see they have a gun-shaped bulge in their pocket."

Lorie Fridell, a criminology professor at the University of South Florida who authored a pioneering study on stop data, said the lower contraband rates for whites are a "warning signal" and should be reviewed by LAPD officials.

"Even though we can never prove or disprove bias, they are a strong red flag for unjustifiable disparity that requires an agency to at least take a closer look at the search practices," said Fridell, who has conducted federally funded training on bias at police departments across the country.

In addition to the traditional analysis involving racial breakdowns of stops and searches, The *Times* used a statistical model called a "threshold test" in collaboration with the Stanford Open Policing Project. The model weighs search rates and contraband recovery rates to determine how much evidence officers require before conducting searches of different racial groups.

The Stanford researchers found that the LAPD generally searched blacks and Latinos based on less evidence than whites.

This was true even when excluding "non-discretionary" searches—including those conducted because of an arrest or as a condition of probation or parole—as the primary reason for the search. In those cases, officers have explicit permission to search, so racial bias is unlikely to be at play, versus when the search is more of a judgment call, experts said.

Even if every search has a legal basis, it is unconstitutional to apply a different search standard to African Americans and Latinos than to whites, said Peter Bibring, senior staff attorney at the ACLU of Southern California and director of police practices for the ACLU of California.

"If that's the kind of policing that they think fits the white community in Los Angeles, if that's the kind that's least intrusive, that's the kind of policing that every Angeleno deserves," he said.

For people who have been stopped and searched by the LAPD, the experience can be humiliating.

In November 2017, Bryant Mangum was driving home in his white BMW with tinted windows when he was pulled over by LAPD officers at gunpoint.

They patted him down and told him to stand facing a fence with his hands behind his back, he told the *Times*.

While one officer searched the car, the other asked whether he had guns or drugs, whether he was in a gang and how he could afford a BMW.

The officers didn't say why they pulled him over and didn't ask permission to search the car, Mangum said. They let him go without a ticket or a warning.

Mangum, 37, is a warehouse foreman who owns a home a block away from East 99th and South Main Streets, where the incident occurred. He has a criminal record, mostly for vandalism from his days as a guerrilla graffiti artist, but his last conviction was in 2006, court records show.

South L.A. Resident Bryant Mangum

South L.A. resident Bryant Mangum has been pulled over and searched many times by Los Angeles police. When he first bought the BMW and it still had paper plates, he was pulled over 10 times in one month, he said.

Mangum believes that officers see a nice car driven by a black man and want to investigate whether he is a gang member or drug dealer. He doesn't ask why he is being stopped or searched, since officers have bristled at questions in the past.

"It's very traumatic—I don't like to drive my car at night," Mangum said. "I can't enjoy it where I live. I'm more worried about cops than criminals."

In Van Nuys, Leo Hernandez said he was stopped by LAPD officers twice in 2015.

Once, the officers told him his Honda Civic was a model often stolen in the area. The other time, they said his tinted windows were too dark and the rosary beads on his mirror illegally obstructed his view.

Both times, the officers asked to search his car, Hernandez said. He agreed, and they found nothing.

"I asked, 'Why am I being stopped? Is it because of how I look?'" Hernandez, 36, who is Latino and works part time for the city's Recreation and Parks Department, said of the tinted windows stop, which resulted in a ticket. "Of course it felt like profiling."

The gaps in search rates between blacks and whites in Los Angeles are wider than those found in other major California cities such as San Diego and Oakland, but smaller than San Francisco, according to the most recent reports available.

Policing experts acknowledge the limitations of the data but say that local law enforcement leaders should take it seriously.

The LAPD was required by a federal consent decree to collect detailed stop and search data but cut back after the decree was lifted in 2013. Until the new state law took effect last July, LAPD officers collected basic information on vehicle and pedestrian stops but almost nothing about searches.

"They have a responsibility to say, 'Here's the nature of the stop data, and here's the nature of the crime in this area,'" said Chuck Wexler, executive director of the Police Executive Research Forum, which researches and recommends policies for police agencies. "I'm not saying the stops are wrong, but they're a starting point for a discussion about the nature of crime in that neighborhood and what does that say about the strategy?"

In response to a lawsuit by the ACLU, the New York City Police Department drastically cut back on stopping and frisking black and Latino pedestrians. The Oakland Police Department has decreased its vehicle stops by nearly half since 2015.

Oakland police officers still stop and search blacks at higher rates than other races. But fewer residents are inconvenienced by traffic stops, while crime has decreased in many key categories.

Pretextual stops are more of a fishing expedition than a targeted crime-fighting effort, according to Oakland police leaders, and officers have been instructed to use them sparingly.

"We've reduced our footprint in the community. And that also heals relationships," said Police Chief Anne Kirkpatrick. "You're not stopping everybody with a broad net."

Print Citations

CMS: Poston, Ben, and Cindy Chang. "LAPD Searches Blacks and Latinos More Often." In *The Reference Shelf: U.S. National Debate Topic: 2020–2021 Criminal Justice Reform,* edited by Micah L. Issitt, 12-18. Amenia, NY: Grey House Publishing, 2020.

MLA: Poston, Ben, and Cindy Chang. "LAPD Searches Blacks and Latinos More Often." *The Reference Shelf: U.S. National Debate Topic: 2020–2021 Criminal Justice Reform,* edited by Micah L. Issitt, Grey House Publishing, 2020, pp. 12-18.

APA: Poston, B., & Chang, C. (2020). LAPD searches blacks and latinos more often. In Micah L. Issitt (Ed.), *The reference shelf: U.S. national debate topic: 2020–2021 criminal justice reform* (pp. 12-18). Amenia, NY: Grey House Publishing.

Study That Claims White Police No More Likely to Shoot Minorities Draws Fire

By Juanita Bawagan
Science, August 15, 2019

Researchers are raising red flags about a recent study on race and deadly encounters with police in the United States, highlighting the difficulties in measuring racial bias. The study claimed that white police were no more likely than their nonwhite colleagues to shoot minorities. But now, other researchers say the study was flawed and that it adds little to the debate over whether minorities have a greater chance of getting shot by police than white civilians.

"It's just a completely indefensible conclusion to draw from the data that's available," says Dean Knox, a political scientist at Princeton University who published a critique of the study this month. To begin to justify such a claim, he says, researchers would need to know how often black and white civilians encounter police officers—something the authors of the original study did not consider in the paper.

Another criticism: The study did not investigate the possibility that all police—white and nonwhite—could be biased in shooting black men, says psychologist Phillip Atiba Goff at the Center for Policing Equity and John Jay College of Criminal Justice in New York City. "It's not a serious framing of bias to think that white people have bias and other people don't," he says.

In the original study, published on 22 July in the Proceedings of the National Academy of Sciences (PNAS), researchers at Michigan State University and the University of Maryland compiled a list of more than 900 fatal U.S. police shootings in 2015 using crowdsourced databases from the *Washington Post* and *The Guardian*. Then, they asked police departments for information about the race of the officers responsible for the shootings. They found black police were more likely to kill black civilians than white civilians. However, the same held true for white and Hispanic officers: Each group of police was likelier to shoot civilians of their own race. That's likely true, the researchers say, because police tend to be drawn from the communities they work in and are thus more likely to have deadly encounters with civilians of the same race. They concluded there were no antiblack or anti-Hispanic disparities across police shootings—which, critics say, should not be used to jump to conclusions of no racial bias.

The finding was picked up by major media outlets and rebounded across the internet, refracted through different political lenses. Without scrutiny, it seemed to undercut one of the central tenets of the Black Lives Matter movement: that unarmed black men have died too often at the hands of police.

Now, Knox and Princeton political scientist Jonathan Mummolo are pushing back against those conclusions with a critique that was published on the preprint server SSRN. They say the PNAS study is "uninformative" about racial bias because it assumes that black and white officers encounter black civilians in equal numbers. They illustrate their critique with a thought experiment in which a black officer encountered 90 black civilians and 10 white, whereas a white officer encountered the reverse. If both officers shot five black civilians and nine white civilians, the raw results seemed to validate the approach of the PNAS study: The white officer was indeed no more likely than the black officer to shoot a minority. But once the encounter rates were taken into account, it was clear that the white officer shot 50% of the black civilians they encountered and only 10% of the whites, revealing obvious racial bias, the authors write.

> **Unarmed black men are 3.5 times more likely to be killed by police than unarmed white men.**

Knox and Mummolo submitted their critique to PNAS as a letter to the editor, but the journal declined to publish it. PNAS did not say why, citing the confidentiality of editorial decisions.

David Johnson, the lead author of the PNAS study and a socio-cognitive psychologist at the University of Maryland in College Park, says the criticisms are largely about how his team framed its research question. He argues that focusing on officer race in fatal shootings is valid, too, and has practical implications. For instance, he says his findings suggest that simply increasing diversity in police forces might not reduce racial disparities in fatal shootings, even if it leads to an increase in public trust. "It's a smaller question, but it's something we can actually answer with the data," Johnson says. He and his co-author have published a formal response to the critique.

Knox and Mummolo say a better way to look for racial bias in police shootings is to compare incident rates to a benchmark, such as population or crime rates. For instance, a 2015 study of police shootings found that unarmed black men are 3.5 times more likely to be killed by police than unarmed white men, even after factoring in local crime rates.

An ideal benchmark, Knox says, would be the numbers of police-civilian encounters in similar circumstances. But these encounter rates are difficult to collect and nearly impossible to compare across jurisdictions. Researchers have begun to use footage from body cameras to examine racial bias in cities such as Oakland, California, but few police departments are willing to share their data. Knox, Mummolo, and their Princeton colleague William Lowe have proposed gathering video footage from highway speed cameras as a way to show what factors lead to driver stops in the first place. License plate numbers could be used to identify the race, age, and gender of the driver, and the footage itself could reveal information that might go unrecorded in administrative data—for example, whether a driver's offensive bumper sticker could have angered the officer.

The question is not just about gathering more data, but the right data, Mummolo says. This year, the Federal Bureau of Investigation launched a "use-of-force" database in an attempt to collect records for nationwide statistics. It's one of many new databases that researchers can use; most, however, still exclude information on incidents and encounters when police did not use force.

Documenting every use of force, Mummolo says, is important but insufficient. "What we're trying to do is develop research designs that allow us to study how police come into contact with civilians in the first place."

Print Citations

CMS: Bawagan, Juanita. "Study That Claims White Police No More Likely to Shoot Minorities Draws Fire." In *The Reference Shelf: U.S. National Debate Topic: 2020–2021 Criminal Justice Reform,* edited by Micah L. Issitt, 19-21. Amenia, NY: Grey House Publishing, 2020.

MLA: Bawagan, Juanita. "Study That Claims White Police No More Likely to Shoot Minorities Draws Fire." *The Reference Shelf: U.S. National Debate Topic: 2020–2021 Criminal Justice Reform,* edited by Micah L. Issitt, Grey House Publishing, 2020, pp. 19-21.

APA: Bawagan, J. (2020). Study that claims white police no more likely to shoot minorities draws fire. In Micah L. Issitt (Ed.), *The reference shelf: U.S. national debate topic: 2020–2021 criminal justice reform* (pp. 19-21). Amenia, NY: Grey House Publishing.

The Bad-Apple Myth of Policing

By Osagie K. Obasogie
The Atlantic, **August 2, 2019**

On a late-fall afternoon in 1984, in Charlotte, North Carolina, Dethorne Graham started to feel ill. He understood what was happening; insulin reactions from diabetes were a regular part of his life. Graham asked his friend William to drive him to a local convenience store where he could buy orange juice to offset the effects. Graham walked in, but left quickly after seeing a long line at the counter.

M. S. Connor, a Charlotte police officer, was nearby. Connor, an African American like Graham, thought it was odd that someone would enter and leave the store so quickly. The officer followed Graham and his friend for about a half mile in his squad car before pulling them over. After speaking briefly with the two men, Connor called for backup.

Graham got out of the car. As he wavered in and out of consciousness, he found himself handcuffed and lying on his stomach on the sidewalk. Graham tried to explain his medical condition, but the group of officers didn't believe him and mistook an insulin reaction as him simply being drunk. The officers pulled him up from behind, slammed his head on the hood of his friend's car, and pinned him facedown, with an officer leaning heavily on each limb. They then picked him up and threw him inside the patrol car. At one point, a friend familiar with Graham's condition ran over to the scene with orange juice to help. Graham begged one of the officers for the drink. She responded: "I'm not giving you shit."

After the clerk at the convenience store confirmed that nothing unusual had happened, the officers drove Graham home. He was left with a broken foot, several lacerations, and what he would later describe as a persistent ringing in his right ear. Little did Graham know as he writhed in pain that this episode would lead, five years later, to one of the most important U.S. Supreme Court decisions in modern history, *Graham v. Connor*. While the decision stemming from this incident is not well known, its influence has been far-reaching.

Since the beginning of the Black Lives Matter movement, in 2013, stories concerning police use of force have been prominent in the news and on social media. Much of the public conversation has focused on a collective exasperation: How is it that police can beat and kill men and women, many of them unarmed, yet rarely be held accountable?

The answer lies in large part in the 1989 *Graham* decision. Graham brought a federal claim against the Charlotte police officers, under a civil-rights statute called 42 U.S.C. §1983, in the U.S. District Court for the Western District of North Carolina. He argued that the excessive use of force against him violated substantive due process, or his right to be free from such abuse under the Fourteenth Amendment—one of the Reconstruction amendments ratified after the Civil War to give African Americans full legal equality with whites.

The trial court, as well as the Fourth Circuit Court of Appeals, sided with the officers. But, in deciding to review the case, the Supreme Court made a surprising move. Until that point, the legal standards through which federal courts reviewed claims of excessive force by state and local police were diverse. Many cases used substantive due process under the Fourteenth Amendment, following an earlier Second Circuit Court of Appeals decision in *Johnson v. Glick*, in which a detained man alleged that a correctional officer had assaulted him. This standard had been criticized, however, for emphasizing officers' subjective mental state—that is, whether the force was applied in "good faith" or "maliciously and sadistically for the very purpose of causing harm."

In the *Graham* decision, the Supreme Court held that substantive due process was not the applicable constitutional standard. Rather, the Court said the proper constitutional test was whether the action was "reasonable" under the Fourth Amendment, which prohibits unreasonable searches and seizures. (Use of force by the police during an arrest or investigative stop is understood to be a type of "seizure.")

The choice was significant. Turning away from the Fourteenth Amendment as a constitutional standard would come to represent a missed opportunity to situate excessive force in minority communities as a long-standing structural problem. The Fourth Amendment was developed at a time when slavery was condoned by the Constitution, and it is largely preoccupied with the relationship between individuals and the government. The Fourteenth Amendment, on the other hand, has its roots in the post–Civil War effort to extend legal equality to former slaves. Particularly through its clause guaranteeing equal protection of the law, it reflects an awareness of how racial groups, not just individuals, can face state persecution. (Although the Fourteenth Amendment's due-process clause is what allows the Fourth Amendment to apply to state and local police, as opposed to only the federal government, the *Graham* decision nonetheless represents a significant retreat from the Fourteenth Amendment's original purpose of protecting racial minorities from state violence and other inequities.)

The Court's decision to embrace a Fourth Amendment perspective that frames excessive force as an isolated interaction between police and individuals would impede federal courts' ability to consider how race and racism can influence an officer's decision to use force. To be sure, before Graham, substantive-due-process claims concerning police violence focused largely on individual liberty rather than structural conditions. But shifting the constitutional standard for excessive force away from the Fourteenth Amendment would prove to hinder courts' ability to consider such abuse as a problem tied to issues of equal protection and racial subordination—in turn limiting the types of claims that victims of police violence could successfully bring. The disproportionate policing of racial minorities and the state-sanctioned violence that often ensues (performed by officers of all racial backgrounds) had been a dire problem in communities of color, and would continue to be. Decades after the *Graham* decision, research would show that black men are three times more likely to be killed by the police than white men. Police violence would come to be understood as a major public-health issue.

Moreover, in articulating the new standard for judging excessive-force cases, the Graham Court didn't do much to describe what "reasonable" means. William Rehnquist, the chief justice at the time, provided a few guideposts, such as paying "careful attention to the facts and circumstances of each particular case, including the severity of the crime at issue, whether the suspect poses an immediate threat to the safety of the officers or others, and whether he is actively resisting arrest or attempting to evade arrest by flight." But he also wrote that reasonableness is difficult to describe, noting that "the 'reasonableness' of a particular use of force must be judged from the perspective of a reasonable officer on the scene, rather than with the 20/20 vision of hindsight."

The vagueness of the standard for "what counts" as excessive force would have sweeping implications. Initially, some believed that its use would favor plaintiffs, because the "reasonableness" test seemed more objective. But this perspective would prove overly optimistic. It has provided limited tactical guidance for how police officers should treat people and how judges and juries should understand claims of police misconduct. Dethorne Graham saw this firsthand. Following the Supreme Court's decision, his case went back to the trial court so that the jury could review the evidence under the new rules. Yet the jury concluded that the police officers' behavior toward him was "reasonable."

Subsequent decisions by the Supreme Court and lower federal courts have continued the *Graham* decision's legacy of ambiguity in considering what constitutes "reasonable" force on the part of officers. Many police departments have also created their own set of administrative rules on when force is appropriate.

But these policies sorely lack specificity. In a study forthcoming in the *Cornell Law Review*, for which I am the lead author, my co-author and I analyzed use-of-force policies from the 75 largest U.S. cities and showed that they regularly fail to provide meaningful instruction to police on when to use force, or how to do so in ways that increase the likelihood that people will survive. For example, only 31 percent of the policies required officers to exhaust alternatives before using deadly force, and only 17 percent had policies that instructed officers to use force that is proportional to a person's resistance. Meanwhile, all of the policies we examined restate Graham's reasonableness standard, many times directly citing the case. The vagueness of this standard creates wide discretion for police and few protections for community members.

Our examination of the case law also showed that when people file lawsuits alleging that police used excessive force, federal courts often reference or defer to police departments' use-of-force policies as the appropriate legal interpretation of "reasonable." For example, in a 2004 case before a federal district court in West Virginia, in which an officer fractured the leg of the plaintiff,

> **Federal courts were influenced by the idea that as long as an officer's behavior does not violate the use-of-force rules created by his own department, his actions are not unreasonable and therefore not unconstitutional.**

Kevin Neiswonger, as he tried to restrain him, the court held that the officer "acted reasonably under the circumstances to protect both Mr. Neiswonger and himself, in accordance with the Morgantown City Police Department's Use of Force Policy," and thus "did not violate Mr. Neiswonger's Fourth Amendment right to be free from unreasonable search and seizure." In this case, as in many others, federal courts were influenced by the idea that as long as an officer's behavior does not violate the use-of-force rules created by his own department, his actions are not unreasonable and therefore not unconstitutional.

This suggests that the ongoing epidemic of police violence is not simply the result of what former Attorney General Jeff Sessions once described as "individuals within a department that have done wrong." Instead, by allowing police to largely define what constitutes excessive force, the Court has limited its own judicial oversight of the system, creating the conditions that allow police to use violence with impunity. As a result, the individual bias often found among police officers can quickly translate into violence against minority communities.

Despite the thousands of lives that have been lost to police violence since the *Graham* decision, the Supreme Court has shown little interest in rethinking its approach. State and local governments, however, have the opportunity to be more proactive. For example, California Governor Gavin Newsom is expected to sign Assembly Bill 392, the California Act to Save Lives, which would change California's current standard regarding police use of deadly force under state law (which looks at whether it was "reasonable") by requiring that police use force only when "necessary." This new term is not clearly defined, and some advocacy groups that fought for the bill have withdrawn their support due to this and other shortcomings. But in shifting from an ambiguous and deferential concept to a more concrete and cautious one, the proposed law seeks to encourage officers to prioritize other ways to resolve situations before using force that often shatters bodies, destroys lives, and fractures communities.

Laws like A.B. 392 wouldn't solve the police-violence crisis alone. Many aspects of policing need reform, such as rules on qualified immunity, which can shield officers who use excessive force, and the level of community participation when police departments develop or revise use-of-force policies. However, A.B. 392, despite its limitations, may offer an instructive case study in whether less permissive rules regarding police use of force can change the culture within police departments and perhaps save lives.

This article is part of our project "The Presence of Justice," which is supported by a grant from the John D. and Catherine T. MacArthur Foundation's Safety and Justice Challenge.

Print Citations

CMS: Obasogie, Osagie K. "The Bad-Apple Myth of Policing." In *The Reference Shelf: U.S. National Debate Topic: 2020–2021 Criminal Justice Reform,* edited by Micah L. Issitt, 22-26. Amenia, NY: Grey House Publishing, 2020.

MLA: Obasogie, Osagie K. "The Bad-Apple Myth of Policing." *The Reference Shelf: U.S. National Debate Topic: 2020–2021 Criminal Justice Reform,* edited by Micah L. Issitt, Grey House Publishing, 2020, pp. 22-26.

APA: Obasogie, O.K. (2020). The bad-apple myth of policing. In Micah L. Issitt (Ed.), *The reference shelf: U.S. national debate topic: 2020–2021 criminal justice reform* (pp. 22-26). Amenia, NY: Grey House Publishing.

2

Prison and Its Alternatives

Critical Resistance logo. The organization, founded by political activist Angela Davis, focuses on dismantling the prison-industrial complex.

Rehabilitation and Punishment

Is the U.S. criminal justice system effective? Do police, the courts, and America's prisons help achieve the goal of making society safer? The most common of the debates involving criminal justice debates focuses on the efficacy of current criminal justice techniques, and usually is based in the different opinions about the purpose of criminal justice. Some believe it is to remove offenders from society and punish them, and that harsher punishments discourage criminal offenses. Others believe that the purpose of criminal justice is to reform and rehabilitate those who have committed criminal acts.

Imprisonment History and Purpose

Imprisonment has a very long history. In a 1921 *Journal of Criminal Law and Criminology* article, Harry Elmer Barnes wrote:

> The prison, viewed as an institution for detaining men against their will, originated in the most remote antiquity. It probably goes back as far as the time of the general practice of cannibalism, when future victims were held in stockades to be fattened or to await their turn in contributing the chief course in the menu of their captors.[1]

While the historical merit of Barnes's assertion that prisons were initially a sort of larder for cannibals is questionable, it is certain that prisons and imprisonment developed quite early in global history. In America, prisons became frequently used in the late 1700s, before which a great many crimes were punished by corporal punishment—using violence and injury as a way of discouraging criminal behavior. Corporal punishment was often dispensed in public, as were executions, as a way to shame criminals, educate citizens on the consequences of certain actions, and provide a form of public and family entertainment.

Until the late eighteenth century, jails were typically used to temporarily house individuals awaiting trial. Jails existed alongside "workhouses," in which prisoners were forced to participate in labor. The workhouses contained potentially dangerous convicts, and provided societies with legalized slavery. They also encouraged corruption, as immoral politicians encouraged imprisonment as a way to bolster the convicted population, which translated into economic benefits. Until the first prison reform movement in the late 1700s, most Americans were in prison because they were in debt, repaying their debt through forced labor.

Most of the original American colonies derived their criminal codes from England, which was developed to serve the needs of the wealthy classes, and the reason that so many in American jails and workhouses were imprisoned for failure to pay their debts. Such a system provides further economic benefits for the wealthy through unfair labor. One notable exception to this approach was the more progressive Quaker philosophy employed by Pennsylvania and New Jersey, which held that criminal justice should be about reforming individuals to rejoin society. After the American Revolution, this approach began spreading through the nation and inspired the first efforts at criminal justice reform.

In an August 1987 issue of *American Heritage*, former prison psychologist Roger T. Pray argues that America "invented" the modern prison. The first prison was created in Philadelphia in 1790 (Walnut Street Prison) and was inspired by a "humanitarian" effort to address crime. Early criminologists had begun to recognize that the widespread and liberal use of capital and corporal punishment seemed to have had little effect on reducing crime rates. Further, in the wake of the Revolution, there was a push to move away from the British way of doing things.[2] The trend in America was for society to reflect the emerging Enlightenment philosophy, and prisons were altered to be more in keeping with this goal. Much of this reform came thanks to the pioneering legal studies of Italian philosopher Cesare Beccaria, an early opponent of capital punishment whose opposition to the treatment of criminals led him to write some of the most famous works on the idea of criminal rehabilitation. In his 1764 *An Essay on Crimes and Punishments*, Beccaria wrote: "The purpose of punishment is not to torment a sensible being, or to undo a crime but is none other than to prevent the criminal from doing further injury to society and to prevent others from committing the like offense."[3]

Beccaria's work inspired many of the Founding Fathers and other jurists and politicians who had an interest in Enlightenment philosophy. His arguments form the foundation for the modern approach to rehabilitation in criminal justice. Beccaria was one of the first to suggest that more severe punishments may actually increase the probability of crime as individuals seeking to avoid punishment commit further crimes to avoid capture. In the Revolutionary era, those who disagreed with Beccaria felt that making the prison system more humane would lead to an increase in crime, and this constituted the conservative criminal justice movement of the late 1700s and early 1800s; indeed, the conservative mindset on the issue has changed little over the centuries that followed. There remain Americans who believe that individuals will avoid behaviors that may result in punishment, despite little evidence to support this.

The prison reform movement in Philadelphia did reduce crime, but penal and criminal justice reformers never gained complete control. Politicians then, as now, frequently opposed efforts to make criminal justice rehabilitative because such efforts are more complex and expensive to a society. Rather, many politicians argue in favor of a "law and order" approach to increase incarceration rates or to lengthen prison sentences in order to remove criminals from society and deter crime. This "tough on crime" strategy remains popular because of its political expediency and relatively low cost, and because of the perceived "common-sense" relationship between punishment and crime prevention.

Time for a New Reform?

One of the most challenging aspects of criminal justice reform is to ensure that federal and state laws are compatible, and that the penalties for certain crimes reflect the best evidence. As of 2020, some of the major issues facing the nation in terms of sentencing reform include the unsustainable growth of the prison population and changing national attitudes about the criminal justice approach to drug use. At the federal level, some believe that federal sentencing is needed to address the overpopulation of the federal prison system, a problem referred to as "mass incarceration."

In 2015, a bi-partisan committee in the U.S. Congress suggested a series of reforms (Sentencing Reform and Corrections Act or SRCA) that altered sentencing guidelines for drug offenders, reduced mandatory minimum sentencing guidelines, and granted judges and juries greater discretion over determining punishments for certain crimes. Though the proposal had high levels of both Republican and Democratic support, efforts stalled because of Republican politicians with deep ties to an anti-prison reform lobby fueled by private prison organizations.[4] In 2019 Congress passed the FIRST STEP Act, which contains some of the provisions present in the SRCA but is not nearly as aggressive. The FIRST STEP Act shortens mandatory minimum sentences for nonviolent drug offenses, limits the use of the federal "three strikes" rule (in which individuals with three convictions receive automatic life sentences), and gives judges greater discretion in sentencing for drug offenses.[5]

Supporters of the FIRST STEP Act call its passage a major victory in the effort to end mass incarceration, but critics argue that the law does not go far enough. Further, it is unclear whether high-profile opponents of the effort, like Senator John Kennedy from Louisiana and Tom Cotton from Arkansas, will ultimately weaken enforcement.

At the extreme end of the debate over prisons is the prison abolition movement, a network of activists, human rights organizations, and criminologists who believe that the incarceration system is either too dysfunctional to be salvaged or that incarceration, in general, serves no purpose and should be eliminated from American society. The prison abolition movement has existed in the United States since the Colonial era, and some of the first generation of criminal justice reformers promoted some version of this idea. In 2019 and 2020, the prison abolition campaign began gaining popular traction, with many mainstream news outlets producing coverage in favor of abolishing the prison system entirely. The prison abolition movement is an important topic in the broader debate because it asks Americans to closely examine the problems with the current system.

According to the Vera Institute of Justice—a nonprofit organization dedicated to studying America's incarceration system—a majority of individuals incarcerated in the states and at the federal level were sentenced for minor violations that included shoplifting, driving violations, or drug use offenses. Polls have routinely showed that Americans overall approve of sentencing and prison reforms, and believe such efforts are necessary. Further, polls indicate that a majority of Americans favor alternative programs and sentencing reform in an effort to rehabilitate those involved in the system.[6] Vera director Nancy Fishman summarized the issue in a 2015 interview with the *New York Times*, saying "It's an important moment to take a look at our use of jails. It's a huge burden on taxpayers, on our communities, and we need to decide if this is how we want to spend our resources."[7]

Works Used

Barnes, Harry Elmer. "Historical Origin of the Prison System in America." *Journal of Criminal Law and Criminology* 12, no. 1 (1921).

Beccaria, Cesare. *An Essay on Crimes and Punishments*. 1764. Online Library of Liberty. Retrieved from http://oll-resources.s3.amazonaws.com/titles/2193/Beccaria_1476_EBk_v6.0.pdf.

"Federal Sentencing Reform." *ABA*. American Bar Association. 2019. Retrieved from https://www.americanbar.org/advocacy/governmental_legislative_work/priorities_policy/criminal_justice_system_improvements/federalsentencingreform/.

Gonchar, Michael. "What Should Be the Purpose of Prison?" *New York Times*. Feb 27, 2015. Retrieved from https://learning.blogs.nytimes.com/2015/02/27/what-should-be-the-purpose-of-prison/.

Grawert, Amex, and Tim Lau. "How the FIRST STEP Act Became Law—and What Happens Next." Brennan Center for Justice. Jan 4, 2019. Retrieved from https://www.brennancenter.org/our-work/analysis-opinion/how-first-step-act-became-law-and-what-happens-next.

"Poll Shows Americans Overwhelmingly Support Prison, Sentencing Reforms." *Senate Judiciary Committee*. Aug 23, 2018. Retrieved from https://www.judiciary.senate.gov/press/rep/releases/poll-shows-americans-overwhelmingly-support-prison-sentencing-reforms.

Pray, Roger T. "How Did Our Prisons Get That Way?" *American Heritage* 38, no. 5 (1987).

Notes

1. Barnes, "Historical Origin of the Prison System in America."
2. Pray, "How Did Our Prisons Get That Way?"
3. Beccaria, *An Essay on Crimes and Punishments*.
4. "Federal Sentencing Reform," *ABA*.
5. Grawert and Lau, "How the FIRST STEP Act Became Law—and What Happens Next."
6. "Poll Shows Americans Overwhelmingly Support Prison, Sentencing Reforms," *Senate Judiciary Committee*.
7. Gonchar, "What Should Be the Purpose of Prison?"

The Case for Abolishing Prisons

By German Lopez
Vox, June 19, 2017

America should abolish prisons. Perhaps not all of them, but very close to it.

That's the argument in a recent, provocative paper by Peter Salib, a judicial clerk to Seventh Circuit Court of Appeals Judge Frank Easterbrook.

According to Salib, the idea behind the criminal justice system should be to punish and deter crimes. But prisons are arguably a very inefficient way to do that. The research shows that long prison sentences have little impact on crime, and a stint in prison can actually make someone more likely to commit crime—by further exposing them to all sorts of criminal elements. At the same time, prisons are incredibly costly, eating up funds that could go to other government programs that are more effective at fighting crime.

So why not, Salib suggests, consider alternative approaches to punishment that can let someone actually pay their debt back to society without forcing taxpayers to shoulder the burden of paying for his full confinement?

Salib gave the example of an accountant who burned down an office building. Instead of locking him up for potentially decades, Salib suggests keeping an eye on him through other means, such as GPS monitoring, and forcing him to work as an accountant to pay back the cost of the office building. This would, he argues, be much better for everyone involved; the office building owner gets paid back for the damage, and society has to pay much less to confine this person.

The idea is a bit discomforting, not least because it sounds like forced labor or slavery. Coupled with the massive racial disparities in the justice system, the idea takes an ugly turn.

But Salib makes two points: First, forced labor is certainly punishing, but prison is very punishing as well—arguably more so.

Second, Salib argues that we can try to make the justice system fairer while changing how it punishes people. "If you think that we shouldn't punish as many minorities as we do now, that's fine," he told me. "I'm not asking about who we should punish; I'm asking about how we punish the people we do punish."

This isn't a wholly new concept. Previously, Dylan Matthews wrote for *Vox* about how we could get rid of prisons by using location-tracking technology to monitor offenders while otherwise letting them live productive lives. And criminal justice experts Mark Kleiman, Angela Hawken, and Ross Halperin previously proposed a "graduated reentry" system that would similarly monitor people convicted of crimes, but incentivize them to slowly re-earn their freedom by proving their rehabilitation—getting a job, following a curfew, not committing other crimes, and so on. This could incentivize the inmate to be productive, while avoiding the higher costs of prison.

Still, Salib makes one of the clearer cases for how this change would be better not just for prisoners, but for society as a whole. You should read the full paper for more detail. But to follow up on some of the lingering questions I had—how his system works for murderers, and what kinds of exceptions he envisions that would still warrant prison—I reached out to Salib. What follows is our full conversation, edited for length and clarity.

German Lopez: What is the main argument in your paper?

Peter Salib: We start with the law and economics premise of criminal punishment, which is that the main thing we're interested in when we punish people is deterring anti-social behavior—imposing costs on people so it's not advantageous for them to make everyone's life worse.

For various reasons having to do with how hard it is to figure out when people are doing bad stuff to sufficiently deter them, the costs have to be sufficiently high. In layman terms that means we usually can't just extract money from them, but we sometimes have to do other things. The way our system usually does that now, if criminal punishment is necessary, is imprisonment.

The argument in the paper is that if our starting premise is the economic premise of minimizing social costs, we should look at other social costs [related to prison].

It turns out prison is really costly. It may be pretty good at deterring the bad acts we want to deter. But it has high administrative costs. It creates a lot of perverse incentives.

And, most importantly, if I'm a guy who would otherwise be a productive member of society and I get put in prison, part of the cost to me of being in prison is that I don't get to earn any money and enjoy the fruits of my labor while I'm in prison. It turns out that's also a cost to society: If there was some other punishment that also allowed me to work in a socially productive way, we could take the money I earned and give it to, say, my victims or, if my victim has already been compensated, the government or a nonprofit that would distribute it to other people who need it. That would be a lot better from a social standpoint.

The second half of the paper says it's not so out there that we could have a different system besides prison. When somebody is convicted of having done some bad stuff we think needs to be deterred, we first exhaust the monetary transfers we could make. So we say you have to keep working to pay your debt to society with actual money to the extent you can.

If it turns out there needs to be additional costs on the person, there are lots of additional things you could do. There are some that are historical, and maybe people think some of those are too horrible and archaic. But if you don't like those, you can pick anything you like. You could have public shaming as a punishment. If you don't think that's harsh enough, you could have other modern-day costly pun-ishments—you could make people eat very spicy peppers on a regular basis or have them do something else that's unpleasant on a regular basis.

The idea is that there are options that don't keep people from working and re-maining a productive member of society. So not a drain, but rather beneficial to others while still being deterred.

German Lopez: The way we usually talk about prison, we mostly talk about the costs to the prisoner. "Now he has to pay for his crime": That's the frame most people think about with prisons. But I think you're right that people tend to overlook some of the other social costs. To give readers a better idea of what some of the so-cial costs of prison are, could you walk me through them?

Peter Salib: Say I'm an accountant. But I have a streak of pyromania, so I burn down a big office building.

Under the current system, I go to prison. Let's say I get sent to 30 years of prison for serious arson. Part of the cost for me is, in addition to being confined to my prison cell and not being able to be with my family and loved ones, I don't get to earn any money while I'm in prison. And when I get out, I have foregone 30 years of my salary. That's a cost to me. But it's also a cost to everyone else.

Imagine if instead of getting sent to prison, the court tells me I have to repay the costs of the office building. But I don't have the savings to do that. If instead of be-ing sent to prison, I was forced to continue working as an accountant to give, say, 80 percent of my earnings for however long to whoever's office building I burned down, that would actually be a lot better to the guy whose office building I burned down.

The fact that I get sent to prison and am prevented from earning any wealth while I'm there is as much taking money out of my victim's pocket as it is taking money out of my pocket.

German Lopez: I could see someone latching onto that framing and arguing that sounds a lot like forced labor or slavery, especially with racial disparities in the criminal justice system. It could have some pretty ugly implications. How would you respond to that?

Peter Salib: I do worry about it. Part of the reason I don't engage with it very much in the paper is, one, the paper is really supposed to be narrowly a law and economics piece. There are other kinds of reasons we might want to do this. There are moral objections to this and some of the alternative punishments being imposed. As a law and economics matter, though, the point is this system is more efficient.

Particularly in regards to racial disparities in incarceration in America, there is a lot of research on that. It is very good. I buy that there are racial disparities that can't be explained or are hard to explain by good reasons.

But there's nothing incompatible with the idea that we should be fairer about who we punish and that we might want to punish them in a different way. I can ac-cept the objection that the American system of criminal punishment is unfair along the racial lines. If you think that we shouldn't punish as many minorities as we do now, that's fine. I'm not asking about who we should punish; I'm asking about how we punish the people we do punish.

The other thing: If you think forced labor is bad because of American slavery, I don't think that's wrong either. I just point out in the paper that prisoners in our current system do work. We do have forced labor for prisoners now. It just turns out there aren't a lot of ways for people who are locked up in a cell to do high-value labor. So that undercompensates people who are victims of crime who could be compensated more if people were using their talents more productively.

German Lopez: There are some crimes that don't have a hard, monetary value attached to them—like murder, where it's hard to measure the value of a human life. So how do you approach those situations?

Peter Salib: It's right that it's very difficult to put a value on a human life. That's given by the fact that most of us would pay potentially any sum of money to prevent our impending death.

The point of this system is not to put a dollar value on a life and then extract that from the murderer. The point of this system is to figure out how much private cost we want to impose on the murderer to keep him from killing the person in the first place. That might be—in fact, likely is—a lot less than the value of a human life. If you think the value of a human life approaches infinity, you probably don't have to impose an infinite amount of costs on a potential murderer to deter him from murdering.

So when we're thinking about how much punishment to inflict, how much private cost to impose on a potential bad actor, we're really thinking less about the losses of the victim—which can be enormous and likely irreparable. The best we can do in a system of criminal law is figure out what threat we need to make to murderers to keep them from murdering. That's the cost we're thinking of.

The idea, then, is that as much of that punishment as possible should be paid in the form of money instead of a form of discomfort, confinement, or things that can't be transferred. As far as we're imposing costs on bad actors like murderers, it's senseless to destroy wealth when we could make those people generate wealth and give it to their victims or give it to their governments.

That's not to fully say we'll ever fully compensate the family of a murder victim. The only idea is that there's no sense in having them lose a loved one and then giving them nothing, because we've locked up the person who did it.

German Lopez: What are some of the other alternatives to prison that you think are plausible, besides forced labor?

Peter Salib: In the system I suggest, the only way there is some economic efficiency is if there is a required labor component. The whole idea is that instead of destroying people's wealth, you let them generate wealth and transfer it—either to victims or the government or someone else who we think would do good things with the money. So that's kind of the baseline.

The idea for additional punishment comes from the fact that if I steal $10,000, you might think that having me pay $10,000 back is good enough to deter me from having stolen it in the first place. But it turns out we only catch some thieves. So if we only catch 50 percent of thieves, and account for my expected value of a $10,000 jewel, the actual [deterrent] value is $20,000—because there's only a 50 percent chance I'll have to pay it back.

> **Long prison sentences have little impact on crime, and a stint in prison can actually make someone more likely to commit crime—by further exposing them to all sorts of criminal elements.**

The idea is that high penalties are required as long as we don't catch that many criminals. So we have people work so they repay victims and society so much as that's possible. But insofar as some people do some socially costly stuff, there will sometimes be a higher required punishment than people can pay for in money. That's where some other sanction comes in. I call these non-monetary sanctions.

The paper is completely agnostic about what and how many non-monetary sanctions we should impose.

In the American colonial days, we had pillory—putting people in the stock and humiliating them. We had flogging. We had tarring and feathering (although it was often extrajudicial, not sanctioned).

The point isn't to endorse those punishments. I think there are valid objections to those punishments — especially because they look a lot like the things that we did to American slaves, and that's very ugly.

The paper says we don't need to do that. You can invent anything you like. Whatever you think is the right way to impose costs on people who've harmed others in society, that's okay.

There are judges out in America who are inventing these kinds of things. They're often a little bit silly. So after someone made his daughter sleep in the doghouse, the judge made him sleep in the doghouse. There's a similar eye-for-an-eye story for a judge who made someone get a very bad haircut.

A lot of people would probably say those are probably not costly enough to impose on many people who do bad things. That's fine too. Pick something between a bad haircut and whatever you think the extreme is.

If you think part of the effectiveness of prison is it confines people, you could have people live in very confining conditions when they're not working. It could be, really, anything that we think, as a society, is humane and effective.

Certainly, punishing people can be hard to stomach. I agree with that. But one thing I put in the paper is prison is really hard to stomach if you're intimately familiar with it. Prison is a place where we send people to be subject to incredible rates of violence, incredible rates of sexual assault, [and] often more limited medical care.

If you object to how brutal prison is, then under my system you can impose something less brutal in the world. But you shouldn't object to moving away from prison to something that seems brutal without also recognizing that prison as we do it now is a pretty nasty place.

German Lopez: I wanted to bring that up. I think there's an underlying bias for the status quo. People don't always think of prison as this brutal place. But as you mentioned, there are high rates of violence and sexual assault. Even if there weren't higher rates of violence, just imagining yourself in a position where you are stuck somewhere for years in this monotonous, terrifying situation, that still seems like a brutal environment to be in. So while flogging seems harsher to me, it's certainly true that prison is harsh. It's bizarre to not consider that when criticizing or vetoing these other forms of punishment you mentioned.

So it seems like the point is that people should think about alternative punishments more seriously and start thinking outside the box for this, acknowledging that prison is by itself fairly harsh and inefficient.

Peter Salib: That's right.

One reason for the status quo bias is we need prisons to keep dangerous people out of society and therefore prevent them from committing crime. But I think alternatives to prison might actually do better on that count.

There's a fair amount of research that there's actually a causal relationship between years of imprisonment and lifetime crimes committed. We think prison as reducing crime, because it takes people who we think would commit crimes and puts them away so they can't commit them. But it actually has the opposite effect: Maybe you can't commit a crime while you're in prison, but you commit a bunch more [crimes] once you get out.

So for many people who commit crimes, it may be possible to stop them from committing more crimes while they're out in the world, working and contributing to society, because we have all this cool technology now that we didn't have before. We have very good location-detection technology. We can really make sure people are where they're supposed to be using biometric technology. We can monitor them. Our smartphones have every kind of data transfer you'd like, from voice to video to pictures to text.

We just have to think outside the box with how we use criminal punishment as a mechanism for preventing future crimes in a way that doesn't involve just putting people in a cage.

German Lopez: Are there exceptions in this system? Are there some people who do need to go to prison?

Peter Salib: There are at least some murderers—I'm thinking of, at the very least, the kind of psychotic serial killers, the Ted Bundys of the world—that probably we really should keep away from society. Insofar as there is some percentage of people who really are an irreparable danger to society, the paper concedes that okay, maybe those people really do need to be locked up.

It might not be everyone who commits a violent crime, but there are certainly some people for who prison is the right answer. But it's almost certainly a small fraction of the millions we incarcerate in America now.

Print Citations

CMS: Lopez, German. "The Case for Abolishing Prisons." In *The Reference Shelf: U.S. National Debate Topic: 2020–2021 Criminal Justice Reform,* edited by Micah L. Issitt, 33-39. Amenia, NY: Grey House Publishing, 2020.

MLA: Lopez, German. "The Case for Abolishing Prisons." *The Reference Shelf: U.S. National Debate Topic: 2020–2021 Criminal Justice Reform,* edited by Micah L. Issitt, Grey House Publishing, 2020, pp. 33-39.

APA: Lopez, G. (2020). The case for abolishing prisons. In Micah L. Issitt (Ed.), *The reference shelf: U.S. national debate topic: 2020–2021 criminal justice reform* (pp. 33-39). Amenia, NY: Grey House Publishing.

How Lessons in Scandinavian Design Could Help Prisons with Rehabilitation

By Yvonne Jewkes and Kate Gooch
The Conversation, January 4, 2019

For many people who end up in prison, efforts at rehabilitation are hampered by historic, pervasive and deeply embedded social inequalities. The bloated prison system in England and Wales has become a dangerous place with little hope of rehabilitating offenders.

The "simple and unpalatable truth" about prisons in the UK, said the chief inspector, is that they have become "unacceptably violent and dangerous places". They are characterised by poor mental health, drug use, and the "perennial problems of overcrowding, poor physical environments [...] and inadequate staffing".

Well-publicised incidents have also shone a spotlight on the dangerous conditions in many jails. One response to this situation which we are investigating is the design and aesthetics of the prison environment. British prisons are often compared unfavourably to those in Scandinavia, where good design is not just expected for the domestic home, but extends to the building of new prisons as well.

For example, officials at Storstrøm Prison in Denmark, which opened in 2017, described it as a "modern, humane, high-security prison that uses architecture to promote prisoners' social rehabilitation". Like Halden Prison in Norway, Storstrøm holds 250 men in buildings that are configured to form a small urban community – with streets, squares and centrally located community buildings.

The cells are unusual in having curved walls and furniture without sharp corners—to both minimise the risk of self harm and ensure optimum use of space. Views of the pleasant landscaping and countryside beyond are provided by two windows on adjacent walls in each cell. One cell window is almost floor to ceiling in height—and neither of the windows have bars on them.

While prisons in the UK are unlikely to truly emulate the Scandinavian model, several governors have sought to introduce innovative design elements into their establishments. The goal is to "normalise" the custodial environment in the hopes that this will help create a "rehabilitation culture".

These include attempts to brighten accommodation units and visiting rooms, with softer furnishings, less overt security paraphernalia and graffiti and street art projects.

Some of the other (previously unthinkable) activities now flourishing in prisons across England and Wales include community music, performing arts projects and lectures. There are sporting opportunities such as parkrun, and numerous examples of voluntary charity work.

Several prison governors have embraced social media to publicise their innovative efforts. Some are commissioning research, employing academic advisers and inviting experts to give lectures to managers, staff and prisoners.

Perhaps the most concerted attempt to create a rehabilitative culture is at the recently opened HMP Berwyn, a £250m medium security prison in North Wales. Despite the standard limitations of prison design, attempts have been made at Berwyn to dramatically improve the physical environment.

This include large photographs and inspirational quotes on the walls, more colourful decor, and soft furniture in areas not usually associated with "soft" or "comfortable", such as the prisoner reception holding cells. Outdoor spaces have been enhanced with seating areas, trees, flowerbeds and bird boxes.

A New Prison Language

Berwyn has also implemented the new lexicon of the rehabilitative prison. Here, the prison's occupants are "men", not "prisoners". Those men are housed in "communities" rather than "blocks" and in "rooms" not "cells". Telephones and laptops have been introduced into these rooms, allowing men to access educational resources and arrange family visits.

Seeking to moderate the possible problems of scale (the prison can accommodate 2,106 men), management is committed to making "big feel small", using the layout to create discrete communities of 88 men (roughly the capacity of most Scandinavian prisons).

Since the beginning of its phased opening in February 2017, Berwyn has not been without controversy with reports of concerns over drugs and safety. And while many of the new initiatives are undeniably well meaning, their ability to rehabilitate remains a moot point. The effects of the efforts made in Berwyn may not be known for some time.

> The cells are unusual in having curved walls and furniture without sharp corners—to both minimize the risk of self harm and ensure optimum use of space.

Some argue that rehabilitation is a two-way social contract. The former offender must be willing to reintegrate into society – but society must do its part as well. The wider community must be open to employing ex-offenders, offering them decent housing, and generally helping them to have a future orientated outlook.

It is only then that the numerous harms done by life long forms of social exclusion—from the crime causing effects of imprisonment, to post-prison stigma—can be overcome and successfully maintained on release.

Print Citations

CMS: Jewkes, Yvonne. "How Lessons in Scandinavian Design Could Help Prisons with Rehabilitation." In *The Reference Shelf: U.S. National Debate Topic: 2020–2021 Criminal Justice Reform,* edited by Micah L. Issitt, 40-42. Amenia, NY: Grey House Publishing, 2020.

MLA: Jewkes, Yvonne. "How Lessons in Scandinavian Design Could Help Prisons with Rehabilitation." *The Reference Shelf: U.S. National Debate Topic: 2020–2021 Criminal Justice Reform,* edited by Micah L. Issitt, Grey House Publishing, 2020, pp. 40-42.

APA: Jewkes, Y. (2020). How lessons in Scandinavian design could help prisons with rehabilitation. In Micah L. Issitt (Ed.), *The reference shelf: U.S. national debate topic: 2020–2021 criminal justice reform* (pp. 40-42). Amenia, NY: Grey House Publishing.

White House Touts Prison Reforms but Throws Cold Water on Sentencing Bill

By C.J. Ciaramella
Reason, March 1, 2018

The White House has sent a list to Congress of its guiding principles for reforming the federal prison system and expanding reentry programs for inmates, the Associated Press reported Tuesday, but it declined to support a bipartisan bill that would overhauling federal sentencing guidelines.

In his State of the Union speech in January, Donald Trump said the White House would press for some reforms to the federal Bureau of Prisons and reentry programs that help inmates transition back into society.

"As America regains its strength, this opportunity must be extended to all citizens," Trump said. "That is why this year we will embark on reforming our prisons to help former inmates who have served their time get a second chance."

The *Washington Times* reported that the principles include, among others, expanding access to prison work programs, encouraging public-private partnerships that assist inmates both pre- and post-release, and prioritizing funding for federal programs with a proven track record of reducing recidivism in state prisons.

Criminal justice groups across the political spectrum have championed prison and reentry reform, including evangelical Christian organizations and business groups. Although Trump's presidential campaign was thick with tough-on-crime rhetoric, advocates found an influential ally in Jared Kushner, Trump's son-in-law and a senior White House adviser.

Kushner has been meeting with state officials, members of congress, and advocacy groups over the past year to discuss possible reforms to the federal prison system and ways to improve reentry programs and job prospects for former inmates. Last month, the White House also hosted a roundtable discussion on prison reform.

Absent from these discussion, however, have been any potential changes to federal sentencing guidelines, a bugaboo for law-and-order Republicans, most notably Attorney General Jeff Sessions.

Senate Judiciary Committee chairman Chuck Grassley (R-Iowa) has been working to pass a bipartisan sentencing reform bill, the Sentencing Reform and Corrections Act, for the past several years. The bill would reduce some federal mandatory minimum sentencing guidelines while eliminating none and adding several new ones. Nevertheless, it is considered by criminal justice reform advocates to be the best shot at passing major legislation on the issue in more than a decade.

The legislation passed out of the Senate Judiciary Committee by a bipartisan vote last month, despite Sessions sending a letter to the committee urging it to vote the bill down. The bill is now waiting to be scheduled for a floor vote in the Senate, but the White House appears to have little to no interest in throwing its weight behind it.

"The sentencing reform part still does not have a pathway forward to getting done," a White House official told reporters on a conference call, according to Reuters. "By doing this in smaller bits and pushing prison reform now, this has a better chance of getting done."

Speaking to Iowa reporters Wednesday, Grassley fired back: "This would be a bipartisan policy win for the Administration, and it seems like a no-brainer to me that we should get this done and the president would be backing it."

Instead, the administration is focusing on the so-called "back end" of the criminal justice system, arguing that improving education and job opportunities for soon-to-be released inmates will give them a better shot at being productive members of society and reduce the risk of them ending up back in prison.

> **Improving education and job opportunities for soon-to-be released inmates will give them a better shot at being productive members of society.**

Conservatives have been emboldened by prison reform experiments in red states such as Texas and Georgia, where Republican officials now boast of lower prison populations, lower crime, and big savings to taxpayers.

The White House guidelines "give broad-stroke best practices to signal to Congress what this administration is willing to do," says Derek Cohen, director of Right on Crime, a conservative criminal justice group that participated in several of the White House meetings.

There are currently two major bipartisan bills in Congress that would address the federal Bureau of Prisons and reentry programs.

In the Senate, John Cornyn (R-Tx.) has introduced the CORRECTIONS Act with Sen. Sheldon Whitehouse (D-R.I.). The bill would expand the ability of federal inmates to earn credits toward time in pre-release custody, as well as require the Bureau of Prisons to provide reentry and anti-recidivism programs to all inmates, among other provisions.

Meanwhile in the House, Rep. Doug Collins (R-Ga.) has introduced the Prison Reform and Redemption Act, which would also expand risk and needs assessments for inmates in federal prisons.

"For effective reform, you basically need everybody on board between the executive and Congress, and I think you're actually seeing that," Cohen says. "The bills vary in some significant ways, but where they overlap, you see the principles that the White House listed. If anything, I'm very optimistic about the future of this legislation and this effort more generally."

Democrats and progressive advocacy groups are less optimistic. Speaking at a forum on criminal justice hosted by *The Atlantic* on Wednesday, Sen. Cory Booker (D-N.J.), a Judiciary Committee member who voted in favor of the Sentencing Reform and Corrections Act, said "the landscape looks horrible to me, and we don't see an appetite for making these kind of changes."

But for conservative criminal justice reformers, having the high-profile support of the Trump White House on an issue like helping inmates get a second shot is reason enough to feel good.

Mark Holden, the general counsel of Koch Industries and another participant in the White House discussions, said in a statement the administration guidelines "will ensure that reforms to our system increase public safety, improve our communities, and strengthen families by creating second chances for individuals who want to become productive members of society."

Print Citations

CMS: Ciaramella, C.J. "White House Touts Prison Reform but Throws Cold Water on Sentencing Bill." In *The Reference Shelf: U.S. National Debate Topic: 2020–2021 Criminal Justice Reform,* edited by Micah L. Issitt, 43-45. Amenia, NY: Grey House Publishing, 2020.

MLA: Ciaramella, C.J. "White House Touts Prison Reform but Throws Cold Water on Sentencing Bill." *The Reference Shelf: U.S. National Debate Topic: 2020–2021 Criminal Justice Reform,* edited by Micah L. Issitt, Grey House Publishing, 2020, pp. 43-45.

APA: Ciaramella, C.J. (2020). White House touts prison reform but throws cold water on sentencing bill. In Micah L. Issitt (Ed.), *The reference shelf: U.S. national debate topic: 2020–2021 criminal justice reform* (pp. 43-45). Amenia, NY: Grey House Publishing.

3 Months into New Criminal Justice Law, Success for Some and Snafus for Others

By Ayesha Rascoe
NPR, April 1, 2019

After spending 15 years in prison for a drug offense, Randy Rader had almost lost hope that he might get out of prison before his release date in 2023.

If Rader's conviction for 5 grams of crack cocaine—his third drug offense—had happened after 2010, he would have received a much shorter sentence. But the 2010 Fair Sentencing Act, which cut down on the disparity between penalties for crack cocaine and powder cocaine, did not apply to those already serving time.

The First Step Act, passed with overwhelming bipartisan support by Congress in December, changed that, making the 2010 statute retroactive.

"They just came and told me, 'You're leaving,'" Rader said. "That was on a Monday. On a Friday, they let me go."

That was just a little more than a week ago. Now back home in Michigan with his mother, Rader is overjoyed to be free, though he's facing some challenges.

His mother lives on a fixed income, and money is tight. He's been rejected for food stamps because of his drug convictions, and he's struggling to even get an ID. His mom set up a GoFundMe page, and they're reaching out to groups that might be able to help Rader get back on his feet.

"I got like $30 to my name, period, and I don't have nothing else, no clothes, no nothing," he said. "I just keep telling myself: Stay focused, even if something blocks my way. Don't worry about it. We're going to figure it out another way."

Rader's struggles get at the heart of another key component of what the First Step Act is supposed to begin to address: preparing prisoners for life after incarceration so they don't return to confinement.

Uneven Implementation of the Law

The White House will be holding a summit Monday evening celebrating the law, which was hailed by President Trump in his State of the Union address this year as proof that the U.S. "believes in redemption."

Activists who backed passage of the law say that certain parts of the act are working as intended, but other parts seem to be facing delays and uncertainty.

"It's been a mixed bag," said Mark Holden, general counsel to Koch Industries, which has been a big supporter of the statute.

More than 500 inmates have been released thanks to the law so far.

Some have been freed based on the retroactive crack cocaine sentencing changes. Others have gotten out due to changes made to the way prisoners can petition for "compassionate release," which allows sentence reductions for severely ill inmates.

"There have been a number of people who have already benefited from the statutory reforms," Holden said. "That is a big deal, people getting out, getting back home."

The First Step Act is supposed to begin to address preparing prisoners for life after incarceration so they don't return to confinement.

Still, Holden and others raised concerns about implementation of key provisions in the law that call for development of rehabilitation and training programs for prisoners aimed at reducing recidivism.

These programs were never expected to be in place for the prisoners such as Rader released in the first months after passage of the law, but the goal is that they will eventually be widely available to the federal prison population.

As a part of the requirement for the expanded programs, the law mandated development of a risk and needs assessment tool that would be used to assess each inmate and determine what types of programs they could participate in and the incentives they could receive.

The tool is critical to imposing the new network of programming, but the Justice Department already has missed one deadline for development.

The attorney general must consult with an outside review committee about how to set up the risk assessment tool. This committee envisioned by the law was supposed to be stood up 30 days after First Step's enactment, but it has not yet been created.

With the committee not yet in place, there are questions about whether the government will meet the July deadline for developing the system.

Kevin Ring, president of Families Against Mandatory Minimums, says there hasn't been much clarity from the administration on the status of these measures.

"All the timelines were ambitious, so it's not surprising that they haven't met them all," Ring said. "It's just it seems to be a bit of a black box. We don't know what's taking so long."

Complicating matters further, Congress passed the law but has not appropriated funds for the initiative.

And the president's budget released earlier this year did not clearly request the $75 million that is needed to support the new criminal justice overhaul.

Despite that, a senior administration official said Trump is committed to working with Congress to fully fund and implement the law.

"We are hoping to get the independent review council in place as soon as possible," the official said.

The official blamed the 34-day government shutdown for contributing to delays but said there would not be a significant holdup.

Another official said the Justice Department is using resources it has on hand to work on the risk assessment tool internally, in the absence of the committee, and expects to meet the July deadline.

But the official acknowledged that Congress will need to provide money or approve shifting funds around in order for the agency to move ahead with the panel and other aspects of the law.

Ensuring that the money is available will be crucial to the effectiveness of the First Step Act, said Nancy La Vigne, head of justice policy at the Urban Institute.

"We always recognized that without proper funding, the First Step Act is really nothing more than window dressing," La Vigne said.

Print Citations

CMS: Rascoe, Ayesha. "3 Months into New Criminal Justice Law, Success for Some and Snafus for Others." In *The Reference Shelf: U.S. National Debate Topic: 2020–2021 Criminal Justice Reform,* edited by Micah L. Issitt, 46-48. Amenia, NY: Grey House Publishing, 2020.

MLA: Rascoe, Ayesha. "3 Months into New Criminal Justice Law, Success for Some and Snafus for Others." *The Reference Shelf: U.S. National Debate Topic: 2020–2021 Criminal Justice Reform,* edited by Micah L. Issitt, Grey House Publishing, 2020, pp. 46-48.

APA: Rascoe, A. (2020). 3 months into new criminal justice law, success for some and snafus for others. In Micah L. Issitt (Ed.), *The reference shelf: U.S. national debate topic: 2020–2021 criminal justice reform* (pp. 46-48). Amenia, NY: Grey House Publishing.

The Case Against Solitary Confinement

By Stephanie Wykstra
Vox, April 17, 2019

Albert Woodfox was held in solitary confinement for more than 40 years in a Louisiana prison before being released in 2016, when he was 69 years old. In his book *Solitary*, published last month, Woodfox writes that every morning, "I woke up with the same thought: will this be the day? Will this be the day I lose my sanity and discipline? Will I start screaming and never stop?"

Thousands of people—at least 61,000 on any given day and likely many thousands more than that—are in solitary confinement across the country, spending 23 hours per day in cells not much bigger than elevators. They are disproportionately young men, and disproportionately Hispanic and African American. The majority spend a few months in it, but at least a couple of thousand people have been in solitary confinement for six years or more. Some, like Woodfox, have been held for decades.

Solitary confinement causes extreme suffering, particularly over prolonged periods of months or years. Effects include anxiety, panic, rage, paranoia, hallucinations, and, in some cases, suicide.

The United Nations special rapporteur on torture, Juan E. Méndez, deemed that prolonged solitary confinement is a form of torture, and the UN's Mandela Rules dictate that it should never be used with youth and those with mental or physical disability or illness, or for anyone for more than 15 days. Méndez, who inspected prisons in many countries, wrote, "[I]t is safe to say that the United States uses solitary confinement more extensively than any other country, for longer periods, and with fewer guarantees."

Many practices in the US criminal justice system are harsh, ineffective, even absurd, from the widespread use of money bail to detain unconvicted people to extremely long sentences and parole terms, and a host of other outrages. But placing people in solitary stands out as a violation of human rights.

Well over a century ago in the US, the practice fell out of favor, partly because of its capacity for psychological harm. Yet starting in the 1980s, its use in prisons and jails exploded again.

Over the past decade, there has been a movement to (again) stop the widespread use of solitary. There have been major steps forward in some states. But there's considerable need for more progress—and wider acknowledgment that this is something that we are all accountable for. As Laura Rovner, a law professor at the University of Denver, put it in a recent talk, "We torture people here in America, tens of thousands of them every day … it's done in our names, with our tax dollars, behind closed doors."

A Brief History of Solitary Confinement

In the 1700s, religious groups, including the Quakers, thought that isolating people in their cells with a Bible would lead to repentance and rehabilitation. The Walnut Street Jail in Philadelphia expanded to include solitary cells in 1790, and other prisons and jails adopted the approach over the subsequent years.

A few decades later, the Eastern State Penitentiary in Pennsylvania opened in 1829, the first prison built entirely to keep people in solitary confinement. When Charles Dickens visited the facility about a decade later and met with people who were held in isolation, he wrote, "I hold this slow and daily tampering with the mysteries of the brain, to be immeasurably worse than any torture of the body."

In 1890, the Supreme Court heard a case in which a person had been held in isolation for a month while awaiting execution. The Court stated that this was "an additional punishment of the most important and painful character, and is therefore forbidden by this provision of the constitution of the United States," adding that experience with solitary confinement over the previous decades had shown the devastating results on people.

By the early 1900s, the practice had largely been abandoned, in part because it was seen as unethical and ineffective, and in part because it was much costlier.

But that was not to be the last word on solitary confinement. Nearly a century later, in the 1980s and '90s, the US prison system again took up the practice in full force.

This shift is commonly traced to October 22, 1983, at a federal prison in Marion, Illinois, when four guards were injured and two were killed by people housed in the prison. Administrators at the facility responded with a long-term "lockdown," in which everyone at Marion was held in their cells for 23 hours per day. The model used at Marion soon spread to other facilities across the country.

The federal and state prison systems began to construct "supermax" prisons, in which a unit of the facility (or the entire facility) is designed to hold hundreds of people in solitary confinement. Pelican Bay State Prison in California was the first newly constructed supermax prison to open, in 1989. Within 15 years, federal and state supermax prisons had opened in 44 states.

Why Solitary Came Back

Why did correctional institutions take up solitary confinement when it had been deemed ineffective and unacceptably cruel 100 years prior?

Researchers often point to a couple of main causes. First, there was a rise in "tough on crime" policies in the '80s and '90s. These policies led to many more people—disproportionately people of color—being locked up for long periods of time. Given subsequent overcrowding, corrections administrations were eager to find ways that, they argued, would increase safety and security for staff and incarcerated people.

In the same period, there was a shift in how incarceration was viewed by corrections staff and policymakers. The opinion that "nothing works" to rehabilitate people became popular, and prison was seen much more as a way to lock away dangerous people. (In an unfortunate turn of events, a researcher whose 1974 systematic review helped popularize the view that "nothing works" later found problems with his analysis and recanted, but his retraction was largely ignored.)

Poor data collection and secrecy surrounding solitary confinement over the years also may have played a role in allowing the practice to proliferate. That said, we do have some data. A Bureau of Justice Statistics analysis of the 2011-'12 National Inmate Survey (in both prisons and jails) estimated that about 18 to 20 percent of incarcerated people spent some time in solitary confinement in the course of a year. A National Institute of Justice report, using the number of people incarcerated in 2013, calculated that about half a million people spent some time in solitary confinement at some point in the year, or 90,000 on a given day.

The most recent nationwide estimate of 61,000 people in solitary on a given day in 2017 comes from a survey of state prisons and a few large urban jails, conducted by the Association of State Correctional Administrators and the Liman Center for Public Interest Law at Yale Law School. As Solitary Watch, a nonprofit that aims to raise awareness about the practice, and the researchers who conducted the survey point out, this estimate is likely to be considerably lower than the total number, given that it omits anyone held in solitary for less than 15 days, as well as those held in other facilities such as local jails, juvenile detention, and immigration detention centers.

Beyond lack of data transparency, many facilities—especially supermax prisons—are also largely closed off to observers. Some prisons forbid anyone who doesn't personally know a person housed there to visit. That restriction even included Méndez, the former UN special rapporteur on torture, who told Solitary Watch that he requested permission to visit prisons in the US for years without success.

What Is It Like in Solitary Confinement?

Researcher Sharon Shalev describes typical solitary confinement conditions in her 2009 book *Supermax: Controlling Risk Through Solitary Confinement*:

> Cells are about 7 or 8 feet by 10 feet in size (slightly bigger than the average bathroom or elevator)

> People are held in their cells for 22.5 to 24 hours per day; when let out, it is into a small, solitary outdoor cage with no recreational equipment

> No group activities or congregating with others

Very few activities or programs

Limited visitors, and then only through a thick glass barrier with no physical contact

Many firsthand accounts from people who have experienced solitary attest to these conditions.

Justice Rountree, who spent five years in solitary and is now an advocate with the New Jersey Campaign for Alternatives to Isolated Confinement, said in a recent panel that compared to regular prison, solitary "feels like losing your freedom."

Rountree and many others describe being kept awake by constant shouting and banging from others in cells. In many cells, there is no window, and sometimes even from the outdoor cage where they are allowed to go (by themselves) for an hour to pace back and forth, they can't see the sky. Shaka Senghor, who spent seven and a half years in solitary, described the smell as "defecation, unwashed armpits … [mingled] with the pepper spray officers use to extract prisoners from their cells." Some have even described how they begin to hallucinate.

Far from isolating only people who have been violent, it's very common for corrections to put people in solitary for trivial reasons. A 2015 report from the Vera Institute of Justice describes how "disruptive behavior—such as talking back, being out of place, failure to obey an order, failing to report to work or school, or refusing to change housing units or cells—frequently lands incarcerated people in disciplinary segregation."

Facilities vary as to what extent they allow people books and other materials while in solitary. Even if reading materials are allowed, they are often censored. In the absence of social connection, many people describe feeling unable to connect normally afterward. Sarah Shourd, who was held in solitary for more than a year in Iran, wrote, "… I couldn't look into another person's eyes without physical discomfort. … A touch on the shoulder made me flinch and tense up."

For some people, particularly teenagers and those with mental illness, this disconnection can be lasting. Kalief Browder was 16 when he was arrested for allegedly stealing a backpack in New York City. His family couldn't afford the bail, and he spent three years at a Rikers Island jail waiting for court hearings, two of them in solitary—where he tried to kill himself a number of times. After his charged were dropped and he went home, he isolated himself, often staying in his bedroom and pacing as he had done in solitary confinement.

At the age of 22, he died by suicide.

What Does Research Show about the Harms of Solitary Confinement?

Research over the past few decades has documented the effects of solitary confinement. In congressional testimony in 2012, psychologist Craig Haney summarized: "Most of the research has reached remarkably similar conclusions about the adverse psychological consequences of solitary confinement."

Haney gives the example of his 2003 study of 100 randomly selected people held at Pelican Bay, the supermax prison in California. Haney found that virtually all of his interviewees reported heightened anxiety, irrational anger and irritability, confused thought processes, and being extremely sensitive to external stimuli. Some 70 percent felt themselves to be on the verge

> **Solitary confinement causes extreme suffering… effects include anxiety, panic, rage, paranoia, hallucinations, and, in some cases, suicide.**

of a nervous breakdown, about 40 percent experienced hallucinations, and just under a third reported suicidal thoughts.

According to Haney, these symptoms closely matched other studies of people held in solitary confinement for a period of months to years, and were much more severe than in general populations of prisons and jails. Haney and other psychologists including Stuart Grassian have long argued that these symptoms develop and increase while people are confined in solitary, rather than merely being preexisting symptoms.

The desperation that people feel in solitary confinement can lead to psychological breakdown, self-harm, and suicide. A 2014 study of New York City jails found that while only about 7 percent of people spent time in solitary confinement, they accounted for nearly half of all acts of potentially fatal self-harm. Studies have shown that a quarter of suicides (or even more) behind bars occur in solitary confinement.

The risks of extreme harm to people in solitary are greater for vulnerable groups, such as those with mental illness and disabilities. In 2012, the American Psychiatric Association released a statement saying that with rare exceptions, people with serious mental illness should not be placed in solitary.

Yet prisons and jails very often do just that. In a Bureau of Justice Statistics analysis of data in 2011-'12, nearly 30 percent of those held in solitary in prisons reported severe psychological distress, with a further 20 to 23 percent reporting mood and anxiety disorders.

There's also widespread agreement among researchers that the risks to young people in solitary confinement are particularly severe. Depriving young people of sensory and social contact has a heightened risk of serious and lasting effects. The federal system and many states are restricting the duration of solitary confinement or banning solitary confinement for youth, but in recent years, the practice has still been common in prisons and juvenile detention facilities in some states.

Not all researchers hold the same view about the harms of solitary confinement. Some are more skeptical about past research showing serious harms, and they question how much we can infer from studies that often lack a comparable control group. In recent years, some researchers have also pointed to a 2011 study in Colorado that purported to show evidence that those in solitary for months to a year fared no worse psychologically than similar people in the general population of the prison.

They also point to two systematic reviews that combine the results of only studies that directly compare those in solitary confinement to those in a control group.

Both reviews claim that after pooling those studies, solitary has only a modest negative impact on mental health. In response, Haney and others have pointed to a number of serious methodological problems with the systematic reviews and with the Colorado study.

Does Solitary Confinement Do What It Purports to Do?

Let's sidestep this debate and ask a different question: What's the evidence that solitary confinement achieves positive results?

Corrections departments have long argued that solitary is effective at maintaining safety and security in prisons. But the evidence does not support this view.

A 2016 report from the National Institute of Justice stated, "There is little evidence that administrative segregation has had effects on overall levels of violence within individual institutions or across correctional systems."

The few studies on the impacts of increased solitary confinement do not show a reduction in violence among people held in the facilities. For example, a 2006 study of three states that opened supermax prisons showed no subsequent statewide reduction in violence among those housed at the prisons.

Furthermore, there's little evidence that solitary meaningfully improves safety for staff in prisons and jails. To be sure, correctional officers have an extremely difficult job, and it's important that they are able to go to work without being in danger. Many who work in corrections believe that solitary confinement plays a role in keeping them safe. As Gary Mohr, director of Ohio Department of Rehabilitation and Correction, wrote, "[O]ur staff, those who work in the trenches of our prisons, firmly believe the use of restrictive housing as a default disciplinary sanction is tied directly to their safety."

However, as in the case with violence in prisons generally, there is no strong evidence that solitary is keeping officers safer. The 2016 National Institute of Justice report found that few studies have focused on the effect of solitary confinement on subsequent misconduct (including violence against staff). A large study in Ohio found no evidence of any effect of solitary on subsequent violent misbehavior. In states like Colorado and North Dakota, which have dramatically reduced the number of people in solitary confinement over the past several years, corrections directors report that there has not been an increase in violent incidents against corrections staff. And while the 2006 study of three states that opened supermax prisons did show a reduction in violent incidents against staff in one of the three states (Illinois), it found no effect in Minnesota and an increase in such incidents in Arizona.

There is a legitimate question of how to protect vulnerable people, such as people with disabilities, LGBTQ people, and others, in prisons. Protecting such populations has often been given as a reason for using solitary.

But there are other options. The Vera Institute, which has worked with corrections departments across a number of states on reducing solitary, reports on effective ways to keep people safe other than solitary confinement. Vera, along with the American Civil Liberties Union and the American Bar Association, recommends keeping people in a safe, separate area of the facility with others, and with full access to programming and services. As far as putting youth in solitary confinement within adult facilities to keep them safe, advocates argue that they shouldn't be in adult prisons to begin with.

Finally, advocates often point out that the vast majority of people housed in solitary will be returning to the community, where they are expected to function. Solitary makes that transition even more difficult.

Abandoning Solitary Confinement. Again.

Over the past decade, there's been a surge of attention and reform on solitary confinement. Advocacy groups have been pushing for change, including the National Religious Campaign Against Torture, California Families to Abolish Solitary Confinement, and the New York Campaign for Alternatives to Isolated Confinement.

The Vera Institute has worked with a number of jurisdictions on reforming their practices. Among the group's recommendations are that solitary confinement should:

> Never be used on vulnerable groups such as those under 18, pregnant women, and those with mental illness or mental/physical disabilities

> Rarely be used as discipline, and then only for violent offenses

> Used with the least restrictive conditions possible, providing access to medical and mental health care outside of the cell, visitors and phone calls, and daily hours of programming with other people

> Never be used directly prior to releasing someone back into the community.

In 2016, President Obama reformed the use of solitary confinement in federal facilities, including banning it for those under 18 and limits on its use for adults. But since the federal system holds about a tenth of the people incarcerated in the US, these reforms only affect a small number of the total held in solitary confinement.

Some reforms have been driven by actions from within prisons and litigation. For example, thousands of people held in Pelican Bay and other prisons in California participated in a series of hunger strikes in 2011 and 2013, protesting their treatment, including the application of indefinite solitary confinement.

In 2012, the Center for Constitutional Rights filed a federal class-action lawsuit (*Ashker v. Governor of California*), resulting in a 2015 settlement that required California's corrections department to release many of those who had been in long-term solitary and to reform their rules.

Other lawsuits in recent years have succeeded in banning and restricting solitary, largely focused on vulnerable groups such as youth, people with mental health issues, and pregnant women. However, as in California, it's been clear that corrections sometimes try to find ways around new rules.

There's also been a wave of legislation at the state level. So far, state bills have largely secured protections for people in vulnerable groups, or have mandated (at the very least) that prisons report data on their use of solitary confinement. However, two states — New York and New Jersey—are considering bills that offer sweeping reforms for everyone who is incarcerated.

Finally, internal change is also taking place within some corrections departments. In 2016, the American Correctional Association—a nonprofit that provides guidelines to corrections departments and facilities across the US—issued new standards on restrictive housing (its term for solitary confinement). These included banning its use for more than 30 days for pregnant women, people with serious mental illness, and young people under 18. Many jurisdictions reported that they were changing their policies as a result of the new guidelines.

A few corrections departments went much further to improve their policies. In 2017, Colorado put into place some of the most progressive policies in the country, limiting solitary confinement to the UN standard of no more than 15 days. North Dakota is another state that has significantly reformed its use of solitary confinement.

When thinking through the movement against solitary confinement, we should see it within the broader context of our criminal justice system. Hugely important changes — such as reforms to bail, parole/probation, and sentencing—will likely go a long way to reducing people in solitary confinement, since there will be fewer people in prisons and jails to begin with. Amy Fettig, the deputy director for the ACLU's National Prison Project and Director of the ACLU's Stop Solitary campaign, told me, "We have to get people out of prison, and we have to get people out of solitary confinement. [Both are] part of a systematic effort ... we're confronting a system that is so profoundly broken in so many ways that you can't fix one problem without fixing the others."

The Supreme Court has stated that what counts as "cruel and unusual punishment" in the Eighth Amendment must "draw its meaning from the evolving standards of decency that mark the progress of a maturing society."

Have our "standards of decency" evolved enough for us to stop this practice?

Print Citations

CMS: Wykstra, Stephanie. "The Case Against Solitary Confinement." In *The Reference Shelf: U.S. National Debate Topic: 2020–2021 Criminal Justice Reform,* edited by Micah L. Issitt, 49-56. Amenia, NY: Grey House Publishing, 2020.

MLA: Wykstra, Stephanie. "The Case Against Solitary Confinement." *The Reference Shelf: U.S. National Debate Topic: 2020–2021 Criminal Justice Reform,* edited by Micah L. Issitt, Grey House Publishing, 2020, pp. 49-56.

APA: Wykstra, S. (2020). The case against solitary confinement. In Micah L. Issitt (Ed.), *The reference shelf: U.S. national debate topic: 2020–2021 criminal justice reform* (pp. 49-56). Amenia, NY: Grey House Publishing.

3
Privatization and Mass Incarceration

Zboralski, via Wikimedia.

Private prisons and prison labor have been controversial since their inception. California's San Quentin Prison, built by inmates of the prison ship *Waban* to house themselves in 1852, is still in operation today and still partly administered privately.

The Incarceration Problem

Since the late twentieth century, America's prison population has been growing at an unsustainable rate, leading to overpopulation and the inability of states and the federal government to effectively manage the prison population. The effort to address this situation has led to the rise of private prisons—corporations that profit from imprisonment—and to an industry that politically promotes more aggressive conviction rates. Many of the debates in criminal justice—racial bias in policing and the courts, sentencing reform, human rights debates, the emergence and development of criminal justice technology—are directly or indirectly connected to mass incarceration, and finding solutions for managing the mass incarceration problem therefore has the potential to significantly alter many of America's perennial criminal justice issues.

The Scope of the Problem

According to the American Civil Liberties Union (ACLU), the incarcerated population in the United States has grown by more than 700 percent since 1970, with more than 2.3 million imprisoned across the country. Though accounting for only 4 percent of the world's population, the United States houses an estimated 22 percent of the world's imprisoned population.[1] While the United States is one of the wealthiest and most prosperous nations in the world, numerous studies prove that, in terms of incarceration rates, the United States is more similar to developing and authoritarian nations than to nations of similar socioeconomic status.

According to a *Washington Post* report, 716 out of every 100,000 Americans is in prison, compared to rates of below 150 per 100,000 in the majority of the world's nations. When comparing the United States only to other nations with similar systems of crime and justice, it is an outlier, imprisoning more people at a more rapid rate than any other developed nation. Further, the International Crime Victims Survey found that the nation's high incarceration rate does not correlate with rates of crime. America has similar rates of crime to most of the nations in Western Europe but has nearly four times the incarceration rate.[2]

The question of who goes to jail in America is complex. One major factor is the incarceration of nonviolent drug offenders, who comprise roughly one fifth or 20 percent of the incarcerated population. A significant number of America's incarcerated are imprisoned for low-level offenses, and more than 25 percent of the prison population spend time in jails and holding facilities because of misdemeanor charges. Further, America's prison population is high in part because individuals who cannot afford bail or legal representation often spend months incarcerated while awaiting trial. A factor contributing to the nation's high incarceration rates is the imprisonment of more low-level offenders than most nations of similar socioeconomic characteristics. However, lowering incarceration rates for low-level offenses will not solve the incarceration problem. Studies indicate that a majority of America's incarcerated population are incarcerated at the state, rather than federal, level and that the majority are incarcerated for violent offenses. For those interested in addressing mass incarceration, therefore, it is important to find ways to lower levels of violent crime incarceration without endangering public safety.[3]

Many factors have contributed to America's mass incarceration problem. Historically, mass incarceration was part of a movement within America's conservative political network to address the rise in violent crime during the late 1960s and early 1970s. At the time, some politicians argued that America needed to invest in social welfare systems to address the underlying roots of criminal activity. Others opted for a stricter focus on "law and order, often called the "get tough on crime" strategy. This approach typically involves increasing penalties for a variety of crimes and adding mandatory minimum sentences in an attempt to make the cost of criminal activity more significant. These policies benefit politicians and appeal to common sense notions about the underlying causes of crime, but have proven ineffective at reducing crime rates. The primary impact of the get tough strategy was a massive increase in the incarcerated population, an increase in longer-term incarceration, and a reduction of investment in social welfare systems to address the factors underlying criminal activity. The United States social services system is underdeveloped in comparison to economically similar nations.

Further, America's mass incarceration problem reflects the nation's other pressing socioeconomic challenges, like income inequality, poverty, and race. America is unique in the degree to which its criminal justice system is monetized. Fees for court costs, drug testing, legal representation, etc., contribute to the incarceration rate by exacerbating low-level offenses. Finding long-term solutions to mass incarceration might therefore require implementing policies that address America's long-standing socioeconomic problems.

Free Market Justice

It is a myth that the privatization of prisons is the key factor in America's mass incarceration problem. Less than 9 percent of America's incarcerated population are in private institutions. The vast majority of prisons and jails are publicly owned. In a 2015 report for the Prison Policy Initiative, Peter Wagner argued that private prisons were not so much driving mass incarceration as they were a "parasite on the publicly owned prison system."[4]

Private prisons have played a role in the American criminal justice system since the nineteenth century. The state of Louisiana was a pioneer, privatizing the state prison system in 1844, only nine years after the state's first prison began operation. Historians have found that this experiment encouraged prison administrators to eliminate provisions designed at enhancing rehabilitation or reformation and reduce resources for prisoners in order to save costs. Prisoners in private prisons were used as slave laborers with prisons taking contracts from labor companies to increase their profit. In the late 1800s, the largest factory in the state of Texas was the nation's first penitentiary, which supplied textiles across the country.[5]

The prison reform movement of the early twentieth century led to reduced emphasis on privatization and an increased emphasis on prison rehabilitation, causing private prisons to fall out of favor. The industry resurged in the 1980s as part of President Ronald Reagan's get tough on crime strategy, which included reducing the costs of criminal justice by eliminating social services. The idea was that private prisons would create a better incarceration system thanks to free-market competition and because such institutions would be governed by individuals incentivized to maintain effectiveness. Further, it was argued that private prisons are more likely to improve over time because management can face fines or other penalties for mismanagement. Several studies indicated that states using private prisons can decrease costs associated with incarceration, but the Bureau of Justice Statistics (BJS) report from 2017 indicated that states have not, over the past fifty years, saved significantly from privatizing incarceration. There is also little evidence to suggest that private prisons are more effectively operated in comparison to public prisons.

Whether or not private prisons are driving mass incarceration, the growth of the private prison system is one of the biggest controversies in criminal justice. Private prison companies and investors lobby for policies that increase incarceration rates. Some critics find such an effort unconscionable given the crisis of mass incarceration that the nation faces. Individuals who favor a rehabilitative rather than punitive approach to criminal justice object to the spread of private imprisonment and the influence of the companies involved in this system.

The financial incentives to increase incarceration rates also expand beyond the companies directly involved in creating and managing private prisons. States and cities profit from the private prison system by renting space to private prison companies. Further, the privatization of the incarceration system has led to an increase in private outsourcing of prison facilities and services. Increasingly, prison food and health care systems have been outsourced to private companies and this has led to major problems, including inadequate medical care. A 2016 study found that the overall U.S. life expectancy would be ten years higher if it weren't for the poor healthcare outcomes in the U.S. prison system.[6] Prisons now regularly seek to profit from prisoners by charging them for healthcare services, telecom services, and some food services, and this has meant transferring some of the costs onto prisoners and their families. Critics of privatization argue that this decreases the likelihood of successful rehabilitation and contributes to a cycle of repeated incarceration, as individuals already facing disadvantages in employment and economic opportunity are faced with further debt and consequent legal problems.

Solutions and Strategies

Mass incarceration is a difficult problem to combat because of the many factors involved. From sentencing guidelines, to the efforts of profiteers lobbying for the for-profit criminal justice industry, to the enduring popularity of the "get tough on crime" philosophy, mass incarceration has numerous causes. This helps explain why no single solution or strategy has been forthcoming. Because so many Americans now profit from the way that the criminal justice system operates, proposals for reforms meet with significant resistance. Some politicians and members of the public have also expressed reluctance to embrace reforms because they fear that changes to the system will lead to systemic dysfunction and potentially increase crime rates. It is also because the problems with the system are so complex and dynamic that debates in the field are important. With politicians often stuck in ideological deadlock, the more that researchers, experts in policy, and social activists debate and explore the problem, the more likely that innovative compromises and solutions may be found and eventually matriculate into American politics.

Works Used

Bauer, Shane. "The True History of America's Private Prison Industry." *Time*. Sep 25, 2018. Retrieved from https://time.com/5405158/the-true-history-of-americas-private-prison-industry/.

Lopez, German. "Mass Incarceration in America, Explained in 22 Maps and Charts." *Vox*. Oct 11, 2016. Retrieved from https://www.vox.com/2015/7/13/8913297/mass-incarceration-maps-charts.

"Mass Incarceration." *ACLU*. American Civil Liberties Union. 2019. Retrieved from https://www.aclu.org/issues/smart-justice/mass-incarceration.

Wagner, Peter. "Are Private Prisons Driving Mass Incarceration?" *Prison Policy Initiative*. Oct 7, 2015. Retrieved from https://www.prisonpolicy.org/blog/2015/10/07/private_prisons_parasite/.

Widra, Emily. "Incarceration Shortens Life Expectancy." *Prison Policy Initiative*. Jun 26, 2017. Retrieved from https://www.prisonpolicy.org/blog/2017/06/26/life_expectancy/.

Ye Hee Lee, Michelle. "Yes, U.S. Locks People Up at a Higher Rate Than Any Other Country." *The Washington Post*. Jul 7, 2015. Retrieved from https://www.washingtonpost.com/news/fact-checker/wp/2015/07/07/yes-u-s-locks-people-up-at-a-higher-rate-than-any-other-country/.

Notes

1. "Mass Incarceration," *ACLU*.
2. Ye Hee Lee, "Yes, U.S. Locks People Up at a Higher Rate Than Any Other Country."
3. Lopez, "Mass Incarceration in America, Explained in 22 Maps and Charts."
4. Wagner, "Are Private Prisons Driving Mass Incarceration?"
5. Bauer, "The True History of America's Private Prison Industry."
6. Widra, "Incarceration Shortens Life Expectancy."

What Democrats Get Wrong about Prison Reform

By John Pfaff

Politico, **August 14, 2019**

Democrats generally agree that to end mass incarceration we must stop punishing drug crimes, especially for marijuana, so harshly. During the most recent Democratic presidential debate, for example, Vice President Joe Biden argued that we shouldn't send people to prison for drug crimes. Senator Cory Booker then talked about marijuana enforcement and "marijuana justice." Governor Jay Inslee discussed pardoning people with drug convictions, while Representative Tulsi Gabbard criticized Senator Kamala Harris for sending people to jail for marijuana crimes when Harris was the district attorney in San Francisco, and Harris defended herself by saying she favors not just decriminalization but legalization of marijuana.

But in their rush to sound strong on criminal justice reform, the candidates left out one important fact.

Drug crime is not what's driving the high prison population in the United States. It's crimes of violence. And this omission has consequences. It means that any "solution" is unlikely to achieve its intended goal and in the meantime society will continue to suffer long-term damage—physical, psychological and economic—from a persistent cycle of unaddressed violent crime.

The numbers are unambiguous.

For all the attention we pay to people convicted of drug crimes, they make up only 15 percent of our state prison populations. Over half the people serving time in state prisons have been convicted of a violent crime; half of those convicted of violence—or more than 25 percent of all prisoners—have been convicted of the most serious crimes: murder, manslaughter or sexual assault. Senator Booker (rightly) disagreed with locking people up for life on drug charges, but that's something that really happens only in the relatively small federal prison system. In state prisons, which hold nearly 90 percent of the nation's 1.5 million prisoners, almost 95 percent of inmates serving long sentences have been convicted of serious violence, not drugs; about half or more of such inmates were convicted of murder or manslaughter.

All this actually understates the extent to which it is our response to violence, not drugs, that drives mass incarceration. That 15 percent number means that 15 percent of the people in prison were convicted of a drug crime; the underlying facts might be more complicated. Someone, say, arrested for assault and found to have drugs on him at the time of the arrest might agree to a deal in which he pleads guilty to just the drug charge. In the data, this person shows up as a "nonviolent drug offender," even if the prosecutor demanded prison time on the drug offense only because of the uncharged violence.

This feature actually lurks in the aggregate national data. The share of people in state prisons for drugs did not really start rising until the mid-1980s, and it then began to decline in the early 1990s. These trends seem far more closely linked to patterns in violent crime—particularly the sharp spike in violence in the mid- to late 1980s and then its steady decline over the 1990s and 2000s—than to changes in drug laws, enforcement or use.

Moreover, the significant role that violent crime plays in boosting prison populations is not just the result of the longer sentences imposed on those convicted of such crimes, although that matters (especially for homicide cases). Violent crimes increasingly explain the total number of people we admit to prison every year, as well. In fact, as of 2011 (the most recent year with good data), state prison admissions for violent crimes were about 15 percent larger than those for drug offenses, a gap that has surely grown in recent years as we continue to reduce sanctions for drugs but not violence.

> **Drug crime is not what's driving the high prison population in the United States. It's crimes of violence.**

Now, to be clear, sending fewer people to prison for drugs is a good idea. Incarceration—especially in the cruel, brutal places that American prisons are—is inarguably harsh and counterproductive for drug cases, even if we accept (as many now no longer do) that drugs, including marijuana, should remain illegal.

But any sort of substantial reduction in prison populations means eventually changing how we punish violence, and unfortunately much of our "drug" talk actually undermines such efforts. We should push to send fewer people to prison for drugs, but we have to do it in a way that doesn't make the inevitable focus on violence more difficult.

This is why the back-and-forth in the debate bothered me. Criminal justice outcomes are driven primarily by city, county and state policies; the federal government's direct role is generally quite slight. But the messaging power of nationally televised debates, not to mention the president's bully pulpit—can matter quite a bit.

And the focus in the debates on drugs likely did more harm than good. Americans already remain quite reluctant to change how we punish violence, in no small part because they misperceive the importance of drugs. A 2016 poll by *Vox*, for example, reported that a majority of Americans incorrectly think about half (not 15 percent) of people in prison are there for drugs. Compounding that misperception, *Vox* reported, a majority of liberals, moderates and conservatives alike said they did not favor reductions in prison time for people convicted of violent crimes but who pose little to no risk of re-offending. Are they less inclined to treat one-time violent offenders more leniently because they erroneously believe high incarceration rates can be solved by dealing with drug crime alone? I would argue that is exactly what's happening. It's understandable that people would reach for a solution that avoids having to deal with complex issues about, say, victims and safety.

Hearing the candidates debate drug policy but ignore violence only reinforces the public's sense that drugs are central to mass incarceration and that violence is not an issue we need to confront.

Both takes are wrong.

Now, of course, given the public's reluctance to think about violence, there's some risk to the politician who runs ahead of the pack to talk about it. But that, then, just creates a nasty vicious circle: The public doesn't want to change how we address violence, so no politician is willing to talk about how we need to change the way we address violence, so the public never learns that we need to rethink our approaches to violence, so attitudes stay fixed. And we remain mired where we are.

And to be clear, changing how we approach violence is not just numerically justified, but actually good policy. The data consistently shows that tough prison sentences provide little additional deterrence over far less aggressive approaches, and often that spending more time in prison actually elevates the risk of future violence and offending, thanks to the traumatic nature of American prisons. Time spent in prison also undermines well-documented pathways out of violence, such as forming stable long-term relationships and gainful employment. And more and more research highlights programs that reduce violence and victimization in more effective—and humane—ways.

On top of being ineffective, prisons impose a vast array of poorly estimated but quite staggering social costs. Each year in prison can reduce life expectancy by up to two years. Prisons impose severe financial and emotional hardships not just on the inmate but on his family and children and friends. Incarceration undermines parenting and relationships, and it is often a vector for diseases and STDs. In some cases, we've sent enough people from a single area to prison that it alters the social and economic dynamics of entire neighborhoods.

Furthermore, a growing number of victims themselves increasingly say that they would prefer policies that focus less on harsh punishment and more on the root causes of crime. One recent survey of hundreds of crime victims, for example, reported that six in 10 favored more spending on prevention and rehabilitation and less on prisons. The growing (if still nascent) popularity of restorative justice programs, which aim to bring together victim, injurer and the broader community to work out how the injurer can make amends—even in cases of serious violence and even homicide—also points out how even those most affected by violence often resist the punitive policies we currently use.

Here's a final example of just how vast our prisons are, and just how unavoidable violence is to any discussion of criminal justice reform. If we freed everyone in prison tomorrow except that 25 percent who are there for murder, manslaughter or sexual assault, we'd still have an incarceration rate higher than that of almost every

European country. Any effort to normalize our outsize reliance on incarceration will have to move past drugs. And we need leaders who are willing to help us get there.

Print Citations

CMS: Pfaff, John. "What Democrats Get Wrong about Prison Reform." In *The Reference Shelf: U.S. National Debate Topic: 2020–2021 Criminal Justice Reform,* edited by Micah L. Issitt, 63-66. Amenia, NY: Grey House Publishing, 2020.

MLA: Pfaff, John. "What Democrats Get Wrong about Prison Reform." *The Reference Shelf: U.S. National Debate Topic: 2020–2021 Criminal Justice Reform,* edited by Micah L. Issitt, Grey House Publishing, 2020, pp. 63-66.

APA: Pfaff, J. (2020). What Democrats get wrong about prison reform. In Micah L. Issitt (Ed.), *The reference shelf: U.S. national debate topic: 2020–2021 criminal justice reform* (pp. 63-66). Amenia, NY: Grey House Publishing.

Who Profits from Our Prison System?

By Michelle Chen
The Nation, August 9, 2018

The US prison system, now home to over 2 million Americans, runs like an economy unto itself: From the cafeteria line to the phone line to the assembly line, a steady stream of money is fueling our incarceration complex. But who profits off prisoners remains a trade secret.

That's why advocates for criminal-justice reform are now harnessing big data to map out the carceral state, exposing the corporate networks that administer and finance the prison industry while driving its expansion. The Corrections Accountability Project of the Urban Justice Center (where, full disclosure, this author once interned) presents a kind of yellow pages of criminal justice, revealing the convoluted, self-serving mechanics of industrialized incarceration.

The prison economy rests on an opaque, often unaccountable economic infrastructure, with its own private-equity financiers, holding companies, and multinational executives. Since the financial transactions driving incarceration are typically private and unregulated, according to CAP director Bianca Tylek, their analysis aims "to help people understand just how big this space is," particularly because, often, "companies spend their money in a way to further entrench or expand the use of our criminal-legal system, and who it ends up touching."

With millions of lives touched by criminal-justice institutions every day—the families and communities of the incarcerated, a sprawling public force, scores of private government contractors—prisons are an increasingly lucrative investment opportunity.

Today, major private corporations administer services ranging from medical-record keeping to surveillance to psychiatric counseling. GEO and CoreCivic provide full-scale management and security services at private state facilities as well as immigration-detention centers. They have lately branched into "Community Corrections," which provides social programming following release, such as court-ordered treatment and halfway houses. Sequel Youth & Family Services provides extensive private juvenile-detention and counseling programs.

Israeli-based Attenti, formerly known as 3M, now operates under private-equity firm Apax Partners, yielding tens of millions from electronic monitoring services. Vocational programs for training inmates in blue-collar trades provide a combination of rehabilitation and behavioral management.

But beyond direct in-house services, the CAP report points to various complex financing entities that fuel a built-in incentive to consolidate, monopolize, and expand the incarceration system and the sentencing and legal processes that keep it humming.

Like any industry-growth model, prisons have fundamental internal incentives to achieve economies of scale by expanding their operations and accruing more state funds. Yet CAP focuses its critique (as does the American Friends Service Committee) on the absence of democratic control and oversight over the commercial operations of mass incarceration, which is often detached from any reasonable public-justice priority and represents a wider pattern of corporate impunity across the criminal-justice system.

Even if prisons are run technically in accordance with official regulations, rights groups are wary of intrinsic profit incentives that border on corporate criminality. For example, Tylek explains, prison-industry lobbyists have been known to actively promote the campaigns of anti-immigration hard-liners, as well as harsh anti-marijuana policies—which in turn fuel fresh "demand" for new prison beds and facilities.

"What we even consider a crime," Tylek says, "is highly shaped by corporate influence.... And the question there becomes, is that how we want crime to be defined, [who decides it] and then who's targeted by that." Harsh policing and sentencing standards for drug-related violations, nonviolent property crimes, and other offenses associated with the young and poor have driven mass incarceration since the 1980s. All the while, Wall Street's white-collar criminals are hardly ever prosecuted—the same kinds of investors who plow money into the prison business, and the same powerful social elite who help drive political discourse that systematically vilifies poor communities, immigrants, and people of color.

> **Prison economy rests on an opaque, often unaccountable economic infrastructure, with its own private-equity financiers, holding companies, and multinational executives.**

Tylek says that the combination of privatization and consolidation over the last three decades, reinforced by the industry's well-funded political champions in Congress and state legislatures, are the product of a private-equity financial network that is "obscured from the public. So they've been able to buy up companies... growing their market share consistently larger." Every time money is wired from an immigration jail through Western Union or blood is drawn by a health-care provider controlled by a private-equity group, it takes a bit off the top. "Their entire business model, is actually dependent on poverty."

The new generation of prison-data mapping elucidates both the commercialization of imprisonment and the social cost of punishment. It doesn't aim to expose any particular smoking gun but rather, to expose how much is at stake in each prison cell, which ultimately represents an individual's life. Naming, mapping, and measuring the system drives forward the public conversation about what society's priorities should be as more communities seek to reform toward a more open, democratic, and humane society. To decarcerate society, we must recognize that we're not just politically implicated in its abuses but economically invested as well.

Print Citations

CMS: Chen, Michelle. "Who Profits from Our Prison System?" In *The Reference Shelf: U.S. National Debate Topic: 2020–2021 Criminal Justice Reform,* edited by Micah L. Issitt, 67-69. Amenia, NY: Grey House Publishing, 2020.

MLA: Chen, Michelle. "Who Profits from Our Prison System?" *The Reference Shelf: U.S. National Debate Topic: 2020–2021 Criminal Justice Reform,* edited by Micah L. Issitt, Grey House Publishing, 2020, pp. 67-69.

APA: Chen, M. (2020). Who profits from our prison system? In Micah L. Issitt (Ed.), *The reference shelf: U.S. national debate topic: 2020–2021 criminal justice reform* (pp. 67-69). Amenia, NY: Grey House Publishing.

Here's Why Abolishing Private Prisons Isn't a Silver Bullet

By Mia Armstrong
The Marshall Project, September 12, 2019

Democratic candidates for president are fed up with the American criminal justice system, and private prisons are a favorite culprit. Cory Booker called them "repugnant." Bernie Sanders wrote that the industry has "racist roots in American chattel slavery." Elizabeth Warren released a plan to ban private prisons and detention facilities and to prohibit contractors from charging for an array of services including phone calls, bank transfers, health care, and probation services. Kamala Harris, a former prosecutor who has faced criticism of her criminal justice record, tweeted recently that "phasing out detention centers and private prisons" would be one of her first acts as president.

And it's not just candidates—JPMorgan Chase, Wells Fargo and Bank of America have all taken steps to end their financial relationships with private prison companies. Universities and cities have launched divestment campaigns. In 2016, the Obama administration announced the Federal Bureau of Prisons would phase out its use of private prisons, though the decision was reversed by the Trump administration shortly after.

Despite their infamy, private prisons house less than a twelfth of the country's prisoners. What is more common is public prisons deciding to outsource services—healthcare, food, communication—to private companies. That's to say, private companies still have a direct impact on the lives of incarcerated people throughout the U.S., but their role is slightly more complicated.

How Many People Are Serving Time in Private Prisons?

In 2017, 8.2 percent of U.S. prisoners—121,420 people—were held in private prisons, according to the most recent data from the Bureau of Justice Statistics. This works out to about 15 percent of federal prisoners and 7 percent of state prisoners at the time. At least 27 states incarcerated people in private facilities, and eight of those states used private facilities to house at least 15 percent of their prison populations (not all states reported data). Montana topped that list with 38 percent of prisoners in private facilities.

Still, across the country the Sentencing Project found that between 2000 and 2016, "the number of people housed in private prisons increased five times faster than the total prison population," while the "proportion of people detained in private immigration facilities increased by 442 percent."

Although private facilities are the exception, not the rule, when it comes to prisons, the opposite is true for immigration detention facilities. According to the Detention Watch Network, more than 70 percent of immigration detainees are held in facilities operated by private companies.

How Do Private Companies Operate within Public Prisons?

We know that the majority of prisoners serve time in publicly run systems. But private companies still loom over their time there. This is because public prisons contract with private companies to provide a variety of services—healthcare, food, transportation, financial services and messaging, phone and video calls, to name a few. Private companies are also making big investments in reentry, electronic monitoring and drug treatment programs.

Which Companies Are We Talking About?

The most dominant companies running corrections facilities in the U.S. are CoreCivic (formerly the Corrections Corporation of America), the GEO Group and Management & Training Corporation (MTC). But there are many other companies involved in the criminal legal system in a variety of different ways. In April, Worth Rises published a report identifying roughly 4,000 private sector companies in this area.

How Did We Get Here?

Private prisons as we know them today started opening up shop in the U.S. in the 1980s, coinciding with booming prison populations. CoreCivic, then Corrections Corporation of America, was founded in 1983 and began operating facilities in Tennessee

This increased capacity thanks to growth of private prisons allowed officials to avoid wrestling with how to reduce prison populations.

in 1984. From there, private prison companies took off, expanding the capacity of increasingly overburdened carceral systems.

This increased capacity thanks to growth of private prisons allowed officials to avoid wrestling with how to reduce prison populations, said Lauren-Brooke Eisen, author of *Inside Private Prisons: An American Dilemma in the Age of Mass Incarceration*.

Still, the practice of using captive labor for private industry has a long history in the U.S. Shane Bauer, who spent four months undercover in a CoreCivic prison, tracks prison privatization back to the mid-19th century South, when Louisiana privatized its penitentiary with a company that used inmates to manufacture clothes for enslaved people.

What Do the Private Prison Companies Say?

Private prison companies argue they save taxpayer dollars, follow government regulations and connect inmates with re-entry resources.

Brandon Bissell, a spokesperson for CoreCivic, said in a statement that criticism of his company and the industry was characterized by "misinformation" and "sends a terrible message to others in the private sector who are working to help our government solve serious problems in ways it could not do alone."

Similarly, the GEO Group emphasized that the company has provided "high-quality services to the federal government under both Democratic and Republican administrations" and that it would "welcome all lawmakers and presidential candidates to visit our facilities, speak with our employees and hear directly from those individuals in our care."

Issa Arnita, a spokesperson for MTC, said in a statement that "getting rid of private prisons would not solve our country's incarceration problem" and noted that the company "supports common sense criminal justice reform like the recently enacted First Step Act" and "uses evidence-based programs to help men and women make lasting changes in their lives."

All three companies said they did not manage facilities that house unaccompanied minors or border patrol holding facilities.

Short of Abolishing Private Prisons, What Other Options Are There?

Some researchers are turning their attention toward restructuring private prison contracts, rather than banning private involvement in the prison sector.

"The reality is that private prisons are a tool, and like all tools, you can use them well or use them poorly," Adrian Moore, vice president of policy at Reason Foundation, said

One alternative is performance-based contracts, which are in place in prison systems in Australia and New Zealand and link payment to measurable good outcomes.

But these models aren't silver bullets either, Eisen said. An ombudsman report raised concerns over confinement conditions at one of the performance-based facilities Eisen visited in New Zealand, even though that facility had met its goal of reducing recidivism.

Print Citations

CMS: Armstrong, Mia. "Here's Why Abolishing Private Prisons Isn't a Silver Bullet." In *The Reference Shelf: U.S. National Debate Topic: 2020–2021 Criminal Justice Reform,* edited by Micah L. Issitt, 70-73. Amenia, NY: Grey House Publishing, 2020.

MLA: Armstrong, Mia. "Here's Why Abolishing Private Prisons Isn't a Silver Bullet." *The Reference Shelf: U.S. National Debate Topic: 2020–2021 Criminal Justice Reform,* edited by Micah L. Issitt, Grey House Publishing, 2020, pp. 70-73.

APA: Armstrong, M. (2020). Here's why abolishing private prisons isn't a silver bullet. In Micah L. Issitt (Ed.), *The reference shelf: U.S. national debate topic: 2020–2021 criminal justice reform* (pp. 70-73). Amenia, NY: Grey House Publishing.

Everything You Don't Know about Mass Incarceration

By Rafael A. Mangual

City Journal, **Summer 2019**

Certain must-pass ideological litmus tests have arisen for the 25 declared candidates (so far) seeking the Democratic Party presidential nomination. Perhaps chief among them is subscription to the belief that the American criminal-justice system is racist and overly punitive. This Democratic unanimity makes sense in light of the criticism that many of the leading candidates have faced from activists, left-wing media, and other, more "woke," presidential hopefuls for their earlier acceptance, or even endorsement, of proactive policing, quality-of-life enforcement, and incarceration as reasonable methods of combating crime.

Joe Biden's role in '90s crime law could haunt any presidential bid, ran a prescient 2015 *New York Times* headline. Doubtless sensing vulnerability, the former vice president and current Democratic front-runner made a Martin Luther King Day speech to Al Sharpton's National Action Network this year, telling the audience that "I haven't always been right" about criminal justice and that "white America has to admit there's still a systematic racism, and it goes almost unnoticed by so many of us."

That hasn't stopped some of Biden's Democratic opponents (not to mention President Trump) from pushing the incarceration button. California senator Kamala Harris, one of his leading rivals, hit Biden for backing the 1994 omnibus crime bill, which, she says, contributed to "mass incarceration in this country." Harris herself, though, has met criticism for being too tough on crime in her days as a prosecutor and as California attorney general. New Jersey senator Cory Booker—one of the most outspoken of the candidates on criminal-justice reform—has also had his reformist credentials questioned, with a recent *Times* story criticizing his "zero-tolerance" approach to crime when serving as Newark's mayor from 2006 to 2013, citing ACLU complaints. But all the Democrats are striking the same chord. "More people [are] locked up for low-level offenses on marijuana than for all violent crimes in this country," Massachusetts senator Elizabeth Warren, another top-tier Biden challenger, declared at last year's We the People Summit. Bernie Sanders, the Vermont senator known best for his left-wing economic populism, has described felon disenfranchisement as racist voter suppression. And South Bend mayor Pete

Buttigieg told *Out* that incarceration is "clearly worsening some of the patterns of racial inequality in our country."

Eight of the declared candidates contributed to a recent compendium published by the Brennan Center for Justice, titled *Ending Mass Incarceration*. The essays provide a useful summation of Democratic talking points on criminal justice. That the United States over-incarcerates is evidenced, reformers say, by the numbers: though it has about 5 percent of the global population, the U.S. houses about a quarter of the prisoners worldwide. America's high incarceration rate, goes another assertion, is driven by the unjust enforcement of "low-level" and "nonviolent" offenses, particularly drug crimes. A further charge: the system is racist, given how much more likely blacks are to be behind bars compared with whites. Finally, they say that sentences have gotten way too long.

True, for a subset of America's prison population, incarceration does not serve a legitimate penological end, either because these individuals have been incarcerated for too long or because they should not have been incarcerated to begin with. Justice dictates that we identify these individuals and secure their releases with haste. But none of the above claims advanced by the presidential hopefuls is correct—and acting on any of them would be disastrous.

Start with drugs. Contrary to the claims in Michelle Alexander's much-discussed 2010 bestseller *The New Jim Crow*, drug prohibition is not driving incarceration rates. Yes, about half of federal prisoners are in on drug charges; but federal inmates constitute only 12 percent of all American prisoners—the vast majority are in state facilities. Those incarcerated primarily for drug offenses constitute less than 15 percent of state prisoners. Four times as many state inmates are behind bars for one of five very serious crimes: murder (14.2 percent), rape or sexual assault (12.8 percent), robbery (13.1 percent), aggravated or simple assault (10.5 percent), and burglary (9.4 percent). The terms served for state prisoners incarcerated primarily on drug charges typically aren't that long, either. One in five state drug offenders serves less than six months in prison, and nearly half (45 percent) of drug offenders serve less than one year.

> Not only are most prisoners doing time for serious, often violent, offenses; they've usually received (and blown) the second chance that so many reformers say they deserve.

That a prisoner is categorized as a drug offender, moreover, does not mean that he is nonviolent or otherwise law-abiding. Most criminal cases are disposed of through plea bargains, and, given that charges often get downgraded or dropped as part of plea negotiations, an inmate's conviction record will usually understate the crimes he committed. The claim that drug offenders are nonviolent and pose zero threat to the public if they're put back on the street is also undermined by a striking fact: more than three-quarters of released drug offenders are rearrested for a non-drug crime. It's worth noting that Baltimore police identified 118 homicide suspects in 2017, and 70 percent had been previously arrested on drug charges.

Not only are most prisoners doing time for serious, often violent, offenses; they've usually received (and blown) the second chance that so many reformers say they deserve. Justice Department studies from 2000 through 2009 reveal that only about 40 percent of state felony convictions result in a prison sentence. A Bureau of Justice Statistics (BJS) study of violent felons convicted over a 12-year period in America's 75 largest counties shows that 56 percent of the offenders had a prior conviction record.

Even though most state prisoners are serious and serial offenders, nearly 40 percent of inmates serve less than a year in prison, with the median time served about 16 months. Lengthy sentences tend to be reserved for the most serious violent crimes—but even 20 percent of convicted murderers and nearly 60 percent of those convicted for rape or sexual assault serve less than five years of their sentences. Nor have sentences gotten longer, as reformers contend. In his book *Locked In*, John Pfaff—a leader in the decarceration movement—plotted state prison admissions and releases from 1978 through 2014 on a graph. If sentence lengths had increased, the two lines would diverge as admissions outpaced releases; in fact, the lines are almost identical.

Getting these facts straight is important, especially since reformers unfavorably contrast the U.S.'s criminal-justice system with those of other nations—Western European democracies, in particular—with significantly lower incarceration rates. Because so few American prisoners are serving time for trivial infractions, aligning America's incarceration numbers with those of, say, England or Germany would require releasing many very serious and frequently violent offenders. Yet many in the decarceration camp have been calling for just such a mass release. The #cut50 initiative, founded by activist and CNN host Van Jones, aims to halve the prison population. Scholars at the Brennan Center have called for an immediate 40 percent reduction in the number of inmates.

Such drastic cuts could produce significant crime increases, as communities lose the incapacitation benefits that they currently enjoy. Already, there's no shortage of cautionary examples. In March, the New York Police Department released a montage of security-camera footage that captured ten gang members in East New York, a Brooklyn neighborhood, as they hunted down and killed a man in broad daylight. The chilling images show the victim, 21-year-old Tyquan Eversley (out on bail, facing a rap for armed robbery), running, as his armed assailants give chase. Eversley gets entangled in barbed wire after jumping a fence into someone's backyard; one of his pursuers hurls what looks like part of a cinder block over the fence at him, as another points his gun over the top and fires five fatal rounds. The rock-slinging thug, according to the NYPD, is 25-year-old Michael Reid, who has since been identified and arrested. Reid, it was subsequently reported, had been recently released from federal custody and was wearing an ankle monitor at the time of the murder.

On the morning of May 25, 2019, according to prosecutors, two men—29-year-old Michael Washington and 23-year-old Eric Adams—drove down a residential street in the Austin neighborhood of Chicago, on the city's South Side. Leaked surveillance video from a police camera showed the car as it passed a small group of people near a parked vehicle. One of them was an unarmed 24-year-old black woman, Brittany Hill, holding her one-year-old daughter, who waved at the car just before the vehicle's occupants opened fire. Hill shielded her child from the bullets but was fatally wounded in the abdomen (just below where she was holding her child) and collapsed in the gutter. Washington was on parole at the time of the shooting, after serving time for a drug charge. Citing prosecutors, the *Chicago Sun-Times* reported that "Washington has nine felony convictions, including for a 2004 second-degree murder charge and a 2001 battery charge that was reduced from attempted murder in a plea agreement." Adams, the second alleged shooter, also had an active criminal-justice status at the time of the shooting. He was on probation following a conviction for aggravated unlawful use of a weapon in 2018. In addition to the gun offense, Adams's Chicago police record includes arrests for public-order offenses relating to marijuana possession and gambling.

With these three men, it's not hard to argue that the criminal-justice system failed the public. All three had troubling criminal histories, signaling a general disregard for law and social norms. Yet they were deemed fit for parole or probation, resulting in two murders. In each case, both the perpetrators and the victims were black. Though the decarceration crowd continues to point to racial disparities in criminal enforcement, the data on criminal victimization suggest that the burden of any crime increase that accompanied large-scale prisoner releases would mostly fall on low-income black communities. Though black men constitute about 7 percent of the population, they accounted for 45 percent of America's 15,129 homicide victims in 2017, FBI numbers show. A BJS study of homicides committed from 1980 to 2008 found that the victimization rate of blacks was six times that of whites. The black homicide-offending rate was about eight times the white rate. These differences, not racial animus, go a long way toward explaining the oft-lamented fact that black men are six times likelier to be incarcerated than white males.

Countless citizens on Chicago's mostly minority South and West Sides have been victimized by offenders like Washington and Adams who'd gotten one too many "second" chances. A January 2017 University of Chicago Crime Lab study found that, of those arrested for homicides or shootings in Chicago in 2015 and 2016, about "90 percent had at least one prior arrest, approximately 50 percent had a prior arrest for a violent crime specifically, and almost 40 percent had a prior gun arrest." On average, someone arrested for a homicide or shooting had nearly 12 prior arrests, the study noted—and almost 20 percent had more than 20 priors. You find more of the same in crime-wracked Baltimore. According to the *Baltimore Sun*, "85 percent of the 118 murder suspects identified by police [in 2017] had prior criminal records," with nearly 36 percent being "on parole or probation" at the time of the alleged crime.

The serial offender isn't just a problem in the highest-crime American cities. Data show that such crime has been occurring in urban jurisdictions across the country for years. The BJS study on violent felons convicted in large counties found that offenders on probation, parole, or released pending disposition of a case constituted 37 percent of those convicted during the 12-year period examined. With so many of the nation's most serious crimes perpetrated by people with an active criminal-justice status—and with 83 percent of released prisoners arrested for a new crime within nine years of getting out—the safety benefits of incapacitation become startlingly clear.

Large-scale decarceration would also undermine the criminal-justice system's retributive function, one of the four penological justifications for incarceration (with rehabilitation and deterrence joining incapacitation to constitute the other three). When I studied criminal law as a first-year law student, my textbook defined "crime" as conduct that, "if duly shown to have taken place, will incur a formal and solemn pronouncement of the moral condemnation of the community." Incarceration, in other words, is more than just a way to protect society from wrongdoers; it's also a key way that society condemns wrong and destructive behavior.

Small wonder that recent polling shows little support for decarceration. A 2016 Morning Consult/Vox poll found that 65 percent of respondents somewhat or strongly opposed "reducing sentences for crimes in general," versus just 24 percent supporting such measures. The same poll reported only 32 percent of respondents strongly or somewhat supporting reduced sentences for nonviolent offenders likely to re-offend, and the support was lower still for easing sentences for violent criminals both likely and unlikely to commit further crimes.

America's incarceration numbers would be even higher if more perpetrators of serious crime were apprehended. Most of the crimes that so many Americans believe—with good reason—should result in time behind bars go unanswered. Either the crimes aren't reported or police prove unable to close the cases.

The FBI tracks and reports on eight "index crimes" committed in the United States. Half of those offenses are violent, and half concern property: murder and nonnegligent manslaughter, rape, robbery, aggravated assault, burglary, larceny theft, motor-vehicle theft, and arson. Since 2010, the U.S. has averaged about 1.2 million violent index crimes and 8.5 million property index crimes yearly. Keeping in mind that many similar crimes never get reported to the FBI, note that police clear just 46.8 percent and 18.9 percent of violent and property index offenses, respectively. Put differently, since 2010, about 5.1 million violent index crimes and 54.9 million property index crimes have gone unpunished—which works out to more than 7.5 million of these offenses yearly. Even assuming that certain criminals commit a disproportionate number of the crimes, one can say with confidence that, in any given year, a large number of people who should be in prison are not.

The U.S. incarcerates more people than any other nation, but international comparisons ignore important differences between other countries and ours. For instance, as is often pointed out by the same Democrats when discussing gun control, the U.S. has significantly higher murder and violent-crime rates than many other developed nations, and those rates of serious crime drive much of the disparity in incarceration—not low-level and nonviolent drug offenses. Likewise, the racial disparities in our prison population are a function of racial disparities in serious criminal offending, not systemic bias. Contrary to the decarceration narrative, most of those imprisoned in America are highly likely to reoffend; most prisoners have committed just the kinds of serious violations that most Americans agree should put them away; and plenty of criminals already walk our streets today who committed their crimes without detection, were released from prison or jail sooner than they should have been, or received too-light sentences, given the level of their actual infractions.

Democrats and their progressive allies are thus wrong that the United States has a mass-incarceration problem. While we should, of course, seek to improve the criminal-justice system's imperfections, voters should resist drastic, far-reaching reforms. The real-world consequences of those reforms would be disastrous, especially for the nation's most vulnerable neighborhoods.

Print Citations

CMS: Mangual, Rafael A. "Everything You Don't Know about Mass Incarceration." In *The Reference Shelf: U.S. National Debate Topic: 2020–2021 Criminal Justice Reform,* edited by Micah L. Issitt, 74-79. Amenia, NY: Grey House Publishing, 2020.

MLA: Mangual, Rafael A. "Everything You Don't Know about Mass Incarceration." *The Reference Shelf: U.S. National Debate Topic: 2020–2021 Criminal Justice Reform,* edited by Micah L. Issitt, Grey House Publishing, 2020, pp. 74-79.

APA: Mangual, R.A. (2020). Everything you don't know about mass incarceration. In Micah L. Issitt (Ed.), *The reference shelf: U.S. national debate topic: 2020–2021 criminal justice reform* (pp. 74-79). Amenia, NY: Grey House Publishing.

Michelle Alexander Is Wrong about Mass Incarceration

By Barry Latzer
National Review, April 4, 2019

Michelle Alexander, famous for her book arguing that mass incarceration is the "new Jim Crow," now has a perch on the op-ed pages of the *New York Times*, where she's been offering her views on the criminal-justice system. Those views have shifted quite a bit—she now at least recognizes that violent crime is a major driver of incarceration—but her policy proposals are just as ill informed as they were when her book caught the zeitgeist in 2010.

The New Jim Crow indicted the criminal-justice system for imposing racially motivated social controls on African Americans through convictions for nonviolent crimes, mainly drug crimes. The aim, according to Alexander, was to undo the civil-rights gains of the 1960s by subjecting blacks to incarceration, probation, and parole:

The seeds of the new system of control were planted well before the Civil Rights movement. A new race-neutral language was developed for appealing to old racist sentiments, a language accompanied by a political movement that succeeded in putting the vast majority of blacks back in their place. Proponents of racial hierarchy found they could install a new racial caste system without violating the law or the new limits of acceptable discourse by demanding "law and order" rather than "segregation forever."

Correctional controls, since they fell disproportionately on blacks, created a new racial caste of people "swept into the system, branded criminals or felons, and ushered into permanent second-class status—acquiring records that [would] follow them for life."

Sounds chilling, but there are huge holes in the argument. First, the racial-conspiracy hypothesis has never been established in historical scholarship and remains the redoubt of a few ideologues. The notion that the buildup of the criminal-justice system, which began in the 1970s but gained steam over the next three decades, was part of a plot to undo the civil-rights movement rather than a response to the massive crime and drug wave that afflicted this country not only is dubious revisionist history, but it overlooks the strong support of black leadership for an expansion of the criminal-justice system. As vividly documented in James Forman's *Locking Up Our Own*, crime terror in the black community led African-American political leaders, including former D.C. prosecutor Eric Holder, to endorse the kind of punitive policies that helped produce mass incarceration.

Those who question the reality of the crime tsunami should consider the homicide statistics, our most accurate crime measure, and the thousands of people who lost their lives at the hands of criminals during these decades. Homicide-victimization rates doubled between 1960 and 1980 and didn't begin a consistent decline until the mid 1990s. From 1970 to 2005, a staggering 673,993 Americans were murdered, more than died in all our wars from World War II on. And these losses don't include the many crime victims injured for life or the billions of dollars in costs.

For those focused on African Americans, the murder statistics are even more disturbing. Though blacks were around 12 percent of the U.S. population, they were nearly half of the homicide victims during this period, and 60 percent of the suspected perpetrators.

This great crime rise was the primary cause of the incarceration expansion. Crime, drugs, and disorder, magnified through mass-media coverage, generated intense public fear, which in turn led to relentless pressure on the politicians to beef up the criminal-justice system. Peter Enns's recent study of public opinion, Incarceration Nation, persuasively demonstrates that it was public support for punitiveness that drove up incarceration rates. . . .

The plain truth is that crime was spinning out of control; our big cities, especially, were becoming seething cauldrons of violence, and the public, frightened out of its wits, demanded a government response.

The New Jim Crow famously repudiated this explanation: Drugs, not violent crime, Alexander said, were responsible for the incarceration buildup:

We ought not be misled by those who insist that violent crime has driven the rise of this unprecedented system of racial and social control. The uncomfortable reality is that arrests and convictions for drug offenses—not violent crime—have propelled mass incarceration.

If "incarceration" means imprisonment, however, this assertion is flat wrong. Among state prisoners, drug-violation sentences were, at their peak, around one-fifth of all sentences, one-fourth for African-American inmates. Sentences for violent crimes, by contrast, were anywhere from 46 to 59 percent of all sentences. (To be sure, drug sentences accounted for more than half of federal inmates, but federal prisoners were a small part of the total prison population, around 7 percent, and the federal prosecutions mainly were of drug dealers, not small-fry street sellers.) Given that the U.S. imprisonment rate roughly quintupled between 1970 and 2010, it is extremely unlikely that drugs could be the full explanation, or anything close to it.

Alexander tries to evade this counterargument by claiming that probation and parole supervision are also part of the system of mass incarceration: "This caste system extends far beyond prison walls and governs millions of people who are on probation and parole, primarily for nonviolent offenses."

But this is unpersuasive. In the first place, probation and parole are alternatives to incarceration and should not be characterized as incarceration in themselves. What's more, if we are to significantly reduce actual incarceration in this country, we will have to increase the use of probation and parole, unless we further reduce crime and arrests, which seems unlikely. (In a recent Times column, Alexander pushes restorative justice as an alternative to prison, but, as I will show, this approach cannot be taken seriously.)

Probation is a sentence, true, but it is a sentence to a restricted freedom, not to jail or prison. It comes with conditions, but they're hardly onerous: e.g., no guns, drug rehab if needed, meet with your probation officer, and, of course, no additional crime. Probation is intended to reduce incarceration, especially for offenders who pose less of a threat to society. Only 20 percent of probationers have been convicted of violent crime, compared with 54 percent of all state prisoners. Alexander spins this to claim that mass incarceration is propelled by nonviolent crime, but the great outcome of probation is mass nonconfinement, not mass incarceration.

Probation sentences usually last six months, maybe a year. What follows the probationer for life, if it isn't expunged, is the record of his conviction. This is as it should be, since in the absence of conviction records we would risk sentencing repeat offenders the same as first offenders. Would Alexander really wipe clean all conviction records?

Alexander says, grimly, that probationers are "swept into the system, branded criminals or felons, and ushered into a permanent second-class status—acquiring records that will follow them for life." That's a pretty disparaging view of a system that gives relatively minor offenders the opportunity to stay out of jail or prison, thereby reducing mass incarceration—real incarceration—for millions of arrested people, provided only that they behave themselves for a short period.

Alexander's discussion of parole is even more deficient. Parole is a sentence reduction, the release of a convicted criminal from prison, also subject to conditions. It too reduces real incarceration. Contrary to Alexander's claims, it does not involve mainly drug and nonviolent criminals. One-third of parolees committed violent crimes, one-third drug crimes, and one-fifth property crimes. Once again, the aim of the policy is rehabilitation. However, as critics observe, parole doesn't work very well. Over 80 percent of those released on parole are rearrested within nine years. Solutions have ranged from providing more services to help parolees reintegrate into society to reducing or ending parole altogether.

I don't have a good answer to this problem. But Alexander doesn't either. Complaints about branding people criminals obviously are irrelevant, as parolees are criminals. And they are probably not harmless youth smoking weed on the streets. To judge by the preceding figures on parolees, they are more likely to be violent and hardened criminals who have served time and may well be incorrigible. Parolees are disproportionately black, but this reflects the disproportionate number of African Americans in prison, not those arrested for minor, nonviolent crimes.

In her November 8, 2018, *Times* column, Alexander discovered a new target, the "newest Jim Crow," as she dubbed it: electronic monitoring (EM) of offenders, who may include parolees, probationers, and those released pre-trial. Once again, Alexander displayed a penchant for opposing the most workable policies for reducing real-world incarceration.

Current release policies are essentially an honor system. When probationers and parolees are discharged, judges admonish them to keep their noses clean, but their putative monitors—probation and parole officers—simply have too many cases to closely oversee anybody. Is it any wonder that violations of the conditions of probation or parole are a major factor in admissions to jail or prison? Such violations alone recently resulted in the incarceration of over 340,000 people in a single year.

Electronic monitoring provides obvious benefits in this situation. Using the same GPS technology found in your cell phone, EM can tell the authorities the precise location, though not the activities, of the subject, who wears a wrist or ankle bracelet. With EM, probation and parole officers will be able to monitor the subject in three different ways. First, the device can alert authorities when the subject has physically entered a prohibited location, such as a victim's or prosecution witness's residence or workplace. Second, contrary to Alexander's concerns that EM will make holding a job more difficult, the devices can remind subjects to go to work or to rehab appointments and alert officers if they do not. Third, since GPS reveals the movement of the subject, along with time information, authorities can compare subjects' whereabouts with the locations of crimes to see whether they match, which would suggest that a subject was present at the scene of a crime.

Alexander is troubled that big corporations benefit financially from electronic monitoring. But there are financial advantages to the taxpayer in outsourcing EM, and besides, current-day probation and parole authorities have all they can do to keep up without technologically supported monitoring. They couldn't possibly manage an expanded EM program.

Alexander also claims that EM doesn't work. To support her claim, she cites a Brookings Institution report that questions the efficacy of "intense supervision" of released parolees and probationers. But nowhere in this report is there a word about EM in particular. Furthermore, there have been studies of EM specifically that have found it very effective. A Florida evaluation supported by the U.S. Justice Department and involving over 5,000 medium- and high-risk offenders placed on electronic monitoring over a six-year period found that approximately one in three would have gone to prison had it not been for the monitoring.

Ultimately, Alexander falls back on race rhetoric: EM is to prison as Jim Crow was to slavery—better, sure, but only by contrast. But EM is not, as Jim Crow certainly was, a race-based barrier to social betterment. It is (let's be honest) an encumbrance, but it is one that can help reduce the appalling failure of today's honor release system. Just keep in mind the system's 83 percent rearrest rate within nine years of parole, and the 340,000 parole and probation failures imprisoned each year.

In her March 3 op-ed, Alexander belatedly discovered violent crime, which accounts, she notes, for 54 percent of those in prison. She now concedes that mass incarceration cannot be addressed without doing something about violent crime. This is a big improvement over her New Jim Crow claim that drug prosecutions were the heart of the problem.

And just what is the prison problem? Alexander insists that the get-tough policies first adopted in the 1980s were an "abysmal failure." This is hard to square

> **Given that the U.S. imprisonment rate roughly quintupled between 1970 and 2010, it is extremely unlikely that drugs could be the full explanation, or anything close to it.**

with a massive decline in African-American violent crime during the period of the great toughening. From 1980 to 2009, the black homicide-mortality rate fell by a whopping 54 percent, from 41 per 100,000 to 19. I don't claim that the increase in incarceration was the full explanation for the crime decline, but certainly it's a big part of the story.

Alexander's second criticism is that prison is "enormously counterproductive." Given the recidivism rate, it is obvious that prison isn't reforming very many offenders. Nonetheless, any full assessment of the prison system also has to take account of the simple and straightforward benefits of incapacitating repeat offenders for the time that they are incarcerated, not to mention the importance of retribution for truly atrocious crimes.

Alexander wants to cut the prison population in half, though she never tells us which crimes will get the benefit of her leniency: rape, murder, robbery, burglary? She does offer an alternative to incarceration—restorative justice (RJ)—but when it comes to the crimes that lead to prison, as opposed to jail for a short term or probation, RJ is pie-in-the-sky.

RJ provides a meeting of crime victims and perpetrators (or as Alexander puts it, "survivors" and "responsible parties") under the direction of a trained facilitator, aimed at arriving at a way for the perpetrator to make the victim whole again, or at least acknowledge her pain.

This certainly has its place, but it will not replace imprisonment. For low-level offenses such as harassment or minor theft, RJ may be effective. It also might be helpful in campus "date rape" situations where "he said, she said" accounts prevent clear findings of responsibility. For most serious crimes, however, especially crimes of violence, RJ can work only as a supplement to incarceration. Not only are serious offenders a danger to the community who must be incapacitated, but their crimes are such that the public's sense of justice requires punishment. Retribution may be out of favor nowadays, but it is an essential ingredient of every criminal-justice system. Alexander claims that 90 percent of victims prefer RJ to imprisonment, but the source for this number is obscure, and in any event, victims aren't representative of the general public. That's one reason we prefer that judges rather than "survivors" impose sentences.

Clearly, whatever the benefits of restorative justice, it will not reduce the prison population by 50 percent—Alexander's target—or anything close. It is likely to be most effective with probationers, who have committed crimes minor enough that they are being released instead of incarcerated. But this is a population that already is unconfined, so it won't help reduce real-world incarceration.

Taken seriously, Michelle Alexander's ideas are pretty thin on facts and real-world solutions. She may have progressed from the catchy shallowness of the New Jim Crow, but she continues to offer little by way of serious criminal-justice reforms.

Print Citations

CMS: Latzer, Barry. "Michelle Alexander Is Wrong about Mass Incarceration." In *The Reference Shelf: U.S. National Debate Topic: 2020–2021 Criminal Justice Reform,* edited by Micah L. Issitt, 80-85. Amenia, NY: Grey House Publishing, 2020.

MLA: Latzer, Barry. "Michelle Alexander Is Wrong about Mass Incarceration." *The Reference Shelf: U.S. National Debate Topic: 2020–2021 Criminal Justice Reform,* edited by Micah L. Issitt, Grey House Publishing, 2020, pp. 80-85.

APA: Latzer, B. (2020). Michelle Alexander is wrong about mass incarceration. In Micah L. Issitt (Ed.), *The reference shelf: U.S. national debate topic: 2020–2021 criminal justice reform* (pp. 80-85). Amenia, NY: Grey House Publishing.

4

The Scientific and Technological Dimensions

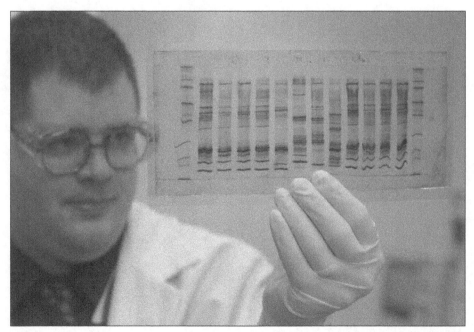

Although many forms of forensic evidence have been called into question, DNA evidence has proven reliable. Above, a chemist reads a DNA profile.

The Technological Edge

Historians increasingly refer to the modern era in history as the "Digital Age" or the "Information Age." The era began with the development of transistors in the late 1940s and has proceeded through an evolving series of ever more transformative innovations. The internet, social media, and the smartphone have become the tools of business, media, and American personal life, a fact made abundantly clear in March of 2020 in the midst of the Covid-19 pandemic that forced many to adjust to a more fully virtual life. Like every other facet of American life and culture, the criminal justice system too has transformed in the increasingly digital world. For one thing, crime is increasingly virtual in nature, with cybercrime, cyberwarfare, and digital identity crimes becoming familiar dangers for American citizens. In some ways, the criminal justice system has been improved by the addition of digital tools and technology, but this evolution has been inconsistent and controversial. The ways in which digital technology has been used by police and the courts has raised serious objections from privacy and civil liberties activists.

New Policing

The use of facial recognition, biometric data, and consumer information is one of the most contentious topics in the campaign for police reform. One of the consequences of the Digital Age has been an overall shift in privacy rights. Companies now regularly profit by collecting and selling data from consumers, and this has left Americans uncertain about who owns and controls their private and consumer data. Since 2010 there have been a number of high-profile cases in which police or agents of the federal government have been accused of utilizing digital data in invasive ways. In February 2020 a *Wall Street Journal* investigative report detailed evidence indicating that local Immigration and Customs Enforcement (ICE) police had been purchasing private user data from cell phone companies to track down undocumented immigrants. While authorities claim such actions are technically legal, the collection of consumer data is another civil liberties concern within the broader debate over ICE and President Trump's immigration policies.[1]

Some of the nation's largest digital giants have been involved in transmitting customer data to police agencies. One such pattern was revealed in a 2019 *New York Times* investigation of how police have been able to access phone location data from a Google database called "Sensorvault," which they then used to track down an accused murderer. In the case in question, the data led police to the correct vehicle, but the wrong suspect was arrested and later released when additional evidence cleared him. The case demonstrated both that cell phone tracking data could potentially provide a major benefit to authorities, but also illustrated the privacy and digital data ownership concerns surrounding police access to consumer data.[2]

Facial recognition is another emerging policing technology that has become increasingly disputed. The technology uses the allometric organization of the face to create a sort of facial blueprint, often called a "facial signature," that can be used to verify a person's identity or to find an individual from among a crowd. Facial recognition technology emerges from the intersection of artificial intelligence and security, and a number of companies, some with military industrial investment, have been developing high-tech tools over the past decade, fueled in part by the effort to locate and prevent violence from domestic and foreign terrorism. Digital facial recognition systems can use facial characteristics to rapidly compare images to locate individuals from mountains of visual data collected by security cameras or posted through the internet.

While facial recognition technology might provide a helpful personal security and computing tool, as well as an aid for business and security technology, a number of critics have raised concerns about privacy and the unauthorized recording of digital imagery. For some, the potential for governments to constantly track citizens is a threat to personal liberty. For others, the advent of new technologies has, in some cases, exacerbated existing imbalances within the justice system. For instance, studies indicate that facial recognition algorithms—the coded instructions that tell computers how to recognize faces—cannot effectively identify nonwhite faces, and this means that the increasing use of facial recognition technology could potentially exacerbate racial disparities in policing.[3]

Other critics are concerned about how police obtain data, arguing that personal and consumer data shared with companies and across social media should be protected from governmental intrusion without due process. Some feel that the courts and government do too little to prevent the unauthorized use and sharing of personal data. Should Americans be willing to allow their society to evolve toward a potential state of constant surveillance by the police or by government agencies? Critics cite the practice in China, where police have used surveillance data and facial recognition to arrest individuals for petty crimes like jaywalking.[4]

There are other examples of governments making similar use of digital data. In March of 2020, for instance, Microsoft announced that the company would be withdrawing investment in the Israeli facial recognition company AnyVision, which has been accused of inappropriately using facial recognition data to conduct surveillance in the West Bank despite objections from human rights groups.[5]

Evidence and Investigation

In 2009, the National Academies of Science (NAS) issued a report on the state of forensic science—defined as the science surrounding tests and techniques used in the process of crime detection and investigation. In the report, the scientists involved evaluated commonly used forensics science techniques and found many to be unreliable and lacking scientific and empirical validity. This sparked a series of developments in the United States, including the establishment of the National Commission of Forensic Science (NCFS) in 2013. From 2013 to 2016, the NCFS engaged in efforts to improve American forensics, but the Trump administration disbanded the NCFS as unnecessary. One of the emerging controversies in the field of criminal justice has to do with whether governments have done enough to improve forensic science in the ten years since the NAS report.

Problems stemming from poor and invalid forensic evidence can be dire. Writing about this issue in *Scientific American* in 2017, a group of scientists discussed Keith Allen Harward, a man who spent thirty-three years incarcerated based largely on evidence involving a "bite mark" that he allegedly left on a murder victim. Bite mark evidence is one of the kinds of forensic evidence once widely used that has since been shown to have little or no scientific value. Harward is one of a number of persons convicted based on now outdated forensics techniques who have since been exonerated because of deoxyribonucleic acid (DNA) evidence.[6]

Examples like Harward's demonstrate the danger inherent in insufficient investigative techniques, in the form of wrongful convictions and executions. While there are independent review organizations in place to evaluate techniques in many facets of American life, the decision to disband the NCFS leaves no such forensic organization in the United States. Critics further argue that the NCFS was disbanded before American forensic science had been improved in keeping with the NAS report. For instance, the United States has not successfully implemented policies to ensure that forensic methods are evaluated before being accepted in court cases.

According to the Center for Statistics and Applications in Forensic Evidence (CSAFE) in 2019 there were several key areas of improvement necessary for the United States to align with the recommendations made by the National Academy of Science in 2009:

- Absences of standardization in operational procedures;

- Lack of uniformity in certification of forensic practitioners or accreditation of crime laboratories;

- Unevenness in techniques, methodologies, reliability, error rates, research and more across forensic science disciplines;

- Variations in reliability of expert interpretation of evidence;

- Lack of rigor to consistently and with high degree of certainty demonstrate a connection between evidence an specific individual or source;

- Lack of research on established limits and measures of performance to address the impact of variability and bias.[7]

While Attorney Generals Jeff Sessions and William Barr have not given any indication that the Trump-led justice department will lead the way toward forensic reform, there have been calls to reform the system from within Congress. In September of 2019, Democratic Representative Mark Takano introduced a bill that would ensure that defendants have access to algorithms used to analyze evidence used in their case. This bill, if passed, would also establish a series of tests and new standards to ensure that all algorithms used in forensic analysis meet certain standards.[8] The recent House bill suggested by Takano does not address all of the problems with the U.S. forensics system but provides for at least a basic set of core standards and enables defense attorneys and accused citizens to obtain information that might be used to challenge questionable forensic evidence.

Forensics is one of the most important and impactful branches of scientific inquiry because the results obtained by forensic specialists can greatly alter the lives of citizens and their families. Accurate or faulty forensics may even be the determining factor in condemning or rescuing thousands from death, either by execution or by criminal violence. Since 2009, the federal and state governments have made significant improvements both at the state and federal level to examine and implement policy changes, but progress in this arena has been halted due to shifting political priorities. The current debate, then, focuses not only on what kinds of solutions might be available to improve standards, but also on whether or not it is important for the American government to continue investing in this effort.

Works Used

"Influencing Forensic Science for a Decade: Remembering the 2009 NAS Report." *CSAFE*. Feb 19, 2019. Retrieved from https://forensicstats.org/blog/2019/02/19/influencing-forensic-science-for-a-decade-remembering-the-2009-nas-report/.

Martin, Nicole. "The Major Concerns around Facial Recognition Technology." *Forbes*. Sep 25, 2019. Retrieved from https://www.forbes.com/sites/nicolemartin1/2019/09/25/the-major-concerns-around-facial-recognition-technology/#446cc4044fe3.

Molla, Rani. "Law Enforcement Is Now Buying Cellphone Location Data from Marketers." *Vox*. Recode. Feb 7, 2020. Retrieved from https://www.vox.com/recode/2020/2/7/21127911/ice-border-cellphone-data-tracking-department-homeland-security-immigration.

"Rep. Takano Introduces the Justice in Forensic Algorithms Act to Protect Defendants' Due Process Rights in the Criminal Justice System." *Takano*. Sep 17, 2019. Retrieved from https://takano.house.gov/newsroom/press-releases/rep-takano-introduces-the-justice-in-forensic-algorithms-act-to-protect-defendants-due-process-rights-in-the-criminal-justice-system.

Sah, Sunita, Arturo Casadevall, Suzanne S. Bell, James Gates Jr., Thomas D. Albright, and M. Bonner Denton. "We Must Strengthen the 'Science' in Forensic Science." *Scientific American*. May 8, 2017. Retrieved from https://blogs.scientificamerican.com/observations/we-must-strengthen-the-science-in-forensic-science/.

Simonite, Timothy. "The Best Algorithms Struggle to Recognize Black Faces Equally." *Wired*. Condé Nast. Jul 22, 2019. Retrieved from https://www.wired.com/story/best-algorithms-struggle-recognize-black-faces-equally/.

Statt, Nick. "Microsoft to End Investments in Facial Recognition Firms after AnyVision Controversy." *The Verge*. Mar 27, 2020. Retrieved from https://www.theverge.com/2020/3/27/21197577/microsoft-facial-recognition-investing-divest-anyvision-controversy.

Valentino-DeVries, Jennifer. "Tracking Phones, Google Is a Dragnet for the Police." *New York Times*. April 13, 2019. Retrieved from https://www.nytimes.com/inter-active/2019/04/13/us/google-location-tracking-police.html.

Notes

1. Molla, "Law Enforcement Is Now Buying Cellphone Location Data from Marketers."
2. Valentino-DeVries, "Tracking Phones, Google Is a Dragnet for the Police."
3. Simonite, "The Best Algorithms Struggle to Recognize Black Faces Equally."
4. Martin, "The Major Concerns around Facial Recognition Technology."
5. Statt, "Microsoft to End Investments in Facial Recognition Firms after AnyVision Controversy."
6. Sah, et al., "We Must Strengthen the 'Science' in Forensic Science."
7. "Influencing Forensic Science for a Decade: Remembering the 2009 NAS Report," *CSAFE*.
8. "Rep. Takano Introduces the Justice in Forensic Algorithms Act to Protect Defendants' Due Process Rights in the Criminal Justice System."

How Robots, IoT and Artificial Intelligence Are Transforming the Police

By Bernard Marr
Forbes, September 19, 2017

It's happened. Arrests have been made thanks to the evidence collected from connected digital devices such as the Amazon dot and a Fitbit. This is just the tip of the transformation that law enforcement will experience because of the Internet of Things (IoT), artificial intelligence and robots. There are certainly benefits to applying this new technology to help fight crime, but it also raises some challenging questions regarding our right to privacy and security breaches.

Internet of Things Used to Help Fight Crime

Law enforcement agencies across the world are getting trained on what to look for at crime scenes and how to handle digital evidence. Gaming consoles, Echo devices and even Fitbits have provided valuable information to help solve crimes. Most people don't comprehend the power of these connected devices to contradict alibis and catch lies. As our reliance on these digital devices for entertainment and convenience continues to grow—watches, phones, televisions, pacemakers and more—there will be a longer trail for detectives to analyze when trying to solve a crime.

It's commonplace now for officers to have body cams on when on patrol. These cameras can provide another set of eyes to sort through an interaction after the fact and studies suggest they can improve self-awareness to prevent unacceptable behavior from officers and those they interact with. Knowing these interactions will be recorded is a big deterrent for bad behavior.

Some squad cars are equipped with GPS projectiles that can be shot via remote control and hook onto the back of an alleged perpetrator's vehicle. These allow officers to know where a suspect is located and therefore prevent high-speed and dangerous car pursuits. Smart sensors have been developed that can be fixed to the inside of an officer's gun to track how the gun is being used including whether it has been unholstered or discharged. This information could prove valuable in criminal trials.

Artificial Intelligence Aids in Predictive Policing

Several law enforcement agencies have dabbled in predictive policing including my

> **Cameras can provide another set of eyes to sort through an interaction. Knowing these interactions will be recorded is a big deterrent for bad behavior.**

customer the UK police in the city of Durham, England. They used a system called Hart (Harm Assessment Risk Tool) that classifies individuals and ranks the probability that they will commit another offense in the future. The system was fed data gathered between 2008-2013 and assesses people based on severity of the current crime, criminal history, flight risk and more. Although Hart's forecasts were accurate a high percentage of the time, there are other studies that warn of using algorithms and predictive software tools because they flag minority defendants as high risk at double the rate of white defendants. One such study from ProPublica shows the human bias that is injected into such formulas because the flawed judgement of humans was used to create the programs in the first place.

Agencies across the world are moving toward more data-driven approaches to solving crimes. Machine learning is particularly skilled at identifying patterns and can be quite useful when trying to discern a modus operandi (M.O.) of an offender. Digital tools can speed up this work and find connections that might take humans much longer to uncover. In the future, these types of algorithms might prove useful to detect serial crimes committed by the same individual or group.

Robo Cops Make Their Debut

There's a new officer in Dubai to help fight crime, but although he wears a police cap, he's 100% robot. Dubai police plan to have robotic officers make up a quarter of the force by 2030. It can speak six languages and is designed to read facial expressions. It has a computer touch screen where people can report a crime. The robot is deployed mainly to tourist spots and is equipped with a camera that sends live images back to police headquarters to identify wanted suspects. Although the robo cop can help deter crime and relieve some tasks from its human counterparts, humans are still expected to make arrests.

Other robots are deployed around the world to collect evidence, investigate and detonate bombs and for crowd control among other tasks. That hasn't stopped more than a thousand robotic experts such as Elon Musk and Stephen Hawking to warn against arming machines without human control.

As with any adoption of artificial intelligence and the Internet of Things, there are questions to ask and answer and concerns to address. Law enforcement agencies across the world are grappling with these and trying to find the right balance to take advantage of the benefits of this technology to fight and solve crime while preserving privacy and security.

Print Citations

CMS: Marr, Bernard. "How Robots, IoT and Artificial Intelligence Are Transforming the Police." In *The Reference Shelf: U.S. National Debate Topic: 2020–2021 Criminal Justice Reform,* edited by Micah L. Issitt, 95-97. Amenia, NY: Grey House Publishing, 2020.

MLA: Marr, Bernard. "How Robots, IoT and Artificial Intelligence Are Transforming the Police." *The Reference Shelf: U.S. National Debate Topic: 2020–2021 Criminal Justice Reform,* edited by Micah L. Issitt, Grey House Publishing, 2020, pp. 95-97.

APA: Marr, B. (2020). How robots, IoT and artificial intelligence are transforming the police. In Micah L. Issitt (Ed.), *The reference shelf: U.S. national debate topic: 2020–2021 criminal justice reform* (pp. 95-97). Amenia, NY: Grey House Publishing.

How the Police Use Facial Recognition, and Where It Falls Short

By Jennifer Valentino-DeVries
The New York Times, June 12, 2020

After a high-speed chase north of Orlando, Fla., sheriff's deputies punctured the tires of a stolen Dodge Magnum and brought it to a stop. They arrested the driver, but couldn't determine who he was. The man had no identification card. He passed out after stuffing something into his mouth. And his fingerprints, the deputies reported, appeared to have been chewed off.

So investigators turned to one of the oldest and largest facial recognition systems in the country: a statewide program based in Pinellas County, Fla., that began almost 20 years ago, when law enforcement agencies were just starting to use the technology. Officers ran a photo of the man through a huge database, found a likely match and marked the 2017 case as one of the system's more than 400 successful "outcomes" since 2014.

A review of these Florida records—the most comprehensive analysis of a local law enforcement facial recognition system to date—offers a rare look at the technology's potential and its limitations.

Officials in Florida say that they query the system 4,600 times a month. But the technology is no magic bullet: Only a small percentage of the queries break open investigations of unknown suspects, the documents indicate. The tool has been effective with clear images—identifying recalcitrant detainees, people using fake IDs and photos from anonymous social media accounts—but when investigators have tried to put a name to a suspect glimpsed in grainy surveillance footage, it has produced significantly fewer results.

The Florida program also underscores concerns about new technologies' potential to violate due process. The system operates with little oversight, and its role in legal cases is not always disclosed to defendants, records show. Although officials said investigators could not rely on facial recognition results to make an arrest, documents suggested that on occasion officers gathered no other evidence.

"It's really being sold as this tool accurate enough to do all sorts of crazy stuff," said Clare Garvie, a senior associate at the Center on Privacy and Technology at Georgetown Law. "It's not there yet."

Facial recognition has set off controversy in recent years, even as it has become an everyday tool for unlocking cellphones and tagging photos on social media. The industry has drawn in new players like Amazon, which has courted police departments, and the technology is used by law enforcement in New York,

> **The biggest controversy in facial recognition has been its uneven performance with people of different races.**

Los Angeles, Chicago and elsewhere, as well as by the F.B.I. and other federal agencies. Data on such systems is scarce, but a 2016 study found that half of American adults were in a law enforcement facial recognition database.

Police officials have argued that facial recognition makes the public safer. But a few cities, including San Francisco, have barred law enforcement from using the tool, amid concerns about privacy and false matches. Civil liberties advocates warn of the pernicious uses of the technology, pointing to China, where the government has deployed it as a tool for authoritarian control.

In Florida, facial recognition has long been part of daily policing. The sheriff's office in Pinellas County, on the west side of Tampa Bay, wrangled federal money two decades ago to try the technology and now serves as the de facto facial recognition service for the state. It enables access to more than 30 million images, including driver's licenses, mug shots and juvenile booking photos.

"People think this is something new," the county sheriff, Bob Gualtieri, said of facial recognition. "But what everybody is getting into now, we did it a long time ago."

A Question of Due Process

Only one American court is known to have ruled on the use of facial recognition by law enforcement, and it gave credence to the idea that a defendant's right to the information was limited.

Willie Allen Lynch was accused in 2015 of selling $50 worth of crack cocaine, after the Pinellas facial recognition system suggested him as a likely match. Mr. Lynch, who claimed he had been misidentified, sought the images of the other possible matches; a Florida appeals court ruled against it. He is serving an eight-year prison sentence.

Any technological findings presented as evidence are subject to analysis through special hearings, but facial recognition results have never been deemed reliable enough to stand up to such questioning. The results still can play a significant role in investigations, though, without the judicial scrutiny applied to more proven forensic technologies.

Laws and courts differ by state on what investigative materials must be shared with the defense. This has led some law enforcement officials to argue that they aren't required to disclose the use of facial recognition.

In some of the Florida cases the *Times* reviewed, the technology was not mentioned in initial warrants or affidavits. Instead, detectives noted "investigative means" or an "attempt to identify" in court documents, while logging the matters as facial recognition wins in the Pinellas County records. Defense lawyers said in interviews that the use of facial recognition was sometimes mentioned later in the discovery process, but not always.

Aimee Wyant, a senior assistant public defender in the judicial circuit that includes Pinellas County, said defense lawyers should be provided with all the information turned up in an investigation.

"Once the cops find a suspect, they're like a dog with a bone: That's their suspect," she said. "So we've got to figure out where they got that name to start."

Law enforcement officials in Florida and elsewhere emphasized that facial recognition should not be relied on to put anyone in jail. "No one can be arrested on the basis of the computer match alone," the New York police commissioner, James O'Neill, wrote in a June op-ed.

In most of the Florida cases the *Times* reviewed, investigators followed similar guidelines. But in a few instances, court records suggest, facial recognition was the primary basis for an arrest.

Last April, for example, a Tallahassee police officer investigating the theft of an $80 cellphone obtained a store surveillance image and received a likely match from the facial recognition system, according to the Pinellas list. The investigator then "reviewed the surveillance video and positively identified" the suspect, she wrote in a court document.

A police department spokeswoman suggested that this step provided a check on the facial recognition system. "What we can't do is just say, 'Oh, it's this guy,' and not even look at it," she said, adding that in this instance "it was a very clear photo." The case is proceeding.

No More "Name Game"

Pinellas County's Face Analysis Comparison & Examination System, or FACES, was started with a $3.5 million federal grant arranged in 2000 by Representative Bill Young, a Florida Republican who led the House Appropriations Committee.

Earlier tests with law enforcement agencies elsewhere had produced meager results, including systems in California that had led to one arrest in four years. Still, the potential was tantalizing. Pinellas's first planned use for facial recognition was in the local jail's mug shot system. After Sept. 11, the program was expanded to include the airport. Eventually, sheriff's deputies were able to upload photos taken with digital cameras while on patrol.

The program received more than $15 million in federal grants until 2014, when the county took over the annual maintenance costs, now about $100,000 a year, the sheriff's office said.

The first arrest attributed to the Florida program came in 2004, after a woman who was wanted on a probation violation gave deputies a false name, local news outlets reported.

The number of arrests ticked up as the system spread across the state and the pool of images grew to include the driver's license system. By 2009, the sheriff's office had credited it with nearly 500 arrests. By 2013, the number was approaching 1,000. Details on only a small number of cases were disclosed publicly.

The latest list, of more than 400 successes since 2014, which *the Times* obtained after a records request, is flawed: Not all successful identifications are logged, and questionable or negative results are not recorded. Still, together with related court documents—records were readily available for about half the cases—the list offers insights into which crimes facial recognition is best suited to help solve: shoplifting, check forgery, ID fraud.

In case after case on the list, officers were seeking ID checks. "We call it the name game," Sheriff Gualtieri said. "We stop somebody on the street, and they say, 'My name is John Doe and I don't have any identification.'"

In about three dozen court cases, facial recognition was crucial despite being used with poorer-quality images. Nearly 20 of these involved minor theft; others were more significant.

After a 2017 armed robbery at an A.T.M. in nearby Hillsborough County, the Pinellas records show, investigators used facial recognition to identify a suspect. They showed the A.T.M. surveillance video to his girlfriend, who confirmed it was him, according to an affidavit. He pleaded guilty.

Instances of violent crime in which the system was helpful—such as the F.B.I.'s tracking a fugitive accused of child rape—typically involved not surveillance images but people with fake IDs or aliases.

In nearly 20 of the instances on the Pinellas list, investigators were trying to identify people who could not identify themselves, including Alzheimer's patients and murder victims. The sheriff's office said the technology was also sometimes used to help identify witnesses.

The most cutting-edge applications of facial recognition in the area—at the airport, for instance—never showed significant results and were scrapped.

"For me it was a bridge too far and too Big Brother-ish," Sheriff Gualtieri said.

Garbage in, Garbage Out

"It comes down to image quality," said Jake Ruberto, a technical support specialist in the Pinellas County Sheriff's Office who helps run the facial recognition program. "If you put garbage into the system, you're going to get garbage back."

The software for FACES is developed by Idemia, a France-based company whose prototype algorithms did well in several recent tests by the National Institute of Standards and Technology.

But the systems used by law enforcement agencies don't always have the latest algorithms; Pinellas's, for example, was last overhauled in 2014, although the county has been evaluating other, more recent, products. Idemia declined to comment on it.

The gains in quality of the best facial recognition technology in recent years have been astounding. In government tests, facial recognition algorithms compared photos with a database of 1.6 million mug shots. In 2010, the error rate was just under 8 percent in ideal conditions—good lighting and high-resolution, front-facing photos. In 2018, it was 0.3 percent. But in surveillance situations, law enforcement hasn't been able to count on that level of reliability.

Perhaps the biggest controversy in facial recognition has been its uneven performance with people of different races. The findings of government tests released in December show that the type of facial recognition used in police investigations tends to produce more false positive results when evaluating images of black women. Law enforcement officials in Florida said the technology's performance was not a sign that it somehow harbored racial prejudice.

Officials in Pinellas and elsewhere also stressed the role of human review. But tests using passport images have shown that human reviewers also have trouble identifying the correct person on a list of similar-looking facial recognition results. In those experiments, passport-system employees chose wrong about half the time.

Poorer-quality images are known to contribute to mismatches, and dim lighting, faces turned at an angle, or minimal disguises such as baseball caps or sunglasses can hamper accuracy.

In China, law enforcement tries to get around this problem by installing intrusive high-definition cameras with bright lights at face level, and by tying facial recognition systems to other technology that scans cellphones in an area. If a face and a phone are detected in the same place, the system becomes more confident in a match, a *Times* investigation found.

In countries with stronger civil liberties laws, the shortcomings of facial recognition have proved problematic, particularly for systems intended to spot criminals in a crowd. A study of one such program in London, which has an extensive network of CCTV cameras, found that of the 42 matches the tool suggested during tests, only eight were verifiably correct.

Current and former Pinellas County officials said they weren't surprised. "If you're going to get into bank robberies and convenience store robberies, no—no, it doesn't work that well," said Jim Main, who handled technical aspects of the facial recognition program for the sheriff's office until he retired in 2014. "You can't ask, like: 'Please stop for a second. Let me get your photo.'"

Print Citations

CMS: Valentino-DeVries, Jennifer. "How the Police Use Facial Recognition, and When It Falls Short." In *The Reference Shelf: U.S. National Debate Topic: 2020–2021 Criminal Justice Reform,* edited by Micah L. Issitt, 98-102. Amenia, NY: Grey House Publishing, 2020.

MLA: Valentino-DeVries, Jennifer. "How the Police Use Facial Recognition, and When It Falls Short." *The Reference Shelf: U.S. National Debate Topic: 2020–2021 Criminal Justice Reform,* edited by Micah L. Issitt, Grey House Publishing, 2020, pp. 98-102.

APA: Valentino-DeVries, J. (2020). How the police use facial recognition, and where it falls short. In Micah L. Issitt (Ed.), *The reference shelf: U.S. national debate topic: 2020–2021 criminal justice reform* (pp. 98-102). Amenia, NY: Grey House Publishing.

How a Hacker Proved Cops Used a Secret Government Phone Tracker to Find Him

By Cyrus Farivar

Politico, June 3, 2018

On a warm summer's day in 2008, police spotted a man walking outside his apartment in Santa Clara, California, one of the many bedroom communities spread across Silicon Valley. Undercover FBI officers saw him outside the building and began following him on foot, radioing to their colleagues nearby. The man saw the agents, and so he began to walk quickly. They followed suit.

After months of tracking him via sting bank accounts and confidential informants, the officers had their man. He had told the apartment complex's manager that he was Steven Travis Brawner, software engineer: a profile that fit right in with many other tenants in the area. But at the time of his arrest, officers didn't know his real name: After watching his activities at a distance, they called him simply the "Hacker." Between 2005 and 2008, federal investigators believed that the Hacker and two other men filed over 1,900 fake tax returns online, yielding $4 million sent to over 170 bank accounts.

The Hacker was found out through the warrantless use of a secretive surveillance technology known as a stingray, which snoops on cell phones. Stingrays, or cell-site simulators, act as false cell phone towers that trick phones into giving up their location. They have become yet another tool in many agencies' toolbox, and their use has expanded with little oversight—and no public knowledge that they were even being used until the Hacker went on an obsessive quest to find out just how law enforcement tracked him that summer day. When he tugged on that thread, he found out something else: that police might be tracking a lot more than we even know on our phones, often without the warrants that are usually needed for comparable methods of invasive surveillance.

The Hacker began breathing more heavily. He may have thought about heading toward the nearby train station, which would take him out of town, or perhaps towards the San Jose International Airport, just three miles away. The Hacker couldn't be sure if there were cops following him, or if he was just being paranoid. But as soon as he saw the marked Santa Clara Police Department cars, he knew the truth, and he started running.

But the Hacker didn't get far. He was quickly surrounded, arrested and searched. The police found the key to the Hacker's apartment. Later, after police obtained a warrant to search his apartment, they found there a folding chair and a folding table that served as a desk. There was no other furniture—his bed was a cot. Law enforcement also found his Verizon Wireless mobile Internet AirCard, and false driver's licenses with the names "Steven Travis Brawner," "Patrick Stout" and more. A 2010 FBI press release later stated that the agency also "seized a laptop and multiple hard drives, $116,340 in cash, over $208,000 in gold coins, approximately $10,000 in silver coins, false identification documents, false identification manufacturing equipment, and surveillance equipment."

Investigators identified the Hacker, via his fingerprints, as Daniel Rigmaiden, previously convicted of state-level misdemeanors. According to an Internal Revenue Service special agent's search warrant, Rigmaiden's computer also included "email regarding leaving the United States for the country of Dominica . . . [and] documents regarding obtaining citizenship in other countries; emails regarding paying off Dominican officials to get Dominican birth certificates and passports; and a Belize residency guide."

Rigmaiden's case dates back several years. In 2007 and early 2008, the IRS identified a bank account at Compass Bank in Phoenix that was receiving fraudulent tax refunds under an LLC as being involved in the possible scheme.

Rigmaiden's indictment was initially sealed, pending cooperation with a federal investigation. But from the start, Rigmaiden declined to cooperate, and moved to represent himself (after firing three attorneys), and the case was subsequently unsealed in 2009.

"The question is what's the law that governs its use?" Eric King, a longtime London-based privacy activist, said when I asked him about the stingray. "We know that the police have them and we know that the police use them, not that they've ever admitted it, and have done so for 10 years. They refuse to engage, they refuse to say that they bought them. We need a public debate around this sort of stuff."

That debate is very slowly starting to happen. And that is due, in large part, to Rigmaiden's unlikely exposure of the stingray.

***

Rigmaiden found out about fraudulent tax return schemes in the mid-2000s. He quickly figured out that tax returns are largely voluntary. The IRS simply doesn't have enough agents and auditors to do a thorough check of everyone. Most IRS personnel do the best they can, but a few slip through the cracks. This meant that Rigmaiden could file a fake tax return for someone who had died, and pocket the refund. He would file dozens at a time, sometimes more, before one would come back with money. His first successful one netted $9,000. "I was going to make a million and then I was going to stop," he said. (He told WNYC's podcast Note to Self in 2015 that he was planning on leaving the country after making the million dollars.)

In late 2007, Rigmaiden moved to Santa Clara. The city, then as now, is home to students and lots of tech workers. He had a comfortable life in an urban area, and lived near a train station and airport should he need to make a quick getaway. But he knew that the longer he stayed in one place, the more exposed to law enforcement he would be. Unbeknownst to the fraudster, federal prosecutors in Arizona—one of the places where he had stashed his money—filed a sealed indictment against Rigmaiden on July 23, 2008.

By the time he was arrested, Rigmaiden had made about $500,000. After Rigmaiden was arrested in California, he was quickly transported to the Florence Correctional Center, about 65 miles southeast of Phoenix. Despite being incarcerated, Rigmaiden could not sit still. He knew that he had been careful. He had used multiple fake identities, with fake documents, and paid in cash. How could law enforcement have not only found him out, but found him in his own apartment, where hardly anyone knew he lived?

Rigmaiden thought there might be something that the government wasn't telling him—there might be some secret surveillance tool afoot. He tried pressing his federal public defenders to listen, but they wouldn't. Within two months, he'd fired one of his lawyers, and then another. In essence, he didn't feel that they were technically sophisticated enough to be able to help him get the answers he needed. Eventually, the accused fraudster got permission to represent himself (pro se), a legally risky move.

Once he was representing himself, he was allowed to use the law library for five hours a day (up from the usual three hours a week). It became a full-time job, immersing himself in legal procedures—but it was likely the most productive way to spend his time behind bars. Fortunately, at the beginning, a fellow inmate and disbarred attorney helped him out with some of the basics, including general court procedure, how to draft a motion and correct legal citation. By October 2009, Rigmaiden had received boxes and boxes (over 14,000 pages in total) of criminal discovery that would help him understand how the government planned to prosecute its case. In the penultimate box, he saw the word "stingray" in a set of notes.

As a prisoner, he wasn't allowed Internet access, but sometimes a "case manager," a sort of guidance counselor, could be convinced to run online searches for inmates who were pursuing legal research. Though this process, Rigmaiden located a Harris Corporation brochure with the StingRay name. Bingo. The device advertised various types of cellular interception.

Although Rigmaiden was pro se, he had a shadow counsel, or a lawyer who was ready to step in if the pro se defendant wished to take on formal counsel. That lawyer had a paralegal, a man named Dan Colmerauer. Rigmaiden could call Colmerauer from a jailhouse pay phone and ask him to run Google searches for him, and tell him the results by phone. Then Colmerauer would print those webpages, and put them in the mail to Rigmaiden, who in turn would have to make handwritten notes about which links to follow and mail that back to Colmerauer. It's how he found out everything he knew about stingrays.

While StingRay is a trademark, stingray has since become so ubiquitous in law enforcement and national security circles as to also often act as the catch-all generic term—like Kleenex or Xerox. A stingray acts as a fake cell tower and forces cell phones and other mobile devices using a cell network (like Rigmaiden's AirCard, which provided his laptop with Internet access) to communicate with it rather than with a bona fide mobile network. Stingrays are big boxes—roughly the size of a laser printer—like something out of a 1950s-era switchboard, with all kinds of knobs and dials and readouts. Stingrays can easily be hidden inside a police surveillance van or another nearby location.

All of our cell phones rely on a network of towers and antennas that relay our signal back to the network and then connect us to the person that we're communicating with. As we move across a city, mobile networks seamlessly hand off our call from one tower to the next, usually providing an uninterrupted call. But in order for the system to work, the mobile phone provider needs to know where the phone actually is so that it can direct a signal to it. It does so by sending a short message to the phone nearly constantly—in industry terminology this is known as a ping. The message basically is asking the phone: "Are you there?" And your phone responds: "Yes, I'm here." (Think of it as roughly the mobile phone version of the children's swimming pool game Marco Polo.) If your phone cannot receive a ping, it cannot receive service. The bottom line is, if your phone can receive service, then the mobile provider (and possibly the cops, too) know where you are.

Rigmaiden eventually pieced together the story of his capture. Police found him by tracking his Internet Protocol (IP) address online first, and then taking it to Verizon Wireless, the Internet service provider connected with the account. Verizon provided records that showed that the AirCard associated with the IP address was transmitting through certain cell towers in certain parts of Santa Clara. Likely by using a stingray, the police found the exact block of apartments where Rigmaiden lived.

This tracking technology is even more invasive than law enforcement presenting a court order for location data to a mobile phone provider, because rather than have the government provide a court order for a company to hand over data, the stingray simply eliminates the middleman. The government, armed with its own stingray, can simply pluck the phone's location (and possibly the contents of calls, text messages or any other unencrypted data being transmitted at the time, depending on the configuration) directly out of the air.

The Harris Corporation, a longstanding American military contractor, won't say exactly how stingrays work, or exactly who it's selling to, but it's safe to say that it's selling to lots of federal agencies and, by extension, local law enforcement. The company's 2017 annual financial report filed with the Securities and Exchange Commission shows that in recent years Harris has increased its sales of surveillance equipment and related tactical radio systems. It works with not only the U.S. military and law enforcement, but also Canada, Australia, Poland and Brazil, among other countries. The company has profited over $1.8 billion from fiscal year 2013 through 2017.

A 2008 price list shows that its StingRays, KingFish and related devices sell for tens to hundreds of thousands of dollars. But like everything else in the tech world, they're getting cheaper, smaller and better all the time.

Like many other enforcement tools, the federal government has used grants to encourage local law enforcement to acquire stingrays in the name of fighting terrorism. But, as the Rigmaiden case shows, over time, particularly as these tools become cheaper and more commonplace—they're used to bust criminal suspects like him.

So far, judges and courts are not in universal agreement over whether locating a person or device, as the stingray helps to do, should require a warrant. Stingrays don't necessarily mean that conversation will be picked up, so wiretap laws, which require warrants, don't apply. In most cases, police officers would need at least a "pen register" court order, named for a kind of technology that allows police to get call logs. The pen register court order has lesser standards than a warrant: Rather than requiring that officers show probable cause, a pen register court order requires that law enforcement only needs relevance to an ongoing investigation. But stingrays are more invasive than pen registers, and as Rigmaiden's case would show, law enforcement didn't have any kind of specified protocol about what it needs to do to use this new technology.

As 2010 rolled around, Rigmaiden decided that he needed allies. He began sending his case details and research file out to various privacy and civil liberties organizations, including the American Civil Liberties Union (ACLU) and the Electronic Frontier Foundation (EFF). There were likely two major red flags that led to him being ignored—he was representing himself without the benefit of counsel, and believed that the government had used some secret surveillance tool against him. They likely thought he was totally nuts—despite the fact that there was already some evidence that the police were using phones as tracking devices. None of the organizations ever responded.

One of the people Rigmaiden sent his file to was Christopher Soghoian, a bearded and ambitious privacy researcher. At the time, Soghoian was a computer science doctoral student always looking for another way to push the envelope, as well as discover how surveillance was actually being conducted in the real world. Years earlier, as a first-year doctoral student at Indiana University, Soghoian figured out by futzing around with Facebook which of his classmates likely moonlighted at local strip clubs. In 2009 and 2010, Soghoian worked at the Federal Trade Commission, and at one point used his government ID to get into a security industry trade show and made a surreptitious recording of Sprint executives bragging about how they'd handed over customers' GPS information to law enforcement eight million times in a single year. In short, Soghoian was the perfect match for Rigmaiden.

On Monday April 11, 2011, while visiting the offices of the EFF in San Francisco, Soghoian received an unsolicited e-mail from Colmerauer.

Dear Mr. Sohoian[sic],

Daniel Rigmaiden instructed me to e-mail you the attached Memorandum. This is in regard to cell phone tracking and locating. He thinks it may be of interest to you but you may have to read past the introduction before understanding why. If you want the exhibits please e-mail Dan Colmerauer at screenwriter2@earthlink.net and make said request. Dictated but not read.

Daniel Rigmaiden

Soghoian tried to get other lawyers that he knew interested, but they saw the extensive pro se filings as a huge red flag. Lots of people think they're being surveilled by the government with secret technology, but hardly anyone can prove it. Soghoian didn't dismiss it out of hand. "My reaction wasn't, 'what is this strange device,'" Soghoian told *The Verge* in 2016. "It was, 'oh I read about this in graduate school.' But I read about it as a thing that was possible, not a thing that the police . . . were using." But the grad student was skeptical.

Still, Soghoian asked Colmerauer to send what he had. What Soghoian received back was a 200-page "meticulously researched" document that had been originally handwritten in a jailhouse library.

Soghoian understood how to get lawmakers' attention—through the media and advocacy organizations. He eventually sent it on to a friendly Wall Street Journal reporter, Jennifer Valentino-DeVries, as she was boarding a plane bound for Las Vegas, where she was going to attend the 2011 DEF CON, the annual hacker conference. On September 22, 2011, Valentino-DeVries' story hit the paper: "'Stingray' Phone Tracker Fuels Constitutional Clash." (It was her first front-page story for the *Journal*.)

This was also the first time that a major American media outlet had reported on the issue, and likely how many lawmakers first heard about the device that had already been in use for years. In short, Rigmaiden unveiled a new chapter in the story of sophisticated surveillance to the public—citizens, journalists, lawyers, judges— that law enforcement had already known for years, mostly without telling anyone.

***

In February 2012, the Electronic Privacy Information Center (EPIC) filed a FOIA request, which resulted in a lawsuit. Its efforts definitively showed that government law enforcement agencies have not been completely upfront about using stingrays when they asked federal magistrate judges for permission to conduct electronic surveillance. In fact, search warrants have generally not been used at all. Most police applications of this era seeking judicial authorization for a stingray did not even mention the name of the device, nor did they describe how it worked.

The Rigmaiden story in the *Journal* hadn't only grabbed the attention of journalists, but also the attention of lawyers. One lawyer, Linda Lye of the ACLU of Northern California, took particular notice. Lye was new to the ACLU, having largely focused on labor and civil rights issues in her previous decade as an attorney. Quickly, Lye pushed the federal court in San Francisco to unseal the court

> **Stingrays, or cell-site simulators, act as false cell phone towers that trick phones into giving up their location.**

orders that had authorized the initial use of the stingray against Rigmaiden, as it was unclear from the Arizona case (where the prosecution against Rigmaiden was unfolding) what the order specifically authorized the government to do.

"What on Earth was this technology?" she told me years later. "It seemed that there would be all kinds of novel and troubling issues. What sort of court authorization was being obtained? How widespread was it? It was also just a very unlikely story."

Initially what drew her in wasn't the technology itself, but the fact that the government was keeping "novel surveillance orders" a secret. In October 2012, Lye and other ACLU and EFF attorneys decided that they would formally jump into the case, not as Rigmaiden's lawyer, but rather as amici, or "friends of the court"—in this case, attorneys who were not party to a case but could file a brief to articulate the broader social concerns it raised. They wrote to the court, noting that this case would "likely result in the first decision to address the constitutional implications" of stingrays.

In early May 2013, the judge ruled in the government's favor on the issue that Lye raised in court, finding that Rigmaiden lacked a "reasonable expectation of privacy" while shrouded under multiple false identities—after all, his AirCard, his apartment and postboxes that he paid for were all done under fake names.

By late January 2014, Rigmaiden and federal prosecutors reached a plea deal: He'd plead guilty and prosecutors would recommend that he be given a sentence of time served. The agreement was signed on April 9, 2014.

While the Rigmaiden case wound down, Soghoian (who had joined the ACLU as its chief technologist) and his colleagues were just getting started. The ACLU, along with other privacy groups, including EPIC and the EFF, spearheaded efforts to speak publicly, file record requests, sue and campaign for meaningful legislative reform.

Several months later, in April 2015, the New York Civil Liberties Union (the New York State chapter of the ACLU) managed to do what no one else could: successfully sue to obtain an unredacted copy of the NDA that the FBI had law enforcement agencies sign when they acquired stingrays. In essence, the document explained that due to the authorization granted by the Federal Communications Commission to the Harris Corporation, any law enforcement agency had to sign an NDA with the FBI. The six-page letter essentially said that agencies that acquired stingrays could not talk about them "in any manner including but not limited to: press releases, in court documents, during judicial hearings, or during other public forums or proceedings."

In May 2015, the FBI issued a bizarre public statement saying that despite the NDA's language to the contrary, it "should not be construed to prevent a law enforcement officer from disclosing to the court or a prosecutor the fact that this technology was used in a particular case."

Later that same month, Washington Governor Jay Inslee signed a bill that passed both houses of the state legislature specifically requiring that law enforcement seek a warrant before using a stingray. Rigmaiden worked on the drafting of this bill with Jared Friend of the ACLU of Washington. (Before its passage, Soghoian even testified in support of the bill.) Months later, California followed suit, with its comprehensive California Electronic Communications Privacy Act, which, among other things, also required a warrant for stingray use.

But the most prominent change regarding stingrays came in September 2015, when the DOJ said it would require a warrant in most situations in which a stingray is used. The policy, which took effect the day it was announced (September 3, 2015), applied to numerous agencies, including the FBI; the Bureau of Alcohol, Tobacco and Firearms; the Drug Enforcement Administration; and the U.S. Marshals Service, among others.

The new state laws and federal policies came as a result of dogged activism by the ACLU and other privacy groups, which all stemmed from Rigmaiden's case. After all, it was Rigmaiden who had initially reached out to Soghoian and presented him with a 200-page memo on a technology that few outside the government had known about. "It was the most well-researched memo I'd ever seen on this technology," Soghoian later told WNYC. "Written by a guy rotting in jail."

Now that lawyers know what to look for and how to challenge them, some of those efforts have been successful. Notably, in March 2016 a state appellate court in Maryland took local law enforcement to task, and ruled unequivocally: "We determine that cell phone users have an objectively reasonable expectation that their cell phones will not be used as real-time tracking devices through the direct and active interference of law enforcement." The three-judge panel in the *State of Maryland v. Andrews* case also noted that such a non-disclosure agreement is "inimical to the constitutional principles we revere."

In other words, judges now seem to be resoundingly echoing the 1967-era Supreme Court language—"reasonable expectation of privacy"—of a landmark privacy case known as *Katz v. United States*, finding that the use of a stingray does require a warrant. But as of this writing, no cases challenging the use of stingrays have reached the Supreme Court, so this legal theory hasn't been cemented just yet, as stingrays continue to be used in everyday law enforcement.

What these judges have realized is that there is now a turning point with respect to smartphones: We carry them with us and they hold all of our secrets. No wonder the police find them valuable during an investigation. But should the police need to get a warrant to find our phones? And what other opportunities for high-tech, low-oversight surveillance might they offer in the future?

Print Citations

CMS: Farivar, Cyrus. "How a Hacker Proved Cops Used a Secret Government Phone Tracker to Find Him." In *The Reference Shelf: U.S. National Debate Topic: 2020–2021 Criminal Justice Reform,* edited by Micah L. Issitt, 103-110. Amenia, NY: Grey House Publishing, 2020.

MLA: Farivar, Cyrus. "How a Hacker Proved Cops Used a Secret Government Phone Tracker to Find Him." *The Reference Shelf: U.S. National Debate Topic: 2020–2021 Criminal Justice Reform,* edited by Micah L. Issitt, Grey House Publishing, 2020, pp. 103-110.

APA: Farivar, C. (2020). How a hacker proved cops used a secret government phone tracker to find him. In Micah L. Issitt (Ed.), *The reference shelf: U.S. national debate topic: 2020–2021 criminal justice reform* (pp. 103-110). Amenia, NY: Grey House Publishing.

Ten Years Later: The Lasting Impact of the 2009 NAS Report

The Innocence Project, February 19, 2019

This week, the Innocence Project commemorates the 10-year anniversary of the groundbreaking report, *Strengthening Forensic Science in the United States: A Path Forward*. The National Academy of Forensic Science (NAS) released the report in 2009, and over the past 10 years, it has served as the foundation for much of our science-driven, policy-based reform and strategic litigation efforts. It established a blueprint for forensic science research, engaged the scientific research community and spurred various meaningful science-based criminal justice reforms. Importantly, it has fostered a new understanding of the intersection of forensic science and the criminal justice system, and it continues to influence an important debate on the courts' gatekeeping responsibilities.

Peter Neufeld, co-founder of the Innocence Project, reflects:

> Science and law have existed in two different worlds with contradictory principles and paradigms. Before the NAS report, forensics was held accountable only to the principles established by the law rather than science. The NAS report called on the scientific community to help the criminal justice system establish the resources and processes needed for forensics to move toward the promise of neutral truth teller. The progress that it set in motion cannot be understated—it is not an exaggeration to say that the report has freed innocent people and saved lives.

John Hollway, associate dean and executive director of the Quattrone Center for the Fair Administration of Justice, adds, "The intellectual rigor of the NAS participants and the depth of their investigation have spurred calls for reform and set an important bar for forensic review of potential evidence in criminal cases."

Citing the "notable dearth of peer-reviewed, published studies establishing the scientific bases and validity of many forensic methods," the NAS report pierced the general perception of the reliability of forensic evidence. The report was the *first* organized voice of research scientists recognizing the limitations of pattern evidence techniques and the urgent need to address these limitations.

The report primarily concluded that, except for nuclear DNA analysis, many commonly used forensic techniques had not undergone the necessary testing to establish sufficient validity and reliability to support claims made in court. The report called for research that would examine the scientific foundations and limitations of several critical forensic disciplines, including: bite mark analysis, microscopic hair analysis, shoe print comparisons, handwriting comparisons, fingerprint examination and firearms and toolmark examinations. According to the report, these forensic methods did not "have the capacity to consistently, and with a high degree of certainty, demonstrate a connection between evidence and a specific individual or source."

Based on its findings, the NAS report made thirteen recommendations, including the creation of an independent, scientific oversight entity for forensic science, investing in research and standards setting, addressing cognitive bias in the practice of forensic testing and educating judges and legal practitioners. The Innocence Project heeded the call of the report and for the last 10 years, has been advocating with other scientific and criminal justice stakeholders for research funding, standards setting and oversight for forensic science practices.

Over the past ten years, the National Institute of Justice has spent more than $123 million on grants to address the research needs outlined in the NAS report, including improving accuracy and reliability of methods and quantifying measures of uncertainty. This investment has yielded evidence that advanced some forensic science disciplines from their status as "reviewed by the NAS report in 2009" to "improved levels of validity." Notably, a 2016 report published by the President's Council on Advisors on Science and Technology concluded that latent print comparison had achieved foundational validity and that firearm comparisons had taken strong steps toward achieving that status. The report also spurred the foundation of the National Commission of Forensic Science in 2013, which operated until 2017.

> **Innocent people have been freed from prison, and consequently, the people who actually committed the crimes have been identified.**

Also since the report's publication, a distinguished group of statisticians, legal scholars and scientists from other fields have collaborated with the Innocence Project on amicus briefs to help educate the courts on the limitations of the forensic techniques outlined above. Dr. Clifford Spiegelman, a signatory of these amicus briefs and a distinguished professor of statistics at Texas A&M, observed:

> Research scientists who challenged foundational aspects of forensic science before the NAS report was published were often dismissed. The report not only provided a critical scientific consensus that supported our concerns, but it is advancing science to change lives. In my home state of Texas, it has led to the courts to abandon bite mark evidence and exonerate Steven Chaney, who spent 28 years in prison for a crime he did not commit.

In addition to Steven Chaney, these efforts have resulted in the exoneration of George Perrot (microscopic hair comparison analysis), Timothy Bridges (microscopic hair comparison analysis) and Alfred Swinton (bite mark).

In July 2013, the Innocence Project, the National Association for Criminal Defense Lawyers (NACDL) and pro bono partner Winston & Strawn LLP, announced a historic partnership with the Federal Bureau of Investigation (FBI) and the Department of Justice (DOJ) to review nearly 3,000 criminal cases in which microscopic hair analysis conducted by the FBI was used to inculpate the defendant(s). This review was spurred by the problems with microscopic hair analysis identified in the NAS report, and by the exoneration, based on DNA evidence, of three men for whom the testimony by FBI hair examiners exceeded the limits of science. More than 90 percent of the first 257 cases reviewed contained one or more types of testimonial errors.

Given the impact of the FBI Hair Review and knowing that research advancing forensic science knowledge will impact the meaning of evidence in cases, the Innocence Project has also advocated for statutory mechanisms to allow individuals to get back into court to prove their innocence based on evolving science or expert repudiation. Chief Justice Bridget McCormack, who supported the implementation of a court rule in Michigan that allows post-judgment motions for relief based on new scientific evidence, acknowledges the far-reaching impact the report has had within both the legal and scientific fields:

Today, forensic science conversations between criminal justice and scientific stakeholders around the world *begin* with the NAS report. The forensic science field has experienced an evolution that would not have been possible without the report's publication. Innocent people have been freed from prison, and consequently, the people who actually committed the crimes have been identified. The forensic science community has partnered with researchers to conduct research, improve forensic testing standards and implement new quality management practices.

In the years ahead, the Innocence Project will continue to work with research scientists, forensic scientists and other criminal justice stakeholders to support scientific advancements in forensic science and to address the need for change in the way evidence is evaluated and applied in the courts. Senior United States District Judge of the United States District Court for the Southern District of New York Jed Rakoff comments:

The National Academies' report on Strengthening Forensic Science was the first serious and objective look at the forensic science evidence that had for decades been routinely received by the courts—and what it revealed was that too much forensic science did not adhere to basic scientific principles and was sometimes little more than guesswork. Still, the impact of the report, modest at first but gathering steam in recent years, might not have been so great if it were not for the fact that the work of the Innocence Project established that questionable forensic science testimony was often associated with wrongful convictions. This one-two punch has slowly but surely caused a growing number of judges to explore with much greater rigor than previously the reliability, and admissibility, of much forensic science testimony that they used to take for granted.

To that end, the Innocence Project pursues mechanisms to ensure the duty to correct forensic science problems and notify defendants through state forensic science commissions, state laws that enable defendants to ask for review of forensic evidence in their cases if science has evolved or an expert retracts their testimony, litigation and amicus opportunities to highlight the application of forensic disciplines used beyond their scientific limits and providing training to legal professionals.

Print Citations

CMS: "Ten Years Later: The Lasting Impact of the 2000 NAS Report." In *The Reference Shelf: U.S. National Debate Topic: 2020–2021 Criminal Justice Reform,* edited by Micah L. Issitt, 111-114. Amenia, NY: Grey House Publishing, 2020.

MLA: "Ten Years Later: The Lasting Impact of the 2000 NAS Report." *The Reference Shelf: U.S. National Debate Topic: 2020–2021 Criminal Justice Reform,* edited by Micah L. Issitt, Grey House Publishing, 2020, pp. 111-114.

APA: The Innocence Project. (2020). Ten years later: The lasting impact of the 2000 NAS report. In Micah L. Issitt (Ed.), *The reference shelf: U.S. national debate topic: 2020–2021 criminal justice reform* (pp. 111-114). Amenia, NY: Grey House Publishing.

Bad Evidence

By Liliana Segura and Jordan Smith
The Intercept, May 5, 2019

In a fluorescent-lit ballroom atop Baltimore's downtown convention center, Lt. Gen. John F. Sattler stepped off the stage and began to pace. He'd had 14 cups of coffee, he boomed, along with a Hershey's bar with almonds. He was not about to stay still.

It was a snowy morning in late February. Sattler, a motivational speaker and retired Marine who once directed strategic planning for the U.S. Joint Chiefs of Staff, was the final panelist at the opening plenary of the 71st Scientific Meeting of the American Academy of Forensic Sciences. The annual conference brings together lawyers, scientists, and forensic practitioners from around the world to discuss the latest research and pressing issues in the field. The plenary sets the tone for the event—past speakers have included U.S. Deputy Attorneys General Sally Yates and Rod Rosenstein—while providing occasional entertainment. At the academy's 2010 meeting in Seattle, the plenary featured a performer called the Physics Chanteuse, who sang provocatively about scientific validity.

A leadership consultant often serving corporate clients, Sattler had no specialized background in forensics. But he was determined to rev up the crowd. He gamely hit upon the theme of the 2019 meeting, emblazoned somewhat awkwardly on its program: Diligence (to the Effort), Dedication (to the Handling of Details), Devotion (to the Field). "If you took those three Ds and you looked at them every morning, you conducted your daily activities with those as your standard, I don't think you could do wrong," he said.

Sattler showed a slide picturing a group of armed Marines. This was the eve of the battle of Fallujah, he said solemnly, where 10,000 warriors came "to drain the swamp and get rid of the terrorists." A year earlier, those same young men (they all happened to be men) were playing high school football and delivering newspapers, he said. Now they were bestowed with "the moral authority to take a life." Such profound responsibility meant they had to be instilled with a clear ethical code—"those moral principles that will guide that decision-making." Likewise, forensics practitioners must ensure their own work was beyond reproach. "In your profession, you live and die—you live and die reputational-wise at a minimum—by getting it right."

Rapidly veering from military scenarios to their application to forensics, Sattler was a bit hard to follow. It was unclear whether anyone was weirded out by his invoking of the Iraq War, a deadly misadventure based on false intelligence, as a vehicle for illustrating ethical decision-making. "Truth matters," he said, only to pivot to a slide of Lance Armstrong.

Nevertheless, some key themes eventually emerged. For one, as forensic scientists have learned all too well, one bad actor can tarnish an entire discipline. Not only must individuals strive to earn the highest level of trust from their peers and subordinate—a measure Sattler calls one's "T-factor"—they should be poised to stand up to bad behavior. It is part of having a "bias for action," Sattler explained—a readiness to move and to keep moving; to be constantly seeking improvement. Settling for the status quo is dangerous, even deadly, he warned. Outside every base in Iraq, "there was a giant sign above the gate as you went out into enemy territory. And it said: 'Complacency kills.' Complacency kills."

As an alternative theme for the 2019 AAFS meeting, "complacency kills" might not have been half bad, at least if anyone had wished to inject some urgency into things. The Baltimore event began amid an ongoing crisis within forensic science that remained woefully unresolved. When we first wrote about the AAFS for *The Intercept* following its 2016 conference in Las Vegas, we encountered an embattled field facing rising public scrutiny over some of its most cherished and longstanding disciplines. Wrongful convictions rooted in junk science, crime labs embroiled in scandal, and a devastating revelation about the FBI's hair microscopy division in 2015 had turned the image of forensics popularized by shows like *CSI: Crime Scene Investigation* on its head. The implications of the FBI scandal were particularly alarming. Hair analysts testifying on the stand had made erroneous statements in at least 33 death penalty cases, according to the agency. "Nine of these defendants have already been executed and five died of other causes while on death row."

But whereas there was some reason in Vegas to feel optimistic about the prospects for reform—the theme that year was "Transformation: Embracing Change"—things have seemed to go backward since then. A report critiquing the scientific validity of certain forensic techniques, released by the President's Council of Advisors on Science and Technology in the fall of 2016, met with aggressive pushback by the FBI and Barack Obama's Department of Justice. Then there was the election of Donald Trump and the elevation of Jeff Sessions, who put a halt on a number of federal initiatives that were just starting to get underway.

Much of the recent upheaval in the forensics world can be traced back to a landmark study released by the National Academy of Sciences in 2009. Titled "Strengthening Forensic Science in the United States: A Path Forward," the report questioned the scientific basis for virtually every forensic discipline used to convict people and send them to prison. With the exception of DNA analysis, it found, "no forensic method has been rigorously shown to have the capacity to consistently, and with a high degree of certainty, demonstrate a connection between evidence and a specific individual or source."

The NAS report was particularly damning for the so-called pattern-matching disciplines, in which an analyst examines a piece of evidence—say a bloody fingerprint found at a crime scene—and tries to match it to a sample belonging to a suspect. At AAFS, where forensic areas are divided into 11 different sections, many members of such fields responded with a mix of denial and defiance. While some practitioners took up the call issued by the NAS report—the fingerprint community, for example, has worked to develop objective comparison methods and determine error rates—others insisted the old ways of doing things were just fine.

In the intervening years, high-profile forensics scandals and a rising tally of exonerations have made it hard for even the most stubborn forensic experts to ignore the problem of junk science. At the 2017 AAFS meeting in New Orleans, a Virginia exoneree named Keith Harward, who spent 33 years in prison for rape and murder based on faulty bite-mark evidence, confronted the forensic dentists of the odontology section. He vowed to show up outside any courthouse where bite-mark evidence is used in the future. "I will contact the media. I will stand on the street corner in a Statue of Liberty outfit with a big sign saying, 'This Is Crap.'"

Nothing to See Here

As the AAFS meeting was getting underway in Baltimore, an article was published on the Innocence Project website, authored by the Honorable Harry Edwards, U.S. circuit judge in Washington, D.C. Titled "10 Year Anniversary of the Landmark Report on Forensic Evidence," it reflected on the progress made since the release of the NAS report—and the work left to do. Edwards is uniquely qualified to take stock of this legacy. He co-authored the report and released it to the world.

Edwards recalled the reaction to the NAS report in 2009. Some disliked that it "challenged established practices," he wrote, a criticism he regards as absurd. "When I explained the situation to my 8-year-old grandson, he asked me, 'Grandpa, does something bad become good just because it has been followed for a long time?' The answer is obvious."

Edwards never set out to be an authority on forensics. It was mainly the esteem of his colleagues that led him to co-chair the committee, formed in 2005, that would produce the NAS report. "I had a reputation of—at least this is what I was told—really fostering collegiality and bringing folks of different views together," he told The Intercept. "That was how I came to be selected. It was certainly not based on any of my experience in science. That was not my world."

As the committee did its research and heard testimony from leading forensic experts, Edwards became alarmed. "I was flabbergasted when I listened to the person that was testifying about bite marks," he recalled. "There were no studies of any consequence on validation, reliability, and I didn't have to be a scientist to understand that what he was saying was fragile, at best." If there was reason to expect some pushback from the members of such disciplines upon the release of the NAS report, other reactions took Edwards aback.

"The group that surprised me the most were prosecutors," he said. "Not just at Department of Justice, but prosecutors generally. Because I would've assumed, in my naïve way, that they would've welcomed a report saying we need more and better research to validate these practices, and to make them better. Because that serves both prosecutors and defendants well. And we got just the opposite. We got a lot of pushback from prosecutors."

"I think a number of them were worried that if you took the report seriously and started doubting some of what they had been doing, this would open cases that they thought were long gone," Edwards continued. For many in law enforcement who relied on longstanding forensic techniques to solve crimes, the NAS report was seen as a threat to their work.

If the 10-year anniversary of the NAS report was a clear opportunity to grapple with its ongoing legacy at AAFS, no one seemed to have told the conference organizers in Baltimore. Instead, they invited to the mainstage a plenary speaker who embodied the kind of skepticism and pushback that so troubled Edwards. They invited Ted Hunt.

A veteran prosecutor from Kansas City, Missouri, Hunt was tapped by Attorney General Sessions to head up the Department of Justice's Forensic Science Working Group—a decidedly opaque pseudo-successor to the very public work of the Obama-created National Commission on Forensic Science, which the Trump administration essentially disbanded. The NCFS included a variety of stakeholders—lawyers, judges, scientists, forensic practitioners, and law enforcement officials—tasked with finding ways to "enhance the practice and improve the reliability of forensic science." Hunt was among those who served on the NCFS, where he clashed with his colleagues on a number of issues — including those designed specifically to improve the reliability of forensic science. "Ted Hunt," one veteran conference attendee concluded, "is the Mike Pence of forensics."

Hunt is neatly-coiffed and trim, with the demeanor of an overcast day. He approached the lectern with an impassive expression and for roughly 30 minutes ambled through a series of platitudes—"we can't let the perfect become the enemy of the good"—inaccurately quoted Carl Sagan and Winston Churchill, and gave lip service to the need for forensic reform while cautioning that getting too wedded to scientific truth could be a problem—"the aspirational may be inspirational, but it's not necessarily operational." And he offered an example to highlight the power of good, old-fashioned, pre-NAS forensics and to excoriate detractors.

Back in 1997, someone broke into a convent in Kansas City through a second-story bathroom window and strangled and sodomized a nun before fleeing the premises. A fingerprint lifted from the window ledge matched a suspect named Jerry Owens; head hairs found in the nun's room were also consistent with Owens. Significantly, Hunt noted, a pubic hair later found on Owens's sock was consistent with the nun's pubic hair; the theory was that Owens picked up the hair after taking his shoes off in the bathroom in order to quiet his steps as he crept through the convent. There was no DNA testing available at the time, Hunt said, "but with the evidence we did have, it didn't matter." Based on the pattern-matching evidence, Owens was convicted and sentenced to two life terms plus 60 years.

But Owens maintained his innocence, persuading a big law firm to take up his cause. The hairs were sent off for DNA testing. "And on that day, science had the final say: The verdict came in and he was a perfect match to each hair," Hunt said. "Post-conviction testing affirmed Owens's guilt and also confirmed the relevance and reliability of the fingerprints and hair evidence offered at trial."

This kind of vindicating result happens all the time in the criminal justice system, Hunt said. "What is uncommon is the fact that you just heard about it." He pulled out an analogy that is a favorite among those who feel that the concerns raised by the NAS and other critical reports are overblown. "How many times do we hear about the planes that land safely at the airport each day? We only hear about the crashes. And then we hear about the same crashes, over and over again, as if the exception is the rule," he said. "In this field, the frequent focus on isolated failures has led to a carefully crafted, constantly reinforced, and patently false narrative that the forensic sky is falling. That's simply not true. Forensic science is not failing, it's flourishing."

Of course, we don't hear about planes making routine, safe landings, because that's what they're supposed to do. And to the extent we hear about the same failures over and over, it's because we need to know why they happened so that we can make improvements to prevent future disasters. The same is true in the criminal justice system, where forensic errors can lead an innocent man to the death chamber. It is impossible to know just how many cases have been negatively impacted by faulty forensics. Nearly half of DNA exonerations to date are in cases tainted by forensic errors. Focusing on mistakes—reviewing them and then applying lessons learned to the broader system—is the point, but not one that Hunt appears to have much patience for.

Instead he blamed critics—undisguised jabs at the Innocence Project, outspoken individuals within the forensics community, and journalist—for the crisis of confidence within the field. "Much of it is … strategic, dishonest, and destructive. Some of it is little more than agenda-driven advocacy in the guise of promoting scientific purity—a genre I call 'forensic science fiction,'" he said. Others promote "what I call 'junk journalism'—media stories full of partisan misinformation, strawman arguments, and half-truths about forensic science."

While Hunt's speech might've provided him a few satisfying zinger moments, it did little to reflect the sobering reality on the ground: Many forensic practices still lack meaningful scientific underpinning even though they are regularly used to prosecute individuals charged with crimes. The federal government has thrown what appears to be an impressive amount of money toward funding foundational research in forensics—more than $200 million since the NAS report was released—but that's hardly enough to cover the amount of ground necessary. In 2014, as one conference presenter noted, the feds funded forensic research at roughly $21 million; that same year the Department of Defense spent more than $41 million on Viagra. And there remain questions—and contention—over what should be researched and to what degree.

As the AAFS meetings over the past few years have made clear, in many ways, the current story of forensics is one of opposing factions: those who believe that science in service of the law needs to be just as strongly supported as pure sciences, and those—including many in law enforcement—who largely believe that things are just fine and that forensic sciences have proven themselves worthy over time regardless of whether their flaws can be drilled down to statistical truths. The question that remains is whether and how these two entrenched sides might find a workable middle ground.

Fighting over Biting

Of all the forensic disciplines and practitioners thrown into turmoil since the release of the NAS report, perhaps no group has melted down so publicly as the forensic dentists involved with bite-mark matching—the process of deciding that a patterned injury left on a victim was made by human dentition and then attempting to match the impression of that injury to the teeth of a suspect. The practice rests on a two-pronged foundation: First, that human dentition, like DNA, is unique; second, that skin is a suitable medium for recording this uniqueness. The problem is that neither premise has been proven true; in fact, scientific research conducted to date has suggested the opposite—and that bite-mark matching is an entirely subjective affair.

The NAS report, and an even more stinging critique of pattern-matching practices released by the President's Council of Advisors on Science and Technology in 2016, were particularly critical of bite marks. The "available scientific evidence strongly suggests that examiners cannot consistently agree on whether an injury is a human bite mark and cannot identify the source of [a] bite mark with reasonable accuracy," reads the PCAST report—a problem the group did not think could be rectified. "PCAST considers the prospects of developing bite-mark analysis into a scientifically valid method to be low. We advise against devoting significant resources to such efforts."

Despite the conclusions of the NAS, the PCAST, and academic researchers in the field—notably, Drs. Mary and Peter Bush, whose findings have been damning—the forensic odontologists have not gone quietly into the night. Instead, for the majority of the last 10 years they have spent considerable energy avoiding serious research into bite-mark matching and have instead focused on attacking their detractors, including skeptics among their ranks. Inevitably, this vitriol has found a public stage during the annual AAFS conference. Lions of the discipline, including David Senn, a professor at the University of Texas at San Antonio, have aggressively pursued dubious ethics complaints against detractors in an effort to get them tossed out of AAFS. Manhattan prosecutor Melissa Mourges, a chief bite-mark apologist, has repeatedly lashed out at Mary Bush, including by making childish public comments about her appearance.

People like Senn and Mourges have consistently come to AAFS conferences with presentations meant to bolster their insistence that bite-mark comparison is a righteous endeavor. In Las Vegas, Mourges pulled out the safely-landing-airplanes analogy to make the case that just because bite-mark analysis isn't perfect—indeed, bite-mark evidence, which is nowhere near as ubiquitous as say, fingerprints, has nonetheless been implicated in 31 wrongful convictions and faulty criminal indictments to date—that doesn't mean it's all bad. In Seattle in 2018, one dentist tried to elevate bite-mark evidence above the need for scientific scrutiny by claiming it was merely an "observational science" and thus not suited to empirical testing—"It's like astronomy, folks! You just can't control it."

That same year, another dentist, Dr. Robert Dorion, opined that the focus on wrongful convictions was "fake news," and suggested that there was a "moral, ethical, and legal obligation" to report on "rightful convictions." In fact, he said, wrongful convictions connected to bite marks "had ceased." When Chris Fabricant, director of strategic litigation at the Innocence Project and a relentless critic of bite-mark evidence, stood with a question challenging Dorion's assertion (Fabricant was then working on two wrongful conviction cases connected to bite marks), the dentist said that his presentation time was up, but that he'd answer the question in 2019 (he didn't). He then tootled off stage—before immediately returning to give a second presentation.

Despite the general intransigence—an insistence that all is fine in the face of plain evidence to the contrary—some key members of the community have broken ranks to embrace an inevitable truth: Junk science has no place in the criminal justice system.

At the 2015 conference in Orlando, two members of the community—Dr. Adam Freeman and Dr. Iain Pretty—presented the results of a study that were undeniably disastrous. Thirty-nine bite-mark analysts certified by the American Board of Forensic Odontology were asked to review 100 case studies and render an opinion on a most basic question: Is this injury a bite mark? The veteran practitioners came to unanimous agreement in just four cases. (Notably, the study did not consider whether the decisions were correct.) The following year the Texas Forensic Science Commission concluded that "there is no scientific basis for stating that a particular patterned injury can be associated to an individual's dentition," and recommended a moratorium on the use of bite-mark evidence.

Prompted by back-to-back blows to the credibility of the practice, a number of previous defenders of bite-mark comparison have begun to change their tune—including Dr. Frank Wright, who stood before his colleagues in Baltimore and offered a mea culpa. Wright, who participated in the Texas commission's bite-mark case review process, noted that for years he had stood before his fellow odontologists to say that bite-mark evidence was valuable. "I stand before you now to say I was wrong."

He said that there were members of the community who had "very strongly requested, if not demanded" that the results of the 2015 study not be made public and revealed that a subsequent study involving a smaller group of the most veteran examiners had yielded even worse results. Looking at the outcome, he said, "the light went off in my head and I said, 'Do we really know what we're doing?'"

Ultimately, Wright said that the entire field of bite-mark comparison had been built on decades of folly: "We learned it because patterns were shown to us and we were told they were bite marks. They went into our memory bank and that's what we compare" casework to, he said. "A 40-year history of confirmation bias as the sole support for bite-mark evidence. It cannot go on."

Wright implored the directors of the American Board of Forensic Odontology to issue their own moratorium on bite-mark comparison, but that did not happen. And there were other signs that not everyone is ready to lay down their dental molds—chief among them, Senn, a veteran leader of the pro-bite-mark tribe that members of the community often refer to as "Sennites." Senn was among a handful of odontologists who orchestrated a 2013 ethics complaint against Dr. Mike Bowers, who has spent the last two decades ringing the alarm over bite-mark evidence. The effort to bounce Bowers from the AAFS ultimately failed. Undeterred, Senn was behind a second set of complaints filed last year aimed at Freeman and Pretty, who have been increasingly outspoken about the practice since 2015. Those complaints were dismissed at the start of the Baltimore conference, which apparently did not please Senn. According to multiple witnesses, he and Freeman got into a heated discussion in the bar of the Baltimore Hilton that culminated in Senn trying to climb over a railing to attack Freeman. It didn't work; Senn got his leg caught mid-climb and had to back down. (Senn did not respond to emailed requests for comment.)

Surprisingly Little Progress

If the crackup within the odontology section exposed a struggle for the future of forensic dentistry, elsewhere in Baltimore things were comparatively drama-free. Many presentations were geared toward improving reliability and guarding against the cognitive bias and bad incentives that can skew the work of forensic practitioners. In criminalistics, a fire marshal from Connecticut warned fire investigators not to veer too far into policing when determining how a fire started. In engineering, a presentation covered how to handle it "when a client's 'pet theory' conflicts with good forensic science practice." The jurisprudence section wrestled with all aspects of wrongful convictions, a regular theme. And members across sections got updates on the Organization of Scientific Area Committees, an ambitious effort underway by the National Institute of Standards and Technology with the ultimate goal of developing standards "to ensure that a sufficient scientific basis exists for each discipline."

All of this made the opening plenary that much more vexing. Among AAFS regulars, the reactions ranged from weary indifference to indignation. Some were less bothered by Hunt's haughty sermon—some version of which they have come to expect from him—than by the speech that preceded it. It was delivered by Bonnie Armstrong, founder and president of an organization called the Shaken Baby Alliance.

Although it remains widely enshrined in medical literature, the diagnosis once known as Shaken Baby Syndrome is a cautionary tale. First coined in 1971 by a pediatric neurosurgeon who identified a "triad" of symptoms as proof that an infant was subjected to violent shaking, the concept has since been thoroughly debunked. Today SBS is an emblem of the kind of junk science that sends innocent people to prison; the National Registry of Exonerations lists 17 cases involving an SBS diagnosis—in 16 of those, it was ultimately determined that there was no crime at all. The most recent exoneration took place last year, in the case of Zavion Johnson, a Sacramento man accused of violently shaking his 4-month-old baby girl to death. Johnson was only 18 years old when he called 911 to report that his child was unresponsive. He spent 10 years in prison before prosecutors finally dismissed the charges against him in January 2018.

A former kindergarten teacher from Texas, Armstrong did not address the controversy over SBS, except as a brief aside about the founding of her advocacy group ("Oh how I wish we'd never used that name"). She began with a harrowing description of being raped by a stranger at a rest stop when she was 13 years old, then moved to the story behind the Shaken Baby Alliance. The organization was inspired by her adoptive daughter, Tiffany, who was brutally attacked by her biological father when she was a baby in 1994. Tiffany had been "shaken violently and beaten with a baseball bat," Armstrong said. Doctors gave a diagnosis of Shaken Baby Syndrome.

Armstrong was certainly sympathetic—and her account deeply disturbing. But her speech raised red flags. For one, there was the rather salient question of how a finding of SBS might relate to a baby being beaten with a baseball bat. More importantly, given the well-documented problems with SBS, why would AAFS place it center stage at an event ostensibly devoted to science?

One attendee, Michael Risinger, a law professor and expert on forensic evidence, walked out during the speech. He was dismayed that there was no one to provide the necessary scientific balance or context. "If the point of this was not to rally the troops to ... evaluate the scientific basis of these things with a sort of rational and truth-conducive neutral eye, then I don't know what the point of it was," he said.

High-profile forensics scandals and a rising tally of exonerations have made it hard for even the most stubborn forensic experts to ignore the problem of junk science.

The presentation reminded Risinger of a past AAFS plenary featuring an "awful film about abused babies," courtesy of the odontology section. Such things might be powerful calls to action—as Armstrong put it, "your work matters"—but they do nothing to contribute to sound science. This was especially disconcerting given the recent backsliding in reform efforts.

To be fair, several academy members pointed out that the plenary session is shaped by whoever is in charge year after year and not necessarily indicative of a larger shift in mission. John Lentini, a top fire scientist and longtime leader within the criminalistics section, said that in fact, AAFS has come a long way. Like forensic techniques themselves, which grew mostly out of the needs of law enforcement rather than the work of scientific researchers, the organization evolved from a prosecutorial mindset. "If you look at the history of AAFS, they've always been a police laboratory organization," Lentini said. In the early 1970s, he said, the organization refused to give fellowship status to Paul Kirk, "one of the great forensic scientists of the 20th century," because he worked for famed criminal defense attorney Lee Bailey. "The academy has certainly reformed because now the highest award in the criminalistics section is the Paul L. Kirk Award," Lentini said. "He didn't get the honor in his lifetime, but they came around to it."

This long slow evolution of what is today the most prestigious forensics organization is a good reminder of just how much time and effort it will take to get forensics as a whole on firmer scientific footing. After all, Risinger points out, some experts were raising the problem of scientific validity back in the 1980s. "The question is, have we made progress in 30 years in attempting to shift things? The answer to that is, yes, but surprisingly little."

Hostility to Reform

The slow progress is not just because of dissenting ranks within forensics. In many ways, the problem has been exacerbated by politics. While Vermont Sen. Patrick Leahy, a former prosecutor, has referred to the revelations of the 2009 NAS report as "rather chilling" and twice introduced a bill to codify some of its recommendations (the bills went nowhere), others have been openly hostile to the mere suggestion that forensic sciences need any meaningful reform. Chief among the naysayers when the NAS report was first released was then-Sen. Jeff Sessions, also a former prosecutor. "I don't think we should suggest that those proven scientific principles that we've been using for decades are somehow uncertain," he said at a hearing in September 2009. Given Sessions's stance—during the hearing he lamented that forensic examinations take so long that they hold up quick prosecutions—it is probably not so surprising that as attorney general he quickly put the kibosh on the forensics commission in favor of the mysterious working group now led by Ted Hunt.

But hostility to reform hasn't been a purely partisan issue. The release of the PCAST report in 2016 was met with even greater misgiving than the NAS report — perhaps in part because the language of the latter was far more judicious, while the PCAST report was blunt: "Without appropriate estimates of accuracy, an examiner's statement that two samples are similar—or even distinguishable—is scientifically meaningless: It has no probative value and considerable potential for prejudicial impact," reads the report. "Nothing—not training, personal experience nor professional practices—can substitute for adequate empirical demonstration of accuracy."

The pushback was swift—including from Obama's own attorney general, Loretta Lynch, who flatly rejected the report's recommendations for shoring up forensic practices. In a statement to the *Wall Street Journal*, Lynch said that her agency remained "confident that, when used properly, forensic science evidence helps juries identify the guilty and clear the innocent," and that the "current legal standards regarding the admissibility of forensic evidence are based on sound science and legal reasoning." The FBI also balked, as did a number of other law enforcement groups, including the National District Attorneys Association, which was particularly harsh. In a statement, the group accused the PCAST of "pervasive bias" and wrote that the report "conveniently overlooks the ancient debate over precisely what constitutes 'science.'"

Minnesota Judge Pamela King was working as a public defender when the NAS report came out during the 2009 AAFS conference in Denver. She had just become a member of the group and says that at the time she really didn't appreciate how important it was, though its release caused quite a stir. The reaction was "very, very mixed," she recalled. "I think there were some academy members who were up-set, felt threatened—really felt like they had committed their careers to doing good work and held themselves to a high degree of professionalism and they really felt that the perspectives that were being offered" by the NAS report "were attacking that." Still others, she said, "were delighted and were really excited" by what the report said and were "hopeful that that would improve the general way that forensic science is utilized and done."

There's been a fair amount of change since the report's release, and the National Commission on Forensic Science, of which King was a member, made a number of recommendations that were adopted—including a ban on practitioners using the phrase "reasonable degree of scientific certainty" when testifying about their con-fidence in the matches they've made. The terminology has no meaning outside the courtroom and yet suggests a strong scientific foundation that cannot be said about most forensic practices. Yet a number of promised reforms have not materialized.

At the 2016 conference in Las Vegas, then-Deputy Attorney General and NCFS co-chair Sally Yates announced that the DOJ would be conducting a "stress test" on various disciplines performed in the FBI lab—not because there were any par-ticular concerns, she was quick to say, but as a means of ensuring "the public's ongoing confidence in the work we do." The decision seemed a prudent one, given the alarming results of a joint review of thousands of FBI hair analysis cases, which revealed that FBI analysts had overstated their conclusions 95 percent of the time. "This doesn't necessarily mean that there were problems with the underlying sci-ence," Yates explained to the plenary audience. "It means that the probative value of the scientific evidence wasn't always properly communicated to juries."

Seven months later, Lynch announced that she was adopting the NCFS recom-mendations on testimonial language, but that wider stress test simply never hap-pened. "We were doing great until the Trump administration came about and … the things that were happening at the federal level, the policy stuff and so on, that came to a screeching halt," said Alicia Carriquiry, a professor of statistics at Iowa State University and director of the Center for Statistics and Applications in Forensic Evidence.

Carriquiry says that conversations happening among stakeholders and the DOJ just fizzled out after Trump was elected and Sessions was brought on board. And the NCFS wasn't the only advisory panel to get the hook. While Trump continued the PCAST on paper, he hasn't appointed any members to it. In December 2018, the DOJ disbanded its Science Advisory Board, which provided input to the department on what types of research—including in forensics—it should fund.

Even gains that had been made in curbing unsupportable testimony have since weakened, she said. "When the DOJ was under the Obama administration there were conversations. In fact, I participated in many of those where we would sit with the DOJ people and think about the type of language that should come out of crime labs and what type of reviews we should be doing of the disciplines," she said. "The second Sessions came on board those initiatives were killed dead."

It wasn't just that things stopped. "Worse, you know. They're trying to walk back many of the things we were making progress on," she said. "For example, we had come to some sort of an agreement about the fact that we were going to do a broad review of the disciplines." But when the Trump administration took over the attitude was, "'What review?' So that was completely done. Then we had come to an agreement on the type of language that should be used in reporting and testimony. That was squashed and the language went back to exactly what it used to be."

Resisting Science

For all the high-stakes political shifts that have stymied reform efforts, the basic problem remains: Some in the forensic science community simply resist the NAS report and what it stands for.

At the 2015 academy meeting in Orlando, the opening plenary hadn't even begun when a controversy broke out over the report. At issue was a question included in the Academy Cup, an annual contest in which members of each section form teams to answer forensics-related trivia. (Question: Who is the anthropology section member behind the hit TV show "Bones"? Answer: Kathy Reichs.) But one true-false question was tripping people up: Is the NAS report authoritative enough to be accepted as evidence in court?

The answer was—and is—yes, says retired New Mexico appeals court Judge Roderick Kennedy, who penned the question. But not everyone agreed, so the emcee polled the group: Who says it's true? No hands went up among the roughly 75 people assembled. False? A sea of hands shot up—"False!" several called out in unison.

Kennedy is not surprised at their reaction—many forensic practitioners don't necessarily understand the rules of court, he says. The NAS report has been admitted as evidence (though perhaps not as often as some defense attorneys would like) and cited by jurists. In December 2018 the notoriously rigid Texas Court of Criminal Appeals gave a firm nod to the report in an exhaustive opinion wherein the court concluded that Steven Mark Chaney had been wrongfully convicted based on bad bite-mark evidence.

The claim that the NAS report was not meant to be authoritative is as old as the study itself. Edwards, the federal judge and coauthor of the report, recalls some prosecutors authoring briefs stating that it "was not intended to have any impact on court proceedings. That's silly, of course." But some have gone even further. In one egregious case, Mourges, the New York prosecutor and defender of bite-mark analysis, brazenly manipulated the language of the NAS report in a 2014 brief seeking to admit bite-mark evidence in a murder trial—transforming its warnings over bite-mark analysis into an endorsement. After the journalist who exposed her linguistic sleight of hand was invited to give remarks at a luncheon held by the jurisprudence section in Baltimore—a speech in which he discussed the deceptive brief—Mourges came to confront him in a room full of lawyers and judges, demanding he "cut the shit."

People like Mourges and Hunt may wish they could censor the media that tarnishes the image of forensic evidence. But just as pep talks from motivational speakers do nothing to address the pressing challenges in the forensics world, silencing journalists won't make the problems go away. To Edwards, who remains proud of the NAS report and its influence, the real problem is that 10 years later, "we're not where we ought to be."

Edwards is dismayed at the shuttering of the NCFS, which "got killed just as it was beginning to get going." But for all its promise, one fundamental problem with the commission was that it was housed at the DOJ, which he called a mistake. One of his "great disappointments," he said, is the failure to fulfill one of the principal recommendations of the NAS report: a "national group that was independent, separate from law enforcement, that oversees forensic science." This group would have a budget "to fund serious research," assess validation and reliability studies, and help to set standards. "That hasn't happened."

Edwards has not given up hope that this might be possible in the future. "If we had one, I think it would work. And I think people would rally behind it. But you've gotta have the political will to set it up. ... Do we have the political will? I don't know."

Print Citations

CMS: Segura, Liliana, and Jordan Smith. "Bad Evidence." In *The Reference Shelf: U.S. National Debate Topic: 2020–2021 Criminal Justice Reform,* edited by Micah L. Issitt, 115-127. Amenia, NY: Grey House Publishing, 2020.

MLA: Segura, Liliana, and Jordan Smith. "Bad Evidence." *The Reference Shelf: U.S. National Debate Topic: 2020–2021 Criminal Justice Reform,* edited by Micah L. Issitt, Grey House Publishing, 2020, pp. 115-127.

APA: Segura, L., & Smith, J. (2020). Bad evidence. In Micah L. Issitt (Ed.), *The reference shelf: U.S. national debate topic: 2020–2021 criminal justice reform* (pp. xxx-xxx). Amenia, NY: Grey House Publishing.

Recent Developments in the Forensic Sciences

By Dr. Victor W. Weedn

United States Attorneys' Bulletin, January 2017

I. Introduction

Forensic science is generally dated to Hans Gross' *Handbuch für Untersuchungsrichter, Polizeibeamte, Gendarmen* (*Handbook for Magistrates, police officials, military policemen*), which was published in 1893, although forensic medicine and forensic toxicology are much older. Edmond Locard established the first crime laboratory in 1910 in Lyon, France. Depending on who is to be believed, the first crime laboratory in the United States was established in Los Angeles or Berkeley, California, in 1923. The FBI laboratory was established in 1932. Throughout the first half of the twentieth century, forensic science laboratories were established throughout the United States. Although the International Association for Identification has origins dating back to 1915, most professional forensic science associations were established during the second half of the century. Initial efforts towards standardization in the field soon followed. Perhaps more importantly, gas chromatography-mass spectrometers (GC-MS) were not in widespread use until the 1970s, and genetic analyzers were not in widespread use until the 1990s. Both are the basic laboratory instruments of modern crime labs. The television show *CSI* captured the attention of the public when it first aired in 2000. Particularly with the rise of databases (fingerprints, DNA, firearms), forensic science laboratories became increasingly powerful and increasingly important to the criminal justice system. The criminal justice system has had to adapt to this new reality; for instance, in addition to appeals based upon unfair process, actual innocence became a basis for appeals in DNA prosecutions. In this article, I will discuss some major developments in forensic science policy over the past several years.

II. 2009 National Academies of Sciences (NAS) Report

In February of 2009, shortly after President Obama took office, the National Research Council (NRC) of the National Academies of Science (NAS), supported by National Institute of Justice (NIJ) funding, published its influential report, *Strengthening Forensic Science in the United States: A Path Forward*. [NAT'L ACAD.

OF SCI., NAT'L RESEARCH COUNCIL, STRENGTHENING FORENSIC SCIENCE IN THE UNITED STATES: A PATH FORWARD (2009)]. The 2009 NAS Report on forensic science was not the first call for forensic science reform in America, but one that captured the attention of policymakers. Judge Harry T. Edwards and statistician Constantine Gatsonis, co-Chairs, speaking for their committee, concluded:

> The forensic science system, encompassing both research and practice, has serious problems that can only be addressed by a national commitment to overhaul the current structure that supports the forensic science community in this country. This can only be done with effective leadership at the highest levels of both federal and state governments, pursuant to national standards, and with a significant infusion of federal funds.

The NAS Report made 13 recommendations (paraphrased here):
1. Create a National Institute of Forensic Sciences (NIFS);
2. Standardize terminology and reporting practices;
3. Expand research on the accuracy, reliability, and validity of the forensic sciences;
4. Remove forensic science services from the administrative control of law enforcement agencies and prosecutors' offices;
5. Support forensic science research on human observer bias and sources of error;
6. Develop tools for advancing measurement, validation, reliability, information sharing, and proficiency testing, and to establish protocols for examinations, methods, and practices;
7. Require the mandatory accreditation of all forensic laboratories and certification for all forensic science practitioners;
8. Laboratories should establish routine quality assurance procedures;
9. Establish a national code of ethics with a mechanism for enforcement;
10. Support higher education in the form of forensic science graduate programs, to include scholarships and fellowships;
11. Improve the medico-legal death investigation system;
12. Support Automated Fingerprint Identification System interoperability through developing standards; and
13. Support the use of forensic science in homeland security.

The NAS Report has been referred to by many courts and was quoted by Justice Scalia in *Melendez-Diaz v. Massachusetts*, 557 U.S. 305 (2009) "to refute the suggestion that this category of evidence is uniquely reliable," but Justice Kennedy in his dissent writes:

> State legislatures, and not the Members of this Court, have the authority to shape the rules of evidence. The Court therefore errs when it relies in such great measure on the recent report of the National Academy of Sciences. *Ante*, at 12–14 (discussing National Research Council of the National Academies, Strengthening Forensic Science in the United States: A Path Forward (Prepublication Copy Feb. 2009)). That report is not

directed to this Court, but rather to the elected representatives in Congress and the state legislatures, who, unlike Members of this Court, have the power and competence to determine whether scientific tests are unreliable and, if so, whether testimony is the proper solution to the problem. . . .

Several bills have been introduced into Congress without passage; it is the Executive Branch that has most vigorously responded to the NAS Report.

III. Subcommittee on Forensic Science (SoFS)

In July 2009, the White House's Office of Science and Technology Policy (OSTP) created a "Subcommittee on Forensic Science" (SoFS) to address the issues raised by the NAS report. The SoFS oversaw five interagency working groups (Accreditation and Certification; Standards, Practices, and Protocols; Education, Ethics, and Terminology; Research, Development, Testing, and Evaluation; and Outreach and Communication), which were responsible for most of the work. SoFS participation spanned 23 federal departments and agencies, and was comprised of nearly 200 federal subject matter experts and 49 individuals representing state and local forensic scientists. This body completed its work December 2012 and published its report, *Strengthening the Forensic Sciences*, in May 2014. [NAT'L SCI. & TECH. COUNCIL'S SUBCOMM. ON FORENSIC SCI., STRENGTHENING THE FORENSIC SCIENCES (2014)]. The report recommended, among other things, the accreditation of forensic science service providers, the certification of forensic examiners and medicolegal personnel, proficiency testing for forensic examiners, and a national code of ethics for forensic service providers.

IV. National Commission on Forensic Science (NCFS)

In 2013, DOJ partnered with the National Institute of Standards and Technology (NIST) to establish the National Commission on Forensic Science (NCFS) as part of the Department's efforts to strengthen and enhance the practice of forensic science.

The Commission is co-chaired by the Deputy Attorney General and the Director of NIST, and consists of 29 voting commissioners and eight *ex officio* non-voting commissioners. The Commission includes federal, state, and local forensic science service providers; research scientists and academics; law enforcement officials; prosecutors, defense attorneys and judges; and other stakeholders from across the country. The work of the commission is supported by several subcommittees: Interim Solutions, Accreditation and Proficiency Testing; Human Factors; Medicolegal Death Investigation; Reporting and Testimony; and Scientific Inquiry and Research.

As a federal advisory committee, NCFS develops recommendations for consideration by the Attorney General. These recommendations are drafted by the subcommittees and then sent to the full body for a vote by all Commissioners. If approved, a copy of the recommendation is delivered to the Attorney General, who typically responds within six months. To date, the Attorney General has agreed to adopt several NCFS's recommendations, either in whole or in part, as discussed in greater depth elsewhere in this issue of the *Bulletin*. For more information, visit https://www.justice.gov/ncfs.

V. NIST Organization of Scientific Area Committees (OSAC)

Also in 2013, DOJ partnered with NIST to create the Organization of Scientific Area Committees (OSAC), which assists development of scientific standards in the various forensic science disciplines. The definitions, protocols, and practices, which comprise the "documentary standards" and guidelines considered by the OSAC, are actually promulgated by various Standards Development Organizations (i.e. ASTM, ASB, NFPA, etc.), but only "approved" standards and guidelines are posted to a National Registry.

The OSAC is composed of five scientific area committees (Biology/DNA, Chemistry/Instrumental Analysis, Crime Scene/Death Investigation, Digital/Multimedia, Physics/Pattern Interpretation) that oversee 25 subcommittees (covering the topic areas of the previous SWGs). The five SACs are overseen by the Forensic Science Standards Board (FSSB). The Human Factors, Quality Infrastructure, and Legal Resource committees also answer to the FSSB.

At the time of this writing, three standards have been posted to the National Registry of OSAC Approved Standards, but many others are in the pipeline. For more information, visit: https://www.nist.gov/forensics/organization-scientific-area-committees-forensic-science.

VI. Microscopic Hair Comparison Analysis (MHCA) Review

In response to a series of exonerations, beginning in late 2012, the DOJ and the FBI, with the collaboration of the Innocence Project (IP) and the National Association of Criminal Defense Lawyers (NACDL), reviewed laboratory reports and scientific testimony provided by FBI laboratory examiners in microscopic hair comparison analysis (MHCA) cases to identify statements that exceed the limits of science.

The review involved over 21,550 closed MHCA cases conducted prior to the year 2000. Of those cases, 3,189 involved a probative association between an evidentiary hair and a known hair sample. Many of these cases involved trials where a transcript of examiner testimony was available for review, although some resulted in guilty pleas prior to trial where only the original lab report was available for review. The majority of the FBI examiner testimony was provided in state court prosecutions.

The FBI, IP, and NACDL agreed to the basis of the MHCA review—namely, that individual statements in reports or testimony that, when viewed alone, did not meet accepted scientific standards, with no assessment of materiality regarding the impact of the report or testimony on the proceeding. The larger context of the complete testimony was not considered, including other language elsewhere that may have mitigated or corrected the overstatement. Language that had more than one interpretation was often conservatively marked as an error.

As part of this process, reviewers categorized potential errors into one of three "types":

- Error Type 1: The examiner stated or implied that the evidentiary hair could be associated with a specific individual to the exclusion of all others.

- Error Type 2: The examiner assigned to the positive association a statistical weight or probability, or provided a likelihood that the questioned hair originated from a particular source, or rendered an opinion on the likelihood or rareness of the positive association that could lead the jury to believe that valid statistical weight can be assigned to a microscopic hair association.

- Error Type 3: The examiner cited the number of cases or hair analyses worked in the lab and the number of samples from different individuals that could not be distinguished from one another as a predictive value to bolster the conclusion that a hair belongs to a specific individual.

An identified error does not necessarily mean that a conviction is invalid or even that the hair analysis evidence contributed to the conviction. DOJ notifies any identified statement errors to prosecutors and defense counsel so they may assess the materiality of the statements. If it is determined by the prosecutor's office that additional testing is necessary, or if a court orders such testing, the FBI provides DNA testing if the relevant evidence is in the government's possession or control.

In April 2015, FBI, IP, and NACDL issued a joint press release in which the FBI acknowledged that at least 90 percent of trial transcripts analyzed as part of the MHCA review contained erroneous statements. [Press Release, Fed. Bureau of Investigation, FBI Testimony on Microscopic Hair Analysis Contained Errors in at Least 90 Percent of Cases in Ongoing Review (April 20, 2015)]. The FBI found that 26 of 28 FBI agent/analysts provided either testimony with erroneous statements or submitted laboratory reports with erroneous statements. The review found that the overstated forensic matches favored prosecutors in over 95 percent of the trials reviewed.

The FBI has not completed their review as of the time of this writing, but it is nearing completion. The Texas Forensic Science Commission has also reviewed Texas state cases involving MHCA, although that review found a smaller percentage of cases with erroneous statements. Several other states are also conducting or preparing to conduct their own MCHA reviews in the future.

VII. Uniform Language for Testimony and Reports (ULTRs)

At the 10th meeting of the NCFS in June 2016, the Department announced that it was developing guidance documents governing the testimony and reports of its forensic experts. This guidance, known as the "Uniform Language for Testimony and Reports" (ULTR), clarifies what scientific statements DOJ's forensic experts may— and may not—use when testifying in court and drafting reports. The FBI currently uses Approved Scientific Standards for Testimony and Reports (ASSTRs) for this purpose.

The Department released draft versions of these guidance documents for public comment in mid2016. [Press Release, Dept. of Justice,

In addition to appeals based upon unfair process, actual innocence became a basis for appeals in DNA prosecutions.

Justice Department Issues Draft Guidance Regarding Expert Testimony and Lab Reports in Forensic Science (June 3, 2016)]. The draft documents were posted in two batches and cover fifteen forensic science disciplines: anthropology, body fluid testing (serology), explosive chemistry, explosive devices, fibers, footwear/tire treads, general chemical analysis, geology, glass, hair, latent fingerprint, metallurgy, mitochondrial DNA, paints/polymers, and toxicology. The Department received hundreds of comments and continues to review and revise the draft ULTRs. Once finalized and adopted, the ULTR documents will apply to all Department personnel, including forensic experts at FBI, ATF, and DEA. The exact timing for the release of the final ULTRs is unknown, although the Department hopes to complete its work in 2017.

Information on the FSDRs may be found on the DOJ forensics website at: https://www.justice.gov/forensics.

VIII. Forensic Science Discipline Reviews (FSDRs)

At the February 2016 meeting of the American Academy of Forensic Science (AAFS), Deputy Attorney General Yates announced that DOJ would review other forensic science disciplines, beyond microscopic hair comparison analysis. She suggested a quality assurance-like review for testimonial overstatements, not triggered by any specific cases or known or suspected problems, but as responsible oversight.

The Department elicited significant input through presentation of the framework, and then a more detailed plan for the Forensic Science Discipline Reviews (FSDR) was presented to the NCFS and posted for public comment, and a Statistician Roundtable was held. After deliberation, the goal of the FSDRs was declared to be "to advance the use of forensic science in the courtroom by understanding its use in recent cases and to facilitate any necessary steps to ensure that expert forensic testimony is consistent with scientific principles and just outcomes." [DEP'T OF JUSTICE, FORENSIC SCI. DISCIPLINE REVIEW OF TESTIMONY (2016)]. The FSDR will compare testimony in a case against the underlying report to ensure that statements conformed with the report. Once the review begins, identified instances of non-conformity will trigger further review and notification of the prosecution and defense.

Information on the FSDRs may be found on the DOJ forensics website at: https://www.justice .gov/forensics.

IX. President's Council of Advisors on Science and Technology (PCAST) Report on Forensic Science

In September 2016, The President's Council of Advisors on Science and Technology (PCAST) issued a report titled *Forensic Science in Criminal Courts: Ensuring Scientific Validity of Feature-Comparison Methods.* [EXEC. OFFICE OF THE PRESIDENT, PRESIDENT'S COUNCIL OF ADVISORS ON SCI. & TECH., FORENSIC SCIENCE IN CRIMINAL COURTS: ENSURING SCIENTIFIC VALIDITY OF FEATURECOMPARISON METHODS (2016).] The report took the position that unless a forensic discipline has been "scientifically validated"—in other words, unless a discipline has a known error rate—then judges should not allow the admission of expert testimony in that discipline. The report examined several specific forensic disciplines and concluded that several, including firearms, shoeprints, complex-source DNA, and bite marks, were not sufficiently validated and, therefore, expert testimony about these disciplines should not be admitted at trial.

Shortly after the report's release, Attorney General Loretta Lynch issued a statement indicating that the Department disagreed with certain findings and that it would not be adopting the report's recommendations related to the admissibility of forensic science evidence. [Gary Fields, *White House Advisory Council Report Is Critical of Forensics Used in Criminal Trials*, Wall St. Journal (Sept. 20, 2016)]. Since then, in a handful of cases, defense attorneys have filed *in limine* motions seeking to exclude the admission of expert forensic testimony. To date, these efforts have been unsuccessful. *U.S. v. Chester* (U.S. Dist Ct, N Dist Ill., Eastern Div; No. 13 CR 00774, Oct. 7, 2016), *IL v. Thompson* (Cook Cnty Cir Ct, 13 CR 426, Oct 25, 2016), *MA v. Legore* (Suffolk Cnty Superior Ct; SUCR 2015-10363, Nov 17, 2016), *MN v. Yellow* (6th Dist Ct; No. 69DU-CR-15-1363, Oct 28, 2016).

X. Forensic Science Research and Development

While all the above has transpired, the forensic science community around the world has continued research and development efforts and made substantial progress. During this administration, technologies introduced in the forensic science community include High Resolution and Q-TOF mass spectrometers, Rapid DNA Identification instruments, Next Generation Sequencers, and 3D laser-doppler crime scene scanners. NIJ alone funds more than $100M of forensic science and DNA-focused programming in forensic science research, forensic science practice improvement, and reduction of backlogs of untested sexual assault kits. In 2015, NIJ distributed $27.5M for research, development, testing, and evaluation; $69.8M for support of publicly-funded laboratories, police departments, and law enforcement agencies; and $6.6M for training and technical assistance. [NAT'L. INST. OF JUSTICE, PROJECTS FUNDED UNDER FISCAL YEAR 2015 SOLICITATIONS (2015)].

The OSTP recently formed a Forensic Science Research and Development Task Force.

XI. Medicolegal Death Investigation

The NCFS has had a Medicolegal Death Investigation (MDI) Subcommittee that submitted several work products approved by the Commission in the area of medicolegal death investigation. The Department contacted the White House OSTP to form a MDI Working Group.

XII. Conclusion

Substantial shifts in forensic science policy have occurred in recent years and will continue to occur for the foreseeable future. Perhaps, these can be summed up as greater attention and scrutiny, as well as a growing national shaping of the standards in the field.

Print Citations

CMS: Weedn, Victor W. "Recent Developments in the Forensic Sciences." In *The Reference Shelf: U.S. National Debate Topic: 2020–2021 Criminal Justice Reform,* edited by Micah L. Issitt, 128-135. Amenia, NY: Grey House Publishing, 2020.

MLA: Weedn, Victor W. "Recent Developments in the Forensic Sciences." *The Reference Shelf: U.S. National Debate Topic: 2020–2021 Criminal Justice Reform,* edited by Micah L. Issitt, Grey House Publishing, 2020, pp. 128-135.

APA: Weedn, V.W. (2020). Recent developments in the forensic sciences. In Micah L. Issitt (Ed.), *The reference shelf: U.S. national debate topic: 2020–2021 criminal justice reform* (pp. 128-135). Amenia, NY: Grey House Publishing.

Forensic Science Isn't "Reliable" or "Unreliable"—It Depends on the Questions You're Trying to Answer

By Claude Roux
The Conversation, September 10, 2019

After recent criticism in the US and the UK, forensic science is now coming under attack in Australia. Several recent reports have detailed concerns that innocent people have been jailed because of flawed forensic techniques.

Among the various cases presented, it is surprising that the most prominent recent miscarriage of justice in Victoria did not rate a mention: the wrongful conviction of Farah Jama, who was found guilty of rape in 2008 before the verdict was overturned in 2009.

This omission is not entirely unexpected. The forensic evidence in the case against Jama was DNA. Despite this fact, the recent media comments have re-emphasised the view that DNA is the gold standard when it comes to forensic techniques. Justice Chris Maxwell, president of the Victorian Court of Appeal, said:

> ...*with the exception of DNA, no other area of forensic science has been shown to be able reliably to connect a particular sample with a particular crime scene or perpetrator.*

How can the same technique simultaneously be the forensic gold standard and contribute to such a dramatic miscarriage of justice? Is forensic science so unreliable that none of it should be admissible in our courts? Of course not, otherwise the criminal justice system would be left relying on much less reliable evidence, such as witness statements and confessions.

Evidence in Context

It makes no sense to assess the reliability of any forensic technique in the abstract. A forensic method is only "reliable" as far as it helps answer the particular questions asked in the context of a particular case. Asking the wrong questions will undoubtedly deliver the wrong answers, even if the best and most fully validated forensic method is applied.

Conversely, some forensic methods are perceived by some commentators to have less intrinsic value or even questionable reliability. But these methods might yield the answer to a crucially relevant question.

A typical example would be an incomplete shoe mark of poor quality left at a crime scene. It might not be possible to assign this mark to a specific shoe, but it might be enough to exclude a particular shoe or to identify the direction in which the perpetrator walked.

Forensic science is much more than merely applying methods or conducting tests – success also depends on the ability to identify and answer a relevant question.

A forensic science system is not like a clinical laboratory, processing samples and producing results for prescribed tests. Rather, good forensic science requires collaboration between investigators, scientists and other stakeholders. The focus should be resolving judicial questions using a scientific approach.

What matters most is the detection, recognition and understanding of the traces left by individuals during an alleged crime. This is a much more complex issue than simply deciding whether or not a particular forensic method is deemed "reliable".

Complex Process

Forensic science is much less cut-and-dried than television dramas might suggest. When a DNA swab or a shoe mark lands on a forensic scientist's lab bench, it has already gone through many steps, each with their own uncertainties.

These uncertainties are unavoidable, because forensic traces typically represent the aftermath of a chaotic event. The only option is to manage these uncertainties through a better understanding of how these traces are generated, persist, degrade, interact with each other, and how the information they hold can be interpreted.

The debate about the reliability of forensic science is not new. It illustrates a more fundamental issue: the lack of understanding of forensic science among the general public (who are potential jurors), and even among highly reputable law practitioners and non-forensic scientists.

Legacy of Reform

The high-profile 2009 US National Academy of Sciences report and the 2016 Obama Administration report, both of which criticised some uses of forensic evidence, prompted an international reaction and several reviews of forensic practices.

They justified more empirical research to support some forensic conclusions. These improvements have been occurring in Australia for some years under the leadership of the National

> **Good forensic science requires collaboration between investigators, scientists, and other stakeholders. The focus should be resolving judicial questions using a scientific approach.**

Institute of Forensic Science and through several academic research programs. And the recent UK House of Lords enquiry into the state of forensic science in England and Wales identified the Australian forensic science model as a leading example.

However, these reports excluded crime scene management from the scientific domain. They provided limited guidance about the challenging topic of interpretation of forensic evidence. This is disturbing because these are the two areas that require most attention if we are serious about improving forensic science outcomes.

As the recent media coverage has shown, evidence interpretation remains a sore point between the legal and scientific communities. Where is the boundary of the responsibility of science versus the law? The fact that the legal community poorly understands forensic evidence is undoubtedly a shared responsibility. Shifting the blame onto forensic science will only exacerbate the problem.

If we think this is all too hard with traditional physical evidence, how does the criminal justice system expect to cope with our rapidly evolving digital society? Digital evidence is typically harder to assess than physical evidence in terms of volume, variety, rapidity, and privacy issues.

Better education, research and collaboration will form a large part of the answer. They will induce a better understanding of forensic science and its fundamental principles, so it can serve justice with confidence.

Print Citations

CMS: Roux, Claude. "Forensic Science Isn't 'Reliable' or 'Unreliable'—It Depends on the Questions You're Trying to Answer." In *The Reference Shelf: U.S. National Debate Topic: 2020–2021 Criminal Justice Reform,* edited by Micah L. Issitt, 136-138. Amenia, NY: Grey House Publishing, 2020.

MLA: Roux, Claude. "Forensic Science Isn't 'Reliable' or 'Unreliable'—It Depends on the Questions You're Trying to Answer." *The Reference Shelf: U.S. National Debate Topic: 2020–2021 Criminal Justice Reform,* edited by Micah L. Issitt, Grey House Publishing, 2020, pp. 136-138.

APA: Roux, C. (2020). Forensic science isn't "reliable" or "unreliable"—It depends on the questions you're trying to answer. In Micah L. Issitt (Ed.), *The reference shelf: U.S. national debate topic: 2020–2021 criminal justice reform* (pp. 136-138). Amenia, NY: Grey House Publishing.

Rep. Takano Introduces the Justice in Forensic Algorithms Act to Protect Defendants' Due Process Rights in the Criminal Justice System

U.S. House of Representatives, September 17, 2019

Washington, D.C.–Today, Rep. Mark Takano (D-Calif.) introduced the Justice in Forensic Algorithms Act of 2019 to ensure that defendants have access to source code and other information necessary to exercise their confrontational and due process rights when algorithms are used to analyze evidence in their case. This legislation will also establish standards and testing to enable a robust conversation about how these algorithms work and whether they are accurate and fair enough to be used in the criminal justice system.

"The trade secrets privileges of software developers should never trump the due process rights of defendants in the criminal justice system," said Rep. Mark Takano. "Our criminal justice system is an adversarial system. As part of this adversarial system, defendants are entitled to confront and challenge any evidence used against them. As technological innovations enter our criminal justice system, we need to ensure that they don't undermine these critical rights. Forensic algorithms are black boxes, and we need to be able to look inside to understand how the software works and to give defendants the ability to challenge them. My legislation will open the black box of forensic algorithms and establish standards that will safeguard our Constitutional right to a fair trial."

Across the country, law enforcement agencies are increasingly using a new type of software to partially automate the analysis and interpretation of evidence in criminal investigations and trials. These forensic algorithms have been used in thousands of criminal cases across the United States over the last decade to analyze everything from degraded DNA samples and faces in crime scene photos to gunshots and online file sharing. People are being convicted based on the results of these potentially flawed forensic algorithms without the ability to challenge this evidence due to the intellectual property interests of the software's developers.

Only the developers know how these algorithms work. Judges consistently side with developers and defendants are being denied the ability to challenge the evidence used against them and evaluate how these algorithms work because of the developers' trade secret protections. This presents a threat to due process rights and

> **These inconsistencies point to the need for greater transparency and understanding of the subjective human decisions involved when this software is being built and used.**

violates the confrontation rights guaranteed for defendants in the Constitution's Bill of Rights, as well as in federal, local, and state law. The *Justice in Forensic Algorithms Act* protects due process rights by prohibiting the use of trade secrets privileges to prevent defendants from challenging the evidence used against them.

There is still much to learn about how effective and trustworthy forensic algorithms really are. A case in upstate New York, where two different probabilistic genotyping programs were used to analyze the same sample demonstrates this subjectivity, one program found a match to the suspect and one said there was no match. These inconsistencies point to the need for greater transparency and understanding of the subjective human decisions involved when this software is being built and used. To address this, the *Justice in Forensic Algorithms Act* directs the National Institute of Standards and Technology (NIST) to establish Computational Forensic Algorithms Standards and a Computational Forensic Algorithms Testing program that federal law enforcement must comply with when using forensic algorithms. By establishing these standards and testing programs, defendants will have access to more information when evaluating the evidence used against them during a criminal proceeding.

Background on the Legislation

The *Justice in Forensic Algorithms Act* opens the black box of forensic algorithms by prohibiting the use of trade secrets privileges to prevent defense access to evidence in criminal proceedings and directing the National Institute of Standards a Technology to establish Computational Forensic Algorithms standards and testing. The bill:

- Ensures defense access by amending the Federal Rules of Evidence to prohibit the use of trade secrets privileges to prevent defense access to evidence they would otherwise be entitled to. Defendants will also receive a report on what software was used in their case and have access to the software so that they can test and reproduce the analysis.

- Directs NIST to establish Computational Forensic Algorithms Standards and a Computational Forensic Algorithms Testing Program and requires federal law enforcement to comply with these standards and testing requirements in their use of forensic algorithms. In developing standards NIST is directed to:

  - collaborate with outside experts in forensic science, bioethics, algorithmic discrimination, data privacy, racial justice, criminal justice reform, exonerations, and other relevant areas of expertise identified through public input;

  - address the potential for disparate impact across protected classes in standards and testing; and

- gather public input for the development of the standards and testing program and publicly document the resulting standards and testing of software.

- Requires Federal law enforcement agencies to comply with standards and testing requirements in their use of forensic algorithms.

Print Citations

CMS: "Rep. Takano Introduces the Justice in Forensic Algorithms Act to Protect Defendants' Due Process Rights in the Criminal Justice Systems." In *The Reference Shelf: U.S. National Debate Topic: 2020–2021 Criminal Justice Reform,* edited by Micah L. Issitt, 139-141. Amenia, NY: Grey House Publishing, 2020.

MLA: "Rep. Takano Introduces the Justice in Forensic Algorithms Act to Protect Defendants' Due Process Rights in the Criminal Justice Systems." *The Reference Shelf: U.S. National Debate Topic: 2020–2021 Criminal Justice Reform,* edited by Micah L. Issitt, Grey House Publishing, 2020, pp. 139-141.

APA: U.S. House of Representatives. (2020). Rep. Takano introduces the justice in forensic algorithms act to protect defendants' due process rights in the criminal justice systems. In Micah L. Issitt (Ed.), *The reference shelf: U.S. national debate topic: 2020–2021 criminal justice reform* (pp. 139-141). Amenia, NY: Grey House Publishing.

5
What the States Are Doing

By Ajay Suresh, via Wikimedia.

Many states have made reforms to the bail system, which disproportionately results in the pretrial incarceration of poor individuals.

The State of Criminal Justice

In his country, reforms that are pioneered in the states often get incorporated into federal policy much later. This is how American government is designed to work. State governments are, by nature, more reflective of immediate needs of their residents and can make changes more rapidly than the federal government. This does not mean that states are necessarily more progressive than the federal government; indeed, there have been many cases in which states have acted on key reforms only when forced to do so by new federal regulations. Regardless, states do better reflect local and regional priorities and, unless hampered by gerrymandering, better reflect the views of state residents as a unique subset of the American population.

The Importance of State Reform

Most of America's incarcerated population is incarcerated at the state, not federal, level. Likewise, most citizens interacting with the criminal justice system will do so through their state. There are more than 1,700 state prisons and 3,100 local jails in America, in addition to eighty facilities serving Native American populations. State laws have contributed to America's mass incarceration problem in several important ways: In 1973, New York State reforms known as the "Rockefeller drug laws" resulted in mandatory fifteen-year sentences for marijuana possession, contributing to higher rates of incarceration than at the federal level; Washington State was the first to adopt a "truth in sentencing" law, requiring individuals to serve at least 85 percent of their sentences before becoming eligible for parole, lowering rates of rehabilitative release.[1]

In addition, fewer than one in forty felony cases result in a trial, with a full 94 percent of criminal cases resolved through plea bargaining. In many cases, individuals who are accused of crimes are pressured to plead guilty under threat of more severe penalties for choosing to appear in court. The threat of mandatory sentences has greatly reduced the number of accused defendants willing to chance a jury trial. In 2011 *New York Times* writer Richard Oppel Jr. discussed a case in which a previously convicted man was offered a sentence of two years plus probation to plead guilty, which he rejected, claiming innocence. However, legislation at the state level meant that he would face a mandatory fifty-year sentence for the same crime if convicted by a jury. That the same crime could yield a two-year sentence by choosing to plead guilty vs. a fifty-year sentence by choosing to go to trial demonstrates the growing power of state prosecutors. Some argue that it shows how the legislative pressure to save costs and increase convictions has led to criminal justice system dysfunction.[2]

Because the state criminal justice systems handle the bulk of America's criminal cases, state laws are the most important frontier in criminal justice reform. Given that the vast majority of Americans, both within and outside of the criminal justice system, agree that major reforms are needed, state reforms stand as the most important way to address problems in the criminal justice system at large.

Trends in State Reforms

In the 2010s, one of the major trends in state-level criminal justice reform was a movement to alter the laws on sentencing. In 2019, California, Delaware, and Oklahoma passed sentencing reform laws, while the federal government's sentencing reform system stalled. Delaware removed "drug free" school zones and other sentencing enhancements, a move that was pioneered by New Jersey, Indiana, and Utah in previous years. Reforms in Oklahoma were even more far-reaching, as the legislature voted to reclassify a number of low-level felony crimes as misdemeanors.[3]

Another recent trend in state-level reforms has been a movement to expand voting rights for individuals convicted of felonies. Colorado, Nevada, New Jersey, and Kentucky were among the states that passed new laws increasing voting rights to individuals on parole or who had completed their felony sentences in good standing. In Kentucky—previously one of only three states with laws calling for the lifetime disenfranchisement felons—the move to restore voting rights came via an executive order from Governor Andy Beshear.

Another area of significant change in state-level reform has seen states struggling to adjust to a national shift in attitudes about marijuana. Both Illinois and New York have passed legislation calling for prior marijuana convictions to be expunged, coming as Illinois passed House Bill 1438, which legalized recreational marijuana use and possession for all residents twenty-one years of age or older. In New York, the state senate approved a bill that decriminalized marijuana and called for marijuana offenses to be punished by a fine rather than a conviction. The state also adopted a measure that allowed individuals with prior marijuana-related convictions to have their records expunged.

Another major debate in state-level criminal justice reform involves the issue of private prison systems. Both Nevada and California banned private prisons through state assembly bills in 2019. Prior to these changes, both states were among the twenty-eight states utilizing controversial for-profit prison services, while twenty-two states had already chosen not to contract out incarceration services. The movement away from private prisons has met with resistance from industry representatives concerned about a loss in profitability and from those who feel that the end of private incarceration will create resource allocation problems for state and public prison facilities. Nevada and California are the fourth and fifth states to pass legislation signifying a movement away from for-profit incarceration with previous bans on private prisons having been passed in Illinois, Iowa, and New York.[4]

Another arena in which states have made progress while federal legislators have stalled is with forensic science reforms. Most states have no independent oversight mechanisms in place for forensic quality control but several states have taken steps to address this issue. In one widely-known case, Harvard University's Criminal Justice Policy Program has been collaborating with the Committee for Public Counsel

Services and the New England Innocence Project to create a state forensic science commission for Massachusetts. While still in an embryonic stage, the Massachusetts program is a great example of how state governments can demonstrate greater flexibility and adaptability. By partnering state and private educational resources, the Massachusetts program can be used as a pilot for systemic forensics reform, and several other states have begun working on similar public-private partnerships to improve forensic science.[5]

States have also made waves is in bail reform, one of the most contentious issues in criminal justice. Advocates have long argued that inconsistent bail systems create a tiered system in which some individuals can purchase their way out of confinement while others without resources are forced to remain locked up. Individuals convicted of relatively low-level crimes who lack monetary resources, are among those most impacted by bail requirements. Defendants who lack financial resources may find themselves in debt and facing additional legal difficulties because of bail payments. With little bail system reform at the federal level, a number of states have enacted their own bail reform bills, with mixed results. The most controversial was New York's, where a law ending bail for misdemeanors and nonviolent felonies went into effect in January 2020. Unlike similar laws passed in California and New Jersey, New York's law takes discretion away from judges and mandates no bail for a specific list of crimes, including assaults that don't result in serious injury, burglary, many drug offenses, and even some forms of arson and robbery. Some individuals have been rearrested for additional offenses after being released without bail. Other state efforts at bail reform have produced little controversy. In New Jersey, for instance, a state law that eliminated cash bail and passed in 2017 resulted in no significant increase in crimes and saw no significant drop in persons returning to court for trial. In both California and Alaska, bail reform laws were passed by state legislatures but were later repealed, largely because of lobbying from representatives of the bail industry seeking to maintain profitability.[6]

The Microcosm and the Macrocosm

The relationship between state and federal laws is complex. When states pass reforms it typically means that federal legislators representing that state are under pressure to pursue similar measures at the federal level. In some cases, state laws and state-led movements for reform can inspire change on the national level, while in other cases state laws can exacerbate existing problems and states are forced to enact reforms through federal law. In some cases, state laws can create blueprints that are later used to craft legislation at the federal level.

The Trump administration has not taken an aggressive lead in the field of criminal justice reform and this reflects the priorities of the administration rather than a broad partisan split on the issue. Across partisan lines, there is widespread agreement that criminal justice reform is needed, though there is less agreement regarding how reforms should be carried out. Given this, the most productive and potentially important debates in the field of criminal justice are occurring in the states, and the laws and policies adopted by the states provide evidence for those interested in evaluating reform efforts to understand how similar measures might work at the national level.

Works Used

Casiano, Louis. "These States Recently Enacted Bail-Reform Laws." *Fox News*. Feb 22, 2020. Retrieved from https://www.foxnews.com/politics/these-states-recently-enacted-bail-reform-laws.

Eisen, Lauren-Brooke. "Criminal Justice Reform at the State Level." *Brennan Center*. Jan 2, 2020. Retrieved from https://www.brennancenter.org/our-work/research-reports/criminal-justice-reform-state-level.

"Forensic Science Reform." *CJPP*. Criminal Justice Policy Program. Harvard Law School. Retrieved from http://cjpp.law.harvard.edu/forensics.

Gorman, Steve. "California Bans Private Prisons and Immigration Detention Centers." *Reuters*. Oct 11, 2019. Retrieved from https://www.reuters.com/article/us-california-prisons/california-bans-private-prisons-and-immigration-detention-centers-idUSKBN1WQ2Q9.

Krehbiel, Randy. "'Retroactivity' Criminal Justice Bill That Reclassifies Felonies Clears Oklahoma House." *Tulsa World*. May 17, 2019. Retrieved from https://www.tulsaworld.com/news/retroactivity-criminal-justice-bill-that-reclassifies-felonies-clears-oklahoma-house/article_a3770284-445a-57ae-b879-18709206e346.html.

Oppel, Richard A. Jr. "Sentencing Shift Gives New Leverage to Prosecutors." *New York Times*. Sep 25, 2011. Retrieved from https://www.nytimes.com/2011/09/26/us/tough-sentences-help-prosecutors-push-for-plea-bargains.html.

Notes

1. Eisen, "Criminal Justice Reform at the State Level."
2. Oppel, "Sentencing Shift Gives New Leverage to Prosecutors."
3. Krehbiel, "'Retroactivity' Criminal Justice Bill That Reclassifies Felonies Clears Oklahoma House."
4. Gorman, "California Bans Private Prisons and Immigration Detention Centers."
5. "Forensic Science Reform," *CJPP*.
6. Casiano, "These States Recently Enacted Bail-Reform Laws."

From Marijuana to the Death Penalty, States Led the Way in 2019

By Daniel Nichanian
The Appeal, December 20, 2019

State legislatures this year abolished the death penalty, legalized or decriminalized pot, expanded voting rights for people with felony convictions, restricted solitary confinement, and made it harder to prosecute minors as adults, among other initiatives.

But criminal justice reform remains an uneven patchwork. States that make bold moves on one issue can be harshly punitive on others. And while some set new milestones, elsewhere debates were meager—and in a few states driven by proposals to make laws tougher.

The Political Report tracked state-level reforms throughout 2019. Today I review the year that was—by theme and with seven maps. And yes, each state shows up.

Death Penalty

While the Trump administration is attempting to restart executions, momentum built against the death penalty at the state level. Five states restricted, halted, or repealed the death penalty over a 10-month period that began in October 2018, when the Washington Supreme Court abolished the death penalty and converted the sentences of the people on its death row.

Then, in March of this year, California Governor Gavin Newsom, a Democrat, imposed a moratorium on executions. Prosecutors can still seek death sentences, though, and people remain on death row.

New Hampshire abolished the death penalty in May, becoming the 21st state to do so. This was a hard-won victory for death penalty abolitionists, who overcame a veto by Republican Governor Chris Sununu with no votes to spare in the Senate thanks to significant gains in the 2018 midterms.

In June, the New Mexico Supreme Court converted the sentences of the last two people on the state's death row. (New Mexico abolished the death penalty 10 years ago.)

Finally, in July, Oregon considerably narrowed the list of capital offenses. This is not retroactive, and leaves 30 people on death row; advocates have asked the governor for commutations.

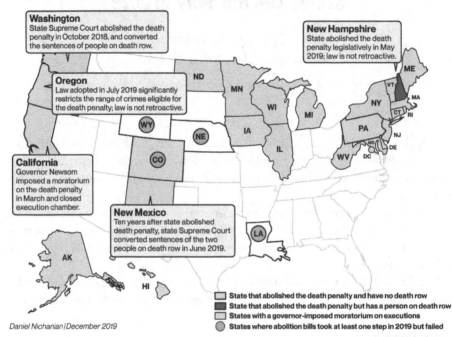

State action against the death penalty

Five states abolished, restricted, or stopped the death penalty between Oct. 2018 and July 2019

THE APPEAL | Political Report.

Washington
State Supreme Court abolished the death penalty in October 2018, and converted the sentences of people on death row.

New Hampshire
State abolished the death penalty legislatively in May 2019; law is not retroactive.

Oregon
Law adopted in July 2019 significantly restricts the range of crimes eligible for the death penalty; law is not retroactive.

California
Governor Newsom imposed a moratorium on the death penalty in March and closed execution chamber.

New Mexico
Ten years after state abolished death penalty, state Supreme Court converted sentences of the two people on death row in June 2019.

☐ State that abolished the death penalty and have no death row
■ State that abolished the death penalty but has a person on death row
☐ States with a governor-imposed moratorium on executions
◯ States where abolition bills took at least one step in 2019 but failed

Daniel Nichanian | December 2019

Other states considered abolition, and Wyoming came the closest—just a few votes short in the state Senate. Also: In Ohio, a bill to ban the death penalty for people with mental illness stalled in the Senate after passing the House; and legislation to require unanimous juries in Missouri failed. Arkansas was a rare state to adopt a law conducive to the death penalty; it made it a felony punishable by up to six years in prison to "recklessly" identify the makers of drugs used for an execution.

Parole and Early Release

The movement against the death penalty was accompanied by a nationwide push against death by incarceration, namely sentences that leave people virtually no chance of ever being released.

In Massachusetts, Pennsylvania, and Vermont, reformers championed bills to abolish sentences of life without the possibility of parole; these bills would have guaranteed that everyone will be at least eligible for release after some lengthy period of incarceration. They did not pass, but they expanded debates around long sentences. Pennsylvania Governor Tom Wolf, a Democrat, commuted the life sentences of eight people this month, reviving a power that had ground to a halt.

Oregon abolished juvenile sentences of life without the possibility of parole, namely for acts that people committed as minors. This increased the number of states that have repealed those sentences to 22 (plus Washington D.C.). But similar bills failed elsewhere, from Democratic-run Rhode Island to Republican-run South

**State action on parole
and early release in 2019**

THE APPEAL | Political Report.

In 2019, Oregon abolished life without the possibility of parole for minors, and expanded opportunities for early release for other lengthy sentences.

In 2019, Illinois re-introduced a parole process for some offenses people commit under the age of 21.

VT (H382)

MA (H3358 S826)

PA (SB942 HB135)

WA

ND

OR

SD

WY

IA

NV

UT

CO

KS

WV

CA

KY

DC

AR

TX

AK

HI

CT
NJ
DE

☐ States that have ended life without parole sentences for offenses committed under the age of 18
Sources: Juvenile Sentencing Project and the Sentencing Project

◯ States where legislation to abolish life without parole sentences for adults was introduced in 2019

December 2019 | Daniel Nichanian

Carolina. Oregon's law also confronted other types of lengthy sentences, creating new opportunities for early release or a revised sentence for people convicted of offenses they committed as minors. This is not retroactive, though, and state advocates are asking lawmakers to revise that.

In Illinois, which eliminated its parole process in 1978 and left many to spend decades in prison with no opportunity for release, a new law changes that paradigm: It will make most people convicted of offenses they committed before the age of 21 eligible for parole. While the law is narrow, advocates told me in April that they see it as a jumping-off point.

Hawaii came close to amplifying these efforts. But Governor David Ige, a Democrat, vetoed a bill to let people suffering from a terminal or debilitating illness request a medical release.

Youth Justice

In 2019, a pair of laws cut the number of teenagers who will be tried as adults. The youth justice system, despite major problems of its own, has a comparatively rehabilitative outlook.

First: mandatory prosecutions. In Oregon, a wide-ranging law repealed all requirements that some minors be prosecuted as adults. Such mandates triggered long sentences for teenagers above 15. (Advocates clinched a supermajority they had long sought for this reform, in a dramatic sequence.) While Florida also ended

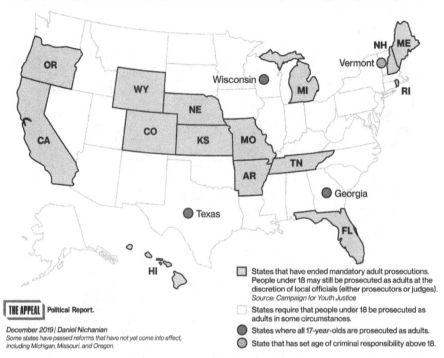

2019 restricted the prosecution of youth as adults
Michigan raised the age to 18. Oregon ended mandatory adult prosecution of minors and narrowed prosecutors' authority.

THE APPEAL | Political Report.

December 2019 | Daniel Nichanian
Some states have passed reforms that have not yet come into effect,
including Michigan, Missouri, and Oregon.

☐ States that have ended mandatory adult prosecutions.
People under 18 may still be prosecuted as adults at the
discretion of local officials (either prosecutors or judges).
Source: Campaign for Youth Justice

☐ States require that people under 18 be prosecuted as
adults in some circumstances.

● States where all 17-year-olds are prosecuted as adults.

● State that has set age of criminal responsibility above 18.

mandatory adult prosecutions this year, Oregon's law took another major step: Rather than empower district attorneys to solely decide when to try minors as adults, it forces them to first obtain a judge's approval.

Second: age eligibility. Michigan raised the age until which teenagers can be in the youth system by one year, to 18. Until now, the state treated every 17-year-old as an adult. Michigan prosecutors retain wide discretion to transfer them into adult court, however.

Michigan's reform left only three states that have passed no law raising the age to 18 (Georgia, Texas, and Wisconsin); each state saw unsuccessful efforts to change that this year. But in some states, the debate has already moved ahead, and advocates are asking why being a day over 18 should cut off access to the youth justice system. In 2016, Vermont passed a law to steer some people up to age 21 to its juvenile system. This year, Massachusetts debated a similar bill with support from three of the state's DAs; and Illinois passed an early-release law that atypically used 21, rather than 18, as its cutoff point.

Also this year: North Dakota raised to 10 from 7 the age at which children can be referred to the juvenile system, Maryland made it harder to detain children under the age of 12, New York made it easier for 16- and 17-year olds to stay in family court, and Washington restricted the detention of children over noncriminal acts like truancy.

Drug Policy

Marijuana legalization reached a new milestone in 2019: Illinois became the first state to create a regulated pot industry legislatively. Until now, this had only been done via popular initiatives.

Illinois also set up a process for people to get old marijuana convictions expunged, and adopted measures to help them enter the pot industry (though advocates warned these are insufficient); some of the revenue will be redistributed to areas with a high share of people with convictions. Here as elsewhere, advocates called such equity provisions essential to repairing some of the harm caused by prohibition, especially against African Americans.

Other states also reformed their marijuana laws to varying degrees. Hawaii, New Mexico, and New York decriminalized the possession of small amounts of marijuana. North Dakota reduced penalties, and removed jail time for first-time offenses. And Florida repealed its ban on smokable medical marijuana. But in Texas, and elsewhere, promising reform efforts stalled.

Colorado and Oklahoma led the way when it came to drug reforms beyond marijuana.

Democratic-governed Colorado made possession of most drugs a misdemeanor rather than a felony, which will reduce penalties and sentences going forward. (Advocates also prioritized a "defelonization" bill in Ohio, though it has yet to move.) Oklahoma already adopted this "defelonization" change in a 2016 referendum; this year, lawmakers made it retroactive. This reform is significant: Republican-governed Oklahoma is only the second state to retroactively defelonize drug possession, after

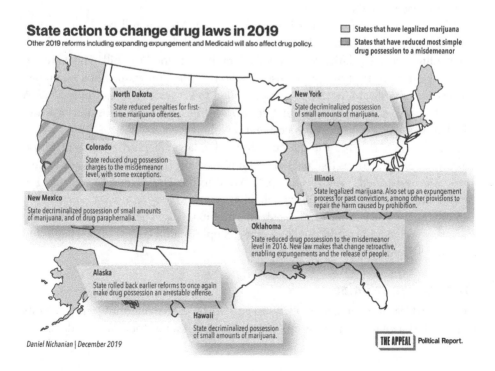

State action to change drug laws in 2019

Other 2019 reforms including expanding expungement and Medicaid will also affect drug policy.

☐ States that have legalized marijuana
☐ States that have reduced most simple drug possession to a misdemeanor

North Dakota
State reduced penalties for first-time marijuana offenses.

New York
State decriminalized possession of small amounts of marijuana.

Colorado
State reduced drug possession charges to the misdemeanor level, with some exceptions.

Illinois
State legalized marijuana. Also set up an expungement process for past convictions, among other provisions to repair the harm caused by prohibition.

New Mexico
State decriminalized possession of small amounts of marijuana, and of drug paraphernalia.

Oklahoma
State reduced drug possession to the misdemeanor level in 2016. New law makes that change retroactive, enabling expungements and the release of people.

Alaska
State rolled back earlier reforms to once again make drug possession an arrestable offense.

Hawaii
State decriminalized possession of small amounts of marijuana.

Daniel Nichanian | December 2019

THE APPEAL | Political Report.

> **State legislatures this year abolished the death penalty, legalized or decriminalized pot, expanded voting rights for people with felony convictions, restricted solitary confinement, and made it harder to prosecute minors as adults.**

California. This will reduce the existing prison population. Hundreds of Oklahomans quickly became eligible for release.

Alaska was a rare state to take a more punitive turn, rolling back earlier reforms to once again make drug possession an arrestable offense. A bill passed by Virginia's GOP-run legislature to make it easier to prosecute overdoses as homicides was vetoed by the state's Democratic governor.

Also: In states like Maine, Idaho, and Nebraska that expanded their Medicaid programs, and where lower-income individuals will have stronger access to health insurance, proponents cast the expansion as a way to combat the opioid crisis and better connect people to treatment for substance use. Kansas's new governor, Democrat Laura Kelly, called for Medicaid expansion to "ease the unsustainable burden on our … criminal justice system;" her push has yet to succeed.

Prison Conditions

New Jersey adopted the country's strictest law against solitary confinement, setting a limit of 20 consecutive days and 30 days over a 60-day period. But this remains beyond the United Nations' "Nelson Mandela Rules," which bar solitary for more than 15 consecutive days.

Advocates pushed for similar legislation in New Mexico and New York. It was not taken up in New York. And in New Mexico, which has high rates of use of solitary confinement, legislative leaders considerably weakened the bill. The state did adopt important restrictions on the use of solitary against pregnant women, minors, and people with disabilities. Connecticut failed to set another major milestone: A bill that would have made it the first state with free phone calls from prisons derailed after a telecommunications corporation lobbied against it.

These events captured the difficulty of getting lawmakers to care about prison conditions. Some reforms that passed exemplify the low bar. "Things we didn't know needed to be banned," Vaidya Gullapalli wrote in the *Daily Appeal* when Oregon banned the use of attack dogs on people in prison.

Perhaps the lowest bar of all: Alabama prohibited its sheriffs from personally pocketing public money allocated to feeding people held in county jails. They could do so legally until now.

Prison Gerrymandering

Nevada and Washington adopted laws to end prison gerrymandering, which counts incarcerated people at their prison's location rather than at their last residence for

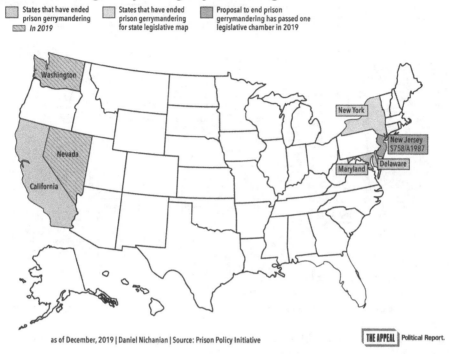

State action against prison gerrymandering

- States that have ended prison gerrymandering
- *In 2019*
- States that have ended prison gerrymandering for state legislative map
- Proposal to end prison gerrymandering has passed one legislative chamber in 2019

Washington

New York

New Jersey S758/A1987

Nevada

Delaware

Maryland

California

as of December, 2019 | Daniel Nichanian | Source: Prison Policy Initiative

THE APPEAL Political Report.

purposes of redistricting. The practice inflates the power of predominantly white and rural areas, where prisons are often located.

Still, despite the backlash against skewed census counts and against gerrymandering, only six states have ended this practice. The clock is ticking, since states draw new maps in 2021.

Rights Restoration and Felony Disenfranchisement

State politicians confronted felony disenfranchisement with new urgency in 2019, in the wake of Florida's historic Amendment 4, which inspired advocates around the state this year, and of the 2018 prison strike, whose organizers demanded voting rights for people in prison.

Florida and Kentucky, two very restrictive states that were each enforcing lifetime voting bans against hundreds of thousands of residents with felony convictions, promoted rights restoration once people complete a sentence. Florida implemented Amendment 4, restoring the voting rights of most people who finish a felony conviction. But state Republicans narrowed implementation in May by requiring payment of outstanding court debt, setting off legal and political battles.

In Kentucky, Democrat Andy Beshear won the governor's race and then promptly restored the voting rights of people who complete sentences for felonies classified as nonviolent. Tens of thousands of people who have completed their sentences will

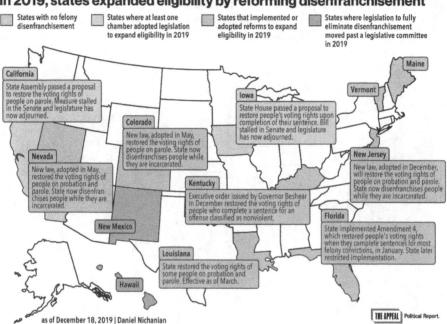

In 2019, states expanded eligibility by reforming disenfranchisement

☐ States with no felony disenfranchisement   ☐ States where at least one chamber adopted legislation to expand eligibility in 2019   ☐ States that implemented or adopted reforms to expand eligibility in 2019   ☐ States where legislation to fully eliminate disenfranchisement moved past a legislative committee in 2019

Maine

California
State Assembly passed a proposal to restore the voting rights of people on parole. Measure stalled in the Senate and legislature has now adjourned.

Vermont

Iowa
State House passed a proposal to restore people's voting rights upon completion of their sentence. Bill stalled in Senate and legislature has now adjourned.

Colorado
New law, adopted in May, restored the voting rights of people on parole. State now disenfranchises people while they are incarcerated.

New Jersey
New law, adopted in December, will restore the voting rights of people on probation and parole. State now disenfranchises people while they are incarcerated.

Nevada
New law, adopted in May, restored the voting rights of people on probation and parole. State now disenfranchises people while they are incarcerated.

Kentucky
Executive order issued by Governor Beshear in December restored the voting rights of people who complete a sentence for an offense classified as nonviolent.

New Mexico

Florida
State implemented Amendment 4, which restored people's voting rights when they complete sentences for most felony convictions, in January. State later restricted implementation.

Louisiana
State restored the voting rights of some people on probation and parole. Effective as of March.

Hawaii

as of December 18, 2019 | Daniel Nichanian

THE APPEAL Political Report.

remain disenfranchised; still, 4 percent of Kentucky's population regained the right to vote with just one stroke of the pen.

Beshear's order leaves Iowa as the only state that enforces a lifetime voting ban over all felony convictions; legislation to reform that rule had momentum, but died in the Iowa Senate. Mississippi's legislature similarly ignored a slate of bills that would have eased its harsh voting rules.

Three states went further to decouple voting and the criminal legal system: They enfranchised all voting-age citizens who are not incarcerated, including if they are on probation or on parole.

Only one state had passed such a reform this past decade (Maryland). But Colorado, Nevada, and New Jersey all did so this year. This brought the number of states that allow all adult citizens who are not incarcerated to vote to 18. (That number includes Maine and Vermont, where people can also vote from prison; they also can in Puerto Rico.) Also: Louisiana implemented a 2018 law that lets some people vote while serving a sentence. The secretary of state did not play an active role informing newly-enfranchised people of their rights, leaving the burden of outreach on grassroots groups.

In some states, advocates focused on ending felony disenfranchisement. This would end the practice of stripping people with felony convictions of their right to vote, including if they are in prison. Lawmakers in eight states plus Washington D.C. filed legislation to that effect. In Hawaii and New Mexico, these bills advanced past a committee; that was already historic since reform on this issue has traditionally been more incremental.

Also: Illinois adopted a law requiring prisons to better inform incarcerated people of their right to vote upon their release. On a parallel issue, California ended its ban on people with felony convictions serving on juries once they have completed their sentences.

Immigration and Local Law Enforcement

In Illinois and New Jersey, Democrats prohibited county governments from entering what may be the most visible form of partnership with ICE: its 287(g) program, which authorizes local law enforcement to act as federal immigration agents within county jails.

These two states join California as the only state to take such a step. This reform did not advance in other Democratic-governed states like Massachusetts and New York, both of which have state or local agencies with 287(g) contracts. In fact, Colorado Governor Jared Polis, a Democrat, threatened to veto such a ban, citing the value of local control.

Another major front regarding local law enforcement's cooperation with ICE was the legality of "detainers," which are ICE's warrantless requests that jails keep detaining people beyond their scheduled release. Colorado Democrats adopted a law that forbids honoring detainers; in New Jersey, Democratic Attorney General Gurbir Grewal did the same, though he allowed for exceptions. Inversely, a law championed by Florida Republicans mandates that local law enforcement honor

The landscape of 287(g) contracts with ICE

Illinois and New Jersey banned local governments from joining ICE's 287(g) program in 2019, joining California

THE APPEAL Political Report.

Daniel Nichanian | December 2019

- States that have banned local or state governments from contracting into ICE's 287(g) program through a law
- State that has banned local or state governments from contracting into ICE's 287(g) program through the attorney general's authority
- States where at least one county has contracted into ICE's 287(g) program (source: ice.gov)
- States whose statewide Department of Corrections has contracted into ICE's 287(g) program

ICE requests; a full-throated effort by the North Carolina GOP to do the same failed because of Democratic Governor Roy Cooper's veto.

Also: Colorado, New York, and Utah cut the maximum sentence for some or all misdemeanors by one day (from 365 to 364). This seemingly-small tweak will shield some people from deportation because noncitizens sentenced to at least one year of detention risk deportation.

Past Records and Expungement

Beyond their immediate sentences or fines and fees, involvement with the legal system restricts people's access to housing, transportation or employment. In response, some states expanded opportunities for people to expunge their criminal records.

Take Delaware, which newly gave people the opportunity to expunge some convictions without first obtaining a pardon. Or West Virginia, which expanded eligibility to cover some felonies.

But most people eligible for expungement do not seek one, as the process is costly and burdensome. As such, one of the year's important trends is the spread of "Clean Slate" laws that automate parts of the expungement process, shifting the burden onto the government.

After Pennsylvania became the first state to adopt such a law in 2018, Utah followed suit this year. California, besides starting to implement a law that automatically clears pot convictions, expanded automation this fall. (California's Clean Slate law is not retroactive, unlike those of Pennsylvania and Utah, but its law is the only one to extend eligibility to some felony convictions.) Michigan and New Jersey have also begun the process of adopting Clean Slate laws.

Elsewhere, lawmakers lessened the tremendous impact that court debt has on the lives of people who cannot afford to pay it. Montana led the way, halting the suspension of driver's licenses over a failure to pay fines and fees, a practice that can trigger mounting legal and economic hardships; Tennessee and Virginia passed more modest versions of this legislation.

California advocates were unsuccessful in their push for a bill that outright banned many fees; Newsom vetoed another bill that would have required judges to determine people's financial ability before imposing fines and fees. In Florida, Republicans tied state politics more tightly to financial obligations by subordinating rights restoration to repayment of fines and fees.

Finally, responding to studies showing that restricting the residency of people convicted of sexual offenses is isolating and fuels homelessness, the GOP-run Wisconsin legislature unanimously passed a bill repealing those restrictions. But Governor Tony Evers, a Democrat, vetoed the bill.

And There's More

On **pretrial procedures**, New York adopted two major changes: It ended the use of cash bail for people charged with misdemeanors and some felonies; it also required that DAs share evidence like witness statements within 15 days of a defendant's first court appearance. These reforms' implementation is a major question heading into 2020 given the resistance of many prosecutors. Also, Colorado prohibited cash bail in low-level cases, and required bond hearings within 48 hours of arrest.

On **policing**, a California law restricted the circumstances in which police officers can use deadly force, though some advocates questioned the reform's scope. California also adopted a three-year moratorium on the use of facial recognition technology in body cameras. And New Jersey mandated that all cases of people killed by police be investigated by the attorney general rather than prosecutors.

On **sentencing**, proponents of reduced sentences had high hopes in Arizona but reforms either died in the legislature or were vetoed by Republican Governor Doug Ducey. By contrast: North Dakota repealed some mandatory minimums, California ended an automatic enhancement statute, Washington slightly narrowed its three-strike law, and Delaware Attorney General Kathleen Jennings, a Democrat, overhauled sentencing guidelines. In South Dakota, the legislature defeated a tough-on-crime push to increase prison admissions.

On **probation**, Minnesota and Pennsylvania considered proposals to cap the length of probation, whose burdens often trip people up on small violations. But Pennsylvania lawmakers gutted the bill so much its champions turned against it; the Minnesota proposal never moved forward in the legislature, but its sentencing commission is now considering adopting it administratively.

On **exonerations**, a new Indiana will provide exonerated individuals $50,000 of restitution for each year they were incarcerated—but only if they agree to forego all litigation against the state.

On **prosecutors**, some lawmakers took steps for DAs to stop operating a black box. Connecticut became the first state to require that prosecutors collect an extensive collection of data about the decisions they are making. Louisiana reduced DAs' power to jail victims of sexual offenses or domestic violence to compel them to testify. And California barred plea deals in which DAs ask defendants to forfeit hypothetical future rights, in response to a strategy that San Diego DA Summer Stephan was implementing.

On **asset forfeiture**, finally, Arkansas adopted the unusual rule of requiring that individuals actually be convicted of a felony before having their assets seized. And while it looked like Hawaii would do the same amid significant problems in the state's system, Ige vetoed the bill.

Preparations are already well underway for 2020 legislative sessions, whether in Virginia, where newly-empowered Democrats are unveiling their agenda, in Maryland, where change in legislative leadership may make criminal justice reform more viable going forward, or in New York.

Print Citations

CMS: Nichanian, Daniel. "From Marijuana to the Death Penalty, States Led the Way in 2019." In *The Reference Shelf: U.S. National Debate Topic: 2020–2021 Criminal Justice Reform,* edited by Micah L. Issitt, 149-160. Amenia, NY: Grey House Publishing, 2020.

MLA: Nichanian, Daniel. "From Marijuana to the Death Penalty, States Led the Way in 2019." *The Reference Shelf: U.S. National Debate Topic: 2020–2021 Criminal Justice Reform,* edited by Micah L. Issitt, Grey House Publishing, 2020, pp. 149-160.

APA: Nichanian, D. (2020). From marijuana to the death penalty, states led the way in 2019. In Micah L. Issitt (Ed.), *The reference shelf: U.S. national debate topic: 2020–2021 criminal justice reform* (pp. 149-160). Amenia, NY: Grey House Publishing.

Voting Rights Restoration Gives Felons a Voice in More States

By Matt Vasilogambros

Pew/Stateline, January 3, 2020

A mistake Rynn Young made decades ago, when he was just a teenager, cost him the right to vote.

Twenty-one years after his drug possession conviction, he got his ballot back when newly elected Democratic Kentucky Gov. Andy Beshear signed an executive order last month restoring voting rights to nonviolent felons after release.

"It's been a very long time coming," Young said at the signing ceremony in Frankfort, Kentucky, surrounded by civil rights leaders. "I've never had the right to vote. My words have always fallen on deaf ears … I appreciate the opportunity for a second chance, just to be heard."

This was one of Beshear's first acts as governor. Two days earlier, he announced at his inauguration that he would restore the right to vote for 140,000 "men and women who have done wrong in the past but are doing right now." His Christian faith, he said, teaches him forgiveness.

"They deserve to participate in our great democracy," he told the inaugural crowd in front of the state Capitol in Frankfort.

Kentucky joined 17 other states that have restored voting rights over the past several decades to felons after they leave prison. In every state except Maine and Vermont, felons are stripped of their voting rights while in prison. In most states, that ban remains for a certain period (Iowa has a lifetime ban, unless reversed by the governor) after they are released, disenfranchising millions of people.

In the past year, however, six states implemented measures restoring voting rights to people with felony convictions.

This shift is part of a broader reaction against the tough-on-crime policies of the 1980s and 1990s. Across the political spectrum, more people are questioning the incarceration of nonviolent offenders and backing anti-recidivism efforts.

"The vast majority of people disenfranchised live in our communities, own homes and pay taxes," said Sarah Shannon, an associate professor of sociology at the University of Georgia who has studied the impact of reinstating voting rights to felons. "They're not behind bars. So, what is it that's stopping us from allowing those folks from fully participating in our democracy?"

Still, strong opposition remains from lawmakers and election integrity advocates who say felons made a choice and must live with the consequences. Other opponents say these measures are ploys by Democrats to gain more voters, a charge Democrats deny.

Long Time Coming

For some former convicts, activists and lawmakers, last year's success was the culmination of years of effort. In New Jersey, for example, Democratic state Rep. Shavonda Sumter has lobbied her colleagues since she took office in 2012, slowly building an appetite for action.

In December, New Jersey enfranchised people with felony convictions. The measure, which applies to people who leave prison but are still on parole or probation, restored the voting rights of 80,000 people.

Sumter, who sponsored the measure, told *Stateline* she is proud to have changed a policy that was "inherently, systematically wrong." African Americans are far more likely to be incarcerated and disenfranchised in New Jersey than residents of other races, according to data compiled by the Sentencing Project, a Washington, D.C.-based criminal justice nonprofit.

"When we start carving people out just because of a crime they committed that had nothing to do with voting, we start stripping them of humanity," Sumter said.

She hopes that on Election Day in November, she can walk around her hometown of Paterson, handing out "I Voted" stickers, and not have disenfranchised constituents tell her they can't accept one.

But Republican state Rep. Hal Wirths, who previously served on a New Jersey parole board, voted against the measure. He says those on parole or probation haven't yet served their sentences and shouldn't be allowed to vote until they do. Around 20 states allow felons to re-register to vote after their parole or probation period and after they've paid any fines.

"I believe in everyone getting second chances," Wirths said. "We all make mistakes. The main thing here is that they haven't finished their sentences yet."

In California and Iowa, measures to restore voting rights to felons made it through one legislative chamber but stalled in the other amid disagreement over whether to include felons with murder or rape convictions. Legislation in New Mexico stalled after making it out of committee, while measures in six other states didn't progress.

Elsewhere, proponents for enfranchising felons have turned to the courts. In Minnesota, four residents with criminal records are suing Democratic Secretary of State Steve Simon, in his capacity as the state's top election official, to reinstate their and other formerly incarcerated residents' voting rights.

Elizer Darris, 35, has never had the right to vote. As a juvenile he was sentenced to life in prison for murder, but his sentence was later reduced and he was freed in 2016. Now, he works as an organizer with the local chapter of the American Civil Liberties Union and he said he wants to help choose the elected officials who make decisions that affect him.

"It's like being invisible," Darris said. "It doesn't make our communities safer to relegate people to the corners."

While he would not comment on the pending lawsuit, Peter Bartz-Gallagher, communications director for Minnesota's secretary of state, said even as Simon is the defendant in this case, he remains in favor of restoring the right to vote to people as soon as they get out of prison. Around 50,000 felons who have finished their sentences remain disenfranchised in Minnesota, he said.

> **Across the political spectrum, more people are questioning the incarceration of nonviolent offenders and backing anti-recidivism efforts.**

"It is an investment in helping people connect with their community," Bartz-Gallagher said. "It leads to a stronger democracy and makes communities safer. This isn't a niche issue. It affects a lot of people who are trying to rebuild their lives."

Some opponents such as the Minnesota Voters Alliance, a St. Paul-based election integrity group, do not think the secretary of state's defense of the state law disenfranchising felons is strong enough. The group has filed a motion to intervene in the lawsuit and join the defense.

Andy Cilek, executive director of the alliance, which calls itself nonpartisan, said the previous support for felon enfranchisement from Simon and Democratic Attorney General Keith Ellison, who will lead the state's defense, make them biased in the case.

Further, Cilek thinks this issue should be resolved through the legislature by amending the state constitution. And he says measures that enfranchise felons really are about helping Democrats boost voter registration.

"That's what it's all about," Cilek said. "There's no doubt about it."

The lawsuit is currently in discovery, which will take several more months, said David McKinney, a staff attorney with the ACLU of Minnesota, which is representing the four plaintiffs in court. After trying for years to get bills through the legislature, McKinney said it's time for the courts to act.

The Case in Florida

The future of a Florida measure that would restore the voting rights of 1.4 million felons is also in the hands of the courts.

After nearly two-thirds of Florida voters passed a constitutional amendment in 2018 that would enfranchise people with felony convictions, Republican lawmakers and GOP Gov. Ron DeSantis have sought to limit the measure. A new law requires that all court fees and fines and other criminal restitutions be paid before people can vote.

This was met by a series of lawsuits from civil rights groups, who argued the measure constituted a poll tax. Daniel Smith, a University of Florida political science professor, testified in October this new law prevents 80% of otherwise eligible felons from voting.

"We thought we were on a good track to get these rights restored, but we've had all of these obstacles thrown in the way," said Patricia Brigham, president of the League of Women Voters of Florida, one of the organizations suing the state. "We're waiting on further court decisions. There is a lot up in the air."

The organization has held several training sessions for lawyers who want to work pro bono to help felons determine whether they can register to vote or have outstanding fines and fees.

In October, a federal judge ruled the state couldn't deny voting rights to people who are "genuinely unable" to pay legal fees. Republicans have argued that these fees are part of a criminal sentence and must be paid before voting rights are restored.

Florida lawmakers are expected to draft new legislation when they return to work this month. In the meantime, DeSantis has asked the Florida Supreme Court to weigh in.

Other states are trying to ease some of that confusion. In Iowa, felons leaving prison will now be handed filled-out forms by the Department of Corrections to make it easier for them to apply to get their voting rights restored by the governor. Previously, discharged inmates had to fill out a complicated form on their own.

Iowa lawmakers failed in 2019 to pass a constitutional amendment that would have restored voting rights for felons. Republican Gov. Kim Reynolds has said she will wait on the legislature instead of signing an executive order.

States will continue to explore ways of giving voting rights back to felons, said the University of Georgia's Shannon. While some states will make sweeping changes applying to all felons, others might limit enfranchisement to people who committed certain crimes. It's unlikely, she said, that many states would go a step further and start giving those in prison voting rights.

Print Citations

CMS: Vasilogambros, Matt. "Voting Rights Restoration Gives Felons a Voice in More States." In *The Reference Shelf: U.S. National Debate Topic: 2020–2021 Criminal Justice Reform,* edited by Micah L. Issitt, 161-164. Amenia, NY: Grey House Publishing, 2020.

MLA: Vasilogambros, Matt. "Voting Rights Restoration Gives Felons a Voice in More States." *The Reference Shelf: U.S. National Debate Topic: 2020–2021 Criminal Justice Reform,* edited by Micah L. Issitt, Grey House Publishing, 2020, pp. 161-164.

APA: Vasilogambros, M. (2020). Voting rights restoration gives felons a voice in more states. In Micah L. Issitt (Ed.), *The reference shelf: U.S. national debate topic: 2020–2021 criminal justice reform* (pp. 161-164). Amenia, NY: Grey House Publishing.

California Set to End Private Prisons and Immigrant Detention Camps

By Steve Gorman
Reuters, October 9, 2019

LOS ANGELES (Reuters)—America's largest state prison system is moving to quit the practice of farming out inmates to lockups run under contract by private companies, following a nationwide decline in the for-profit incarceration business.

California Governor Gavin Newsom is expected to sign legislation this week designed to effectively ban private, for-profit corporations from running prisons or immigration detention facilities.

Sponsors of the measure say it will end a brief but hapless experiment in privately outsourced incarceration begun as a means to ease overcrowding—an endeavor Newsom branded an outrage when he took office in January.

Bill supporters say private prisons, driven to maximize shareholder profits, lack proper oversight or incentives to rehabilitate inmates, and have contributed to a culture of mass incarceration by making it cheaper to lock up people.

> **Sponsors of the measure say it will end a brief but hapless experiment in privately outsourced incarceration begun as a means to ease overcrowding.**

They point to research cited in a 2016 U.S. Justice Department Office of Inspector General report that found private prisons spend less on personnel, and are less safe, than public institutions.

"This is a total and complete failure, and it's hurting and abusing Californians," said state Assemblyman Rob Bonta, a chief author of the bill.

The facilities at stake are low-security lockups operated by one of two leading U.S. private prison companies, Florida-headquartered GEO Group (GEO.N) or Tennessee-based CoreCivic (CXW.N).

Defending their business model, the companies say they provided a vital service when detentions in California's prisons more than doubled the system's capacity, sparking lawsuits that led to court-ordered cuts to inmate populations.

"For 10 years, we provided safe, secure housing and life-changing re-entry programing for inmates that had faced extreme overcrowding," CoreCivic spokeswoman Amanda Gilchrist said.

Separately, GEO Group cited its record as "an innovator in the field of rehabilitative services" and said the bill worked against the state's goal of lowering inmate
recidivism.

Significant Loopholes

Inmate advocacy groups say the legislation does not go far enough, pointing to what
they call significant loopholes, including an exemption for facilities that provide
"educational, vocational, medical or other ancillary services" to inmates.

"I cannot think of any prison that does not provide those services," said Kara
Gotsch, director of strategic initiatives for the Sentencing Project, a criminal justice
reform group.

Several states, including New York, Illinois and Nevada, have adopted similar
bans on private prisons, and nearly half of all states have no such facilities, Gotsch
said.

The bill sets the stage for the three remaining private prisons in California, col-
lectively housing about 1,400 inmates, to close four years from now, when their
contracts with the state Department of Corrections and Rehabilitation expire.

Perhaps more significantly, the federal Immigration and Customs Enforcement
(ICE) agency stands to lose four privately-run detention facilities in California next
year that hold roughly 4,000 people, unless the ban is challenged in court.

ICE has not taken a public position on the bill. But assuming the measure were
adopted, detainees would simply be transferred to facilities outside California, the
agency said in a statement.

The impact "would be felt almost exclusively by residents of California, who
would be forced to travel greater distances to visit friends and family in custody,"
ICE said.

The average daily population at issue in those facilities accounts for less than a
tenth of the 52,000 ICE holds nationwide, it said.

Small Fraction

The bill, which secured its final passage by the state legislature last month, bans
any new or renewed California contracts with private, for-profit prisons, starting in
January.

Four detention facilities privately operated for ICE would be put out of business
even sooner, when their contracts with the federal government expire next year,
Bonta said.

California had already been moving in this direction, terminating in June its
contact with a privately-run correctional center in Arizona—the last of several such
out-of-state facilities—followed by last month's closure of a 700-bed facility in Mc-
Farland, California, near Bakersfield.

The state's share of inmates in private facilities is a small fraction of its total
prison population of nearly 126,000.

By comparison, Texas, which became the first state to outsource incarceration to private companies in 1985, had far more inmates than any other state in for-profit facilities in 2017, nearly 13,000, or 7.8 percent of its total, said Gotsch of the Sentencing Project.

Print Citations

CMS: Gorman, Steve. "California Set to End Private Prisons and Immigrant Detention Camps." In *The Reference Shelf: U.S. National Debate Topic: 2020–2021 Criminal Justice Reform,* edited by Micah L. Issitt, 165-167. Amenia, NY: Grey House Publishing, 2020.

MLA: Gorman, Steve. "California Set to End Private Prisons and Immigrant Detention Camps." *The Reference Shelf: U.S. National Debate Topic: 2020–2021 Criminal Justice Reform,* edited by Micah L. Issitt, Grey House Publishing, 2020, pp. 165-167.

APA: Gorman, S. (2020). California set to end private prisons and immigrant detention camps. In Micah L. Issitt (Ed.), *The reference shelf: U.S. national debate topic: 2020–2021 criminal justice reform* (pp. 165-167). Amenia, NY: Grey House Publishing.

NYPD Overhauls Rules for DNA Evidence in Criminal Cases

By Ben Chapman

The Wall Street Journal, February 20, 2020

The New York Police Department is updating its rules for the collection and use of DNA evidence, a critical tool that has come under scrutiny for its growing role in criminal investigations and prosecutions, Commissioner Dermot Shea said.

The changes, which include easier processes for the removal of DNA samples from a digital index and limits on the collection of samples from juveniles, aim to build trust with the community and are part of a series of reforms, Mr. Shea said in an interview Wednesday.

Mr. Shea's move comes as police departments around the country seek to balance privacy and civil-rights concerns as DNA takes on an increasingly important role in investigations and prosecutions.

"I think it's incumbent upon us to make sure that we're being as fair as possible," Mr. Shea said at NYPD headquarters. "Anytime you dig your heels in and say, 'It's our way or the highway,' I think you should pause and reflect a little on what you're doing."

DNA evidence is used by the NYPD in hundreds of cases each year, police officials said. One recent, high-profile example is the killing of Barnard College student Tessa Majors, where police say DNA linked Ms. Majors to at least one of the suspects charged in her death.

Partly in response to concerns raised by New York lawmakers and defense lawyers, the NYPD is undertaking a number of changes to increase transparency and fairness in its use of such evidence, Mr. Shea said.

The NYPD will begin by conducting an audit of the Local DNA Index System, a database of roughly 82,000 samples from crime scenes and individuals maintained by the Office of Chief Medical Examiner.

Any sample that is more than two years old and isn't linked to a continuing case or conviction will be flagged for removal, police officials said.

The department also will streamline processes for people seeking to have samples of their DNA removed from the index, officials said. Individuals acquitted in criminal cases involving DNA may have their samples removed from the index by providing proof of disposition. Previously, a court order was required.

New limits will be placed on the collection of samples from juveniles, NYPD officials said, so that investigators may only collect DNA samples in cases where they are being investigated for felonies, sex crimes, firearm crimes or hate crimes.

New rules for investigators will ensure that when a sample is obtained by consent, a parent or guardian would be notified and can object to the collection, officials said.

The consent form for the collection of DNA samples also will be updated to state that individuals may refuse to provide samples and to specify that the samples may be kept in an index for future use.

DNA is becoming increasingly common in criminal trials, where juries have grown to expect such evidence, said Rachel Singer, chief of the forensic science unit in the Brooklyn district attorney's office. "It's the 'CSI' effect," she said.

> **Any sample that is more than two years old and isn't linked to a continuing case or conviction will be flagged for removal.**

In 2019, the Local DNA Index System yielded roughly 1,550 DNA matches linking samples to individuals in active criminal investigations, police said. At the Brooklyn district attorney's office, about half of the 490 matches made in 2019 resulted in indictments, Ms. Singer said. DNA also helps investigators clear suspects from crimes, she added.

But some law-enforcement practices involving DNA, such as the collection of samples from suspects without their consent and the collection of masses of samples in investigations, are troubling, said New York state Sen. Brad Hoylman, a Democrat who represents parts of Manhattan.

He has sponsored a bill in Albany that would prohibit local agencies such as the NYPD from maintaining DNA databases, while still permitting the use of DNA in investigations.

Terri Rosenblatt, supervising attorney of the DNA Unit at the Legal Aid Society, New York City's largest criminal defense group, said the NYPD's changes don't go far enough to enact meaningful reform.

"The changes are meaningless," Ms. Rosenblatt said. "The New York City Police Department's plan still violates the law and continues genetic stop-and-frisk."

The New York City Council is to hold a hearing Tuesday in Manhattan on the NYPD's use of DNA, where lawmakers and police officials will discuss the city's database, said the council's Public Safety Committee Chair Donovan Richards, a Democrat from Queens.

"We want to hear a lot more about their methods and how they put people in" the DNA database, Mr. Richards said.

Corrections & Amplifications: The Local DNA Index System is maintained by the New York City Office of Chief Medical Examiner and stores data collected by the New York Police Department. An earlier version of this story incorrectly said it was the NYPD's index.

Print Citations

CMS: Chapman, Ben. "NYPD Overhauls Rules for DNA Evidence in Criminal Case." In *The Reference Shelf: U.S. National Debate Topic: 2020–2021 Criminal Justice Reform,* edited by Micah L. Issitt, 168-170. Amenia, NY: Grey House Publishing, 2020.

MLA: Chapman, Ben. "NYPD Overhauls Rules for DNA Evidence in Criminal Case." *The Reference Shelf: U.S. National Debate Topic: 2020–2021 Criminal Justice Reform,* edited by Micah L. Issitt, Grey House Publishing, 2020, pp. 168-170.

APA: Chapman, B. (2020). NYPD overhauls rules for DNA evidence in criminal case. In Micah L. Issitt (Ed.), *The reference shelf: U.S. national debate topic: 2020–2021 criminal justice reform* (pp. 168-170). Amenia, NY: Grey House Publishing.

Chicago Judge Says His Bail Reforms Were a Success. But Independent Reviews Show Flaws and More Crimes.

By Scott Shackford
Reason, February 20, 2020

Chicago's bail reforms may not have had the rosy outcomes indicated by a top county judge's analysis, which independent researchers say is downplaying the new crimes that have resulted from allowing defendants to await trial outside of jail.

Those are the results of an analysis by a group of *Chicago Tribune* reporters in a new investigative piece as well as a just-published data analysis paper by University of Utah professors Paul Cassell and Richard Fowles.

In 2017, Cook County Chief Judge Timothy Evans implemented an order reforming how the Chicago area courts handled pretrial detention. The goal was to reduce the demands for cash bail, which tend to keep people trapped behind bars on the basis of poverty rather than risk. Cook County met its goal of detaining fewer defendants before their trials. The number of defendants who secured pretrial release between 2016 and 2018 jumped from 71.6 percent to 80.5 percent. When cash bail was ordered, the amount demanded was much lower than before. Cook County's jail population dropped from 7,443 to less than 6,000.

Last May, Evans released a report that showed releasing more defendants from jail did not put the community at greater risk of crime. A high proportion of defendants (83 percent) charged with felonies and released under the new system returned to court as ordered and did not commit new crimes while released. In all, Evans' report painted a positive picture that matched the narrative of those who support bail reform: That court systems in Cook County were accurately sorting defendants based on the risk they posed to public safety and their likelihood of showing up to trial, rather than simply leaving everyone in jail simply because they couldn't afford to pay what the courts ordered.

But further examination of Evans' data paints a less rosy picture. Last week, *The Chicago Tribune* reported that Evans' report left out hundreds of violent crime charges filed after the bail reforms were implemented. The reporters say he did this by including certain violent crimes (murder, attempted murder, non-negligent manslaughter, forcible rape, robbery, and aggravated battery) and excluding incidents like domestic violence, assault with a deadly weapon, battery, reckless homicide, and others. If Evans' report had included all these other crimes, the *Chicago Tribune* calculates the number of violent crimes allegedly committed by released defendants would jump from 147 to 578. The largest chunk of these charges—231 of them—were for domestic battery.

> **The cost of new crimes committed by a percentage of defendants free before trial financially outweighs the savings of freeing people who aren't dangerous.**

Furthermore, Evans' report stated that only three defendants who had been released under the new pretrial system had subsequently been charged with homicide. But the *Tribune* identified 21 defendants accused of murder who had been released during the 15 months of bail reform the report reviewed. Their exclusion from Evans' report is supposedly a result of incomplete records and some odd reporting decisions like only counting the first new charge a defendant received after being released (two of the defendants were arrested for another charge, then released, and then allegedly killed people); or not counting them because their initial charges weren't felonies (five murder defendants had been bonded out on misdemeanor charges).

In a separate review, Cassell and Fowles reanalyzed Evans' data and found other problems.

For one thing, there's a significant flaw in how Evans measured new crime charges prior to his bail reforms and afterward. When calculating the crime rate, Evans' report evaluated the "before" defendants for an average of 243 days and the "after" defendants for an average of just 154 days. This is a significant methodological problem because reducing the time frame in the post-reform evaluation gives these defendants less time to commit new crimes. Cassell and Fowles argue that this difference of nearly 100 days may well mean that, in actuality, the post-reform crime rate among those released might be even higher. Cassell and Fowles' report observes, "the second group will, other things being equal, undoubtedly commit fewer additional crimes simply because they have had less time to commit such crimes."

The two attempts to estimate what the crime rate might actually be if the report monitored the post-change pool for the same time frame. It's a challenging calculation, they note, because they couldn't find any studies showing month-to-month re-arrest rates among those released pretrial. So they used some modifications in stats from the Bureau of Justice Statistics for recidivism rates among those who have been released from prison, combined with some pretrial recidivism rates from Cook County's data. They conclude that in all likelihood, Cook County's report undercounted new crimes committed by released defendants by about 1,200. When they correct for the time frame, Cassell and Fowles estimate that there was actually a 45 percent increase in the number of new crimes caused by defendants who had been released.

It's important to make it clear that this is a mathematical model, and Cassell and Fowles aren't specifically detailing a bunch of concrete new crimes that have been committed by these defendants. But part of the problem here is that the court has been reluctant to share the data Evans used with *Chicago Tribune* reporters, which required the newspaper to file a petition with the Illinois Supreme Court. Evans has since agreed to share his data with the newspaper.

Cassell and Fowles write that their goal is not to kill off bail reforms or scare courts away from implementing them. Rather, they are concerned about biases in self-analysis that "always lurks when an entity implementing reform later studies whether that reform is successful. In this case, it appears that many dangers stemming from the court's expansion of pretrial release were not carefully assessed by the court's own subsequent study."

These kinds of independent assessments are extremely valuable in part because these reforms are still relatively new and they make a number of people very, very nervous. Part of that fear results from deliberate scaremongering by those who have a financial or political stake in protecting a harsh status quo, like bail bond companies and jail officials.

But as the Cassell and Fowles report notes, poorly managed pretrial reforms can backfire and cause additional harms. If you agree, for example, with the argument for reform—that it's a violation of a person's rights to keep them locked up before they're convicted only because they cannot pay bail—you must also consider the risk they pose to the rights of other people if they are released before trial. In a city like Chicago, it is mostly poor people whose rights are violated by the bail requirement *and* mostly poor people whose rights are violated by the defendants who commit additional crimes before their trials.

If, on the other hand, you make a utilitarian argument that keeping people locked up because they're too poor to pay bail but aren't dangerous is much more expensive than letting them return home, Cassell and Fowles note that the cost-benefit analysis changes if the person commits new crimes before trial. While there are established financial harms to pretrial detention (lost jobs and housing) and established benefits to letting them out to continue to work and care for families, the economic impact of a homicide wipes out the financial benefits of letting more people out of jail.

At some point, the cost of new crimes committed by a percentage of defendants free before trial financially outweighs the savings of freeing people who aren't dangerous. Data-driven bail reform is supposed to prevent a few bad defendants from spoiling it for everyone, yet Cassell and Fowles argue that it does not appear to be working as intended in Chicago: "Given equal weight to the benefits the pool of such defendants receive when compared to the costs inflicted on victims seems dubious."

The report ends not trying to bash reforms but warning that court systems need to really explore the impact of pretrial release data and make sure they're not perpetuating new harms: "To be sure, such pretrial release reforms can have significant benefits. But only if both benefits and costs are accurately measured can a sound decision be made about which way the scales tip and whether the 'reform' was truly an improvement."

Print Citations

CMS: Shackford, Scott. "Chicago Judge Says His Bail Reforms Were a Success: But Independent Reviews Show Flaws and More Crimes." In *The Reference Shelf: U.S. National Debate Topic: 2020–2021 Criminal Justice Reform,* edited by Micah L. Issitt, 171-174. Amenia, NY: Grey House Publishing, 2020.

MLA: Shackford, Scott. "Chicago Judge Says His Bail Reforms Were a Success: But Independent Reviews Show Flaws and More Crimes." *The Reference Shelf: U.S. National Debate Topic: 2020–2021 Criminal Justice Reform,* edited by Micah L. Issitt, Grey House Publishing, 2020, pp. 171-174.

APA: Shackford, S. (2020). Chicago judge says his bail reforms were a success: But independent reviews show flaws and more crimes. In Micah L. Issitt (Ed.), *The reference shelf: U.S. national debate topic: 2020–2021 criminal justice reform* (pp. 171-174). Amenia, NY: Grey House Publishing.

Big Risks in Discovery Reform: N.Y.'s New Law Tips the Balance Way Too Far in Favor of Defendants

By Seth Barron and Ralf Mangual
New York Daily News, June 3, 2019

Police Commissioner James O'Neill has spoken up about serious problems in the bail-reform legislation that was passed as part of the state budget. The Legislature curtailed the ability of judges to assign bail regardless of the risk to public safety or the record of the accused.

The commissioner is right; Albany needs to fix its bail-reform legislation to give judges more discretion over who walks free after being arrested for serious crimes. But our lawmakers also need to redo another set of criminal-justice reforms they rushed through without considering all the consequences.

The new standards for discovery that Albany imposed on prosecutors risk endangering witnesses and crime victims.

Discovery is the process through which prosecutors turn over evidence so someone accused of a crime can mount a capable defense. The new laws mandate that the prosecution must reveal all its evidence within 15 days of arraignment.

Currently, discovery is required before a trial starts, which only happens in about 3% of all cases. To be sure, this measure will equip defendants with information about the evidence against them before deciding whether to take a plea bargain, and give them more time to prepare a trial defense. Ensuring that defendants are not coerced into accepting plea deals is a worthwhile goal.

But the new law goes too far, as all five borough district attorneys have testified.

One of the primary reasons why witnesses are hesitant to cooperate with an investigation is confidentiality. Brooklyn DA Eric Gonzalez explains, "if you talk to any assistant district attorney, they will tell you that one of the first questions they are asked by victims and witnesses is: 'Will the defendant know who I am?' 'Will they know where I live?'"

Prosecutors will no longer be able to assure witnesses that their identity will be protected, even in the case of grand jury testimony, which the new law will now require be disclosed. (While there's a provision to ask a judge for a protective order to shield a name, that would come after cops and prosecutors talk to witnesses to make an arrest and build a case.)

Manhattan DA Cy Vance put it this way: "Having to hand defendants a roster of who has spoken out against them just 15 days after their first appearance, absent a protective order, is a seismic change that undoubtedly will dissuade witnesses who live in all neighborhoods from reporting crime."

It gets worse. The new law increases the likelihood of defendants being granted access to the locations—stores, bank vaults, bedrooms—where they are accused of committing crimes. In a section entitled, "Order to grant access to premises," the law stipulates that the defense may apply for "access to an area or place relevant to the case in order to inspect, photograph, or measure same." A judge can exercise discretion about access, but the provision appears to establish a presumption of material necessity for "preparation of the case" by the defense.

> **District attorneys who oppose the reforms are not lock-'em-up conservatives.**

Acting Queens DA John Ryan asks, "How do we tell a burglary complainant that the defendant may have the right to come into her house with an investigator to take pictures?" Beyond taking pictures, the law seems to permit the defendant to "inspect" the premises, presumably to undertake his own investigation of the crime scene. Thus a suspected home invader and rapist could be permitted to poke around the same room where he committed his crimes.

This new law, which favors defendants to the extreme, was largely drafted by public defenders. But the district attorneys who oppose the reforms are not lock-'em-up conservatives. Gonzalez and Vance are two of the most progressive prosecutors in the country. They refuse to prosecute farebeating and marijuana arrests and believe in cutting jail and prison populations as a means of achieving social justice.

Albany needs to fix these new laws now.

Print Citations

CMS: Barron, Seth, and Ralf Mangual. "Big Risks in Discovery Reform: N.Y.'s New Law Tips the Balance Way Too Far in Favor of Defendants." In *The Reference Shelf: U.S. National Debate Topic: 2020–2021 Criminal Justice Reform,* edited by Micah L. Issitt, 175-176. Amenia, NY: Grey House Publishing, 2020.

MLA: Barron, Seth, and Ralf Mangual. "Big Risks in Discovery Reform: N.Y.'s New Law Tips the Balance Way Too Far in Favor of Defendants." *The Reference Shelf: U.S. National Debate Topic: 2020–2021 Criminal Justice Reform,* edited by Micah L. Issitt, Grey House Publishing, 2020, pp. 175-176.

APA: Barron, S., & Mangual, R. (2020). Big risks in discovery reform: N.Y.'s new law tips the balance way too far in favor of defendants. In Micah L. Issitt (Ed.), *The reference shelf: U.S. national debate topic: 2020–2021 criminal justice reform* (pp. 175-176). Amenia, NY: Grey House Publishing.

New York Police Try To Pin Gang Witness's Death on Criminal Justice Reforms

By Scott Shackford
Reason, February 6, 2020

When Wilmer Maldonado Rodriguez, 36, was found dead Sunday in New Cassel, New York, police and prosecutors quickly went to work—not just on solving the crime, but on trying to blame recent reforms to how information is shared with criminal defendants.

Rodriguez had been attacked and stabbed, allegedly by members of gang MS-13, in 2018, and he had agreed to testify against his attackers. He died right as the cases move forward against three alleged assailants. If MS-13 was responsible, there are a number of ways it could have tracked down Rodriguez. But Nassau County police and prosecutors were quick to the lay the blame on the "discovery" laws that came into effect with the new year.

Discovery rules guide how evidence must be shared between police, prosecutors, and defense attorneys. Until this year, New York had notoriously secretive rules that allowed prosecutors to withhold evidence from the defense until the last possible moment. Prosecutors and police insisted this was necessary to protect witnesses from retaliation. Defense attorneys pointed out that this also prevented them from preparing for trial, and that it was used to force defendants to accept plea deals without knowing what evidence the state had against them.

> **Under the revised laws, prosecutors are still able to ask judges for protective orders to seal the identities of witnesses.**

The changes that New York just implemented put the state in line with most of the rest of the country, but you wouldn't know that from the screaming. Nassau County Police Commissioner Patrick Ryder held a press conference Wednesday to blame the new discovery rules for Rodriguez's death. According to *Newsday*, Ryder said that harassment of Rodriguez began after the new discovery law forced prosecutors to give Rodriguez's name to defense attorneys.

But Ryder eventually had to acknowledge that there was no evidence linking the new rules to Rodriguez's death. Under the revised laws, prosecutors are still able to ask judges for protective orders to seal the identities of witnesses if releasing the information could put them in danger. Prosecutors had done so here, and a judge had kept the information sealed until December. Then the judge disclosed the names to defense attorneys, but under orders not to share the names until the trials began.

So the only way the new discovery rules could be responsible for Rodriguez's death would be if the defense attorneys violated the judge's orders and shared them with the defendants. That's quite an accusation to be making without evidence. And indeed, after saying we "don't know if the defense counsel turned that info over to the defendants," Ryder later in the day issued a statement acknowledging there was "no direct link between the death of Wilmer Maldonado Rodriguez and criminal justice reform." Attorneys representing two of the defendants have denied sharing the witnesses' names with their clients.

Even though there's no evidence at this point linking the murder to the reforms, Nassau County District Attorney Madeline Singas still put out a statement subtly attacking the changes: "This case underscores the importance of safeguarding the identities of witnesses and victims of crime and our hearts are with Mr. Maldonado's family and friends as we grieve his loss."

To reiterate, New York's new discovery laws aren't taking case information-sharing into some wild, unheard-of space. It puts it in line with the vast majority of other states (including Texas and Florida, not exactly known for coddling defendants) by requiring that this information be disclosed to defense teams. The new rules should not be "controversial." They're the national norm. But police and prosecutors are using this unfortunate death to make it appear as though these rules are outrageously lax and a danger to the community. Don't fall for it.

Print Citations

CMS: Shackford, Scott. "New York Police Try to Pin Gang Witness's Death on Criminal Justice Reforms." In *The Reference Shelf: U.S. National Debate Topic: 2020–2021 Criminal Justice Reform,* edited by Micah L. Issitt, 177-178. Amenia, NY: Grey House Publishing, 2020.

MLA: Shackford, Scott. "New York Police Try to Pin Gang Witness's Death on Criminal Justice Reforms." *The Reference Shelf: U.S. National Debate Topic: 2020–2021 Criminal Justice Reform,* edited by Micah L. Issitt, Grey House Publishing, 2020, pp. 177-178.

APA: Shackford, S. (2020). New York police try to pin gang witness's death on criminal justice reforms. In Micah L. Issitt (Ed.), *The reference shelf: U.S. national debate topic: 2020–2021 criminal justice reform* (pp. 177-178). Amenia, NY: Grey House Publishing.

How a Criminal Justice Reform Became an Enrichment Scheme

By Jessica Pishko

Politico, July 14, 2019

ALEXANDRIA, La.—Bruce Kelly has been treasurer of Rapides Parish for three years and was assistant treasurer for 27 before that. A man in his 50s with a bald head and bulldoggish demeanor, Kelly is responsible each year for ensuring that the local government—run by a nine-member elected body called, in Louisiana tradition, a police jury—has enough money to sustain basic functions like paying government salaries, feeding inmates, and maintaining records and inventory for the 131,000-person parish, nestled in the heart of Louisiana.

But in early 2018, Kelly faced a crisis: The district attorney's office, led by the elected DA, Phillip Terrell, was requesting more than $2.5 million in parish funds. This was more than it had ever asked for in all the years Kelly had been at this job, and Kelly didn't have the money. In fact, the parish was facing a budget shortfall of $427,000; even its "rainy day fund" had been used up.

In the parish seat of Alexandria, where abandoned storefronts compete with a grand hotel built by a lumber mogul, many downtown streets desperately needed paving. The main courthouse needed a new air conditioner, to replace one installed in the 1960s. The county jail was overcrowded. The poverty rate in Rapides hovers around 20 percent—average for Louisiana, but above the national rate.

As Kelly reviewed the request, he pulled previous records and found that something had changed in the DA's budget. Over the past three years, the DA's intake from court fines had dropped from $900,000 to about $500,000 in 2017. According to Kelly's calculations, the number of traffic tickets issued—the DA office's primary source of fine income—had also dropped, from an average of 12,000 per year to 7,000. Kelly found it curious that the DA's office was requesting so much money from the parish, while seemingly cutting down on one of its main money sources.

And there were signs that the DA's office, despite its big ask, wasn't short on cash: It had a fleet of new cars with leather seats. Kelly went through old state audits and other public information, and came to the conclusion that Terrell's office was bringing in plenty of money but keeping it for itself.

He was right. Under Terrell, the DA's office, as shown by public documents, had ramped up its "pretrial diversion" program, also sometimes called "pretrial intervention," or PTI. As the website for the Rapides Parish DA's office explains, the program provides "nonviolent offenders an opportunity to avoid conviction and incarceration" through "tailored" agreements in which the offenders pay money in exchange for their charges being dropped and their cases dismissed. In the program's simplest form, instead of receiving and paying speeding tickets, offenders were paying fees not to get tickets. And those fees were going directly to the DA's office—whose website features a prominent MAKE A PAYMENT button.

Diversion programs, which exist in almost every state in the country, are a popular criminal-justice reform, often used to keep people accused of nonviolent crimes out of jail, and to prevent their cases from clogging the courts. In general, district attorneys can decide whether to offer diversion. In Rapides Parish, the program came with a twist: The district attorney also got to keep the money from those diversion fees. Typically, the fees go into a general parish fund, just like fines levied in a courtroom. Not in Rapides. Based on the records he had examined, Kelly believed Terrell was diverting cases—which had the effect of depriving the parish of fine money—and keeping the fees for the DA's office. As his department got more money, the parish got less.

In March 2018, the parish leadership and Kelly filed a lawsuit against the DA's office, asking a court to force the DA's office to hand over some of its PTI proceeds. In 2017, according to the suit, Terrell's office had brought in $2.2 million through PTI fees—more than 10 times what the previous DA had captured from diversion fees annually—by charging dismissal fees that ran from about $250 for traffic tickets, $500 for misdemeanors and $1,200 to $1,500 for felonies. Those rates were substantially higher than those of the previous district attorney, according to Kelly. Documents released by the DA's office indicate that the money Terrell was pulling in from pretrial diversion was used for conference fees, postage, office supplies, computers, as well as "capital outlay" and almost $90,000 for unspecified "fringe" expenditures. Kelly, who ran the parish's general budget, was on the hook for the courthouse's failing A/C.

Terrell's office and his attorney did not respond to requests for comment for this article. But the DA made his position clear in a monthslong fight with the police jury. A former local judge and city prosecutor who was placed on probation shortly after his 2014 election (an employee of his had used client funds to pay her bills), Terrell argued to the police jury that he could make as much as he wanted through PTI because the law didn't say otherwise. In a deposition related to the court proceedings, Terrell also said his office needed the money: It was "woefully underfunded to accomplish our mission."

As his lawyer, Terrell hired Hugo Holland, a tough-on-crime prosecutor who loves the Confederacy, his hunting dogs and Lee Harvey Oswald. According to local news reports, Holland had threatened the police jury members with investigations into their own use of funds if they did not agree to drop their feud with Terrell. When that didn't work, Terrell filed a countersuit, arguing that the DA's office did not owe any money to the police jury. Terrell's office referred to the police jury's lawsuit in court papers as "politically driven."

This lawsuit in central Louisiana might appear to be a local skirmish, but its trajectory tells a bigger story. Nationwide, pretrial diversion has come under fire for hurting the poor, who can't always afford to pay their way out

> **Nationwide, pretrial diversion has come under fire for hurting the poor, who can't always afford to pay their way out of their charges.**

of their charges; there also have been reports of politically connected individuals receiving more lenient diversion offers in Alabama, Louisiana and elsewhere. But what becomes clear from the court documents in the Rapides Parish case and from interviews with people in the parish, as well as documentation about PTI programs that Louisiana district attorneys filed with the state Supreme Court, is that diversion comes with another, less-recognized risk: It can operate in a gray legal area that gives DAs a chance to siphon money from the budgets of often cash-strapped local governments.

In Louisiana, the problem is exacerbated by the fact that the state is one of a few that doesn't directly fund most criminal court operations—meaning parish court systems, including public defenders' offices, depend heavily on the kinds of fees and fines that Terrell's office was cutting down on in favor of diversion. The state's public defenders are already chronically underfunded, to the point that some have refused to take on new cases. (The Rapides public defender, Deirdre Fuller, did not return requests for comment.)

Rapides is just one example of many in Louisiana in which elected DAs seem to have enriched their offices through PTI. But it is an important one: The dueling lawsuits between the parish jury and the DA have raised the question of how far DAs can go in using diversion and who has the authority to set stricter rules around it.

***

Over the past quarter-century, advocates, community leaders and elected officials on both sides of the political aisle have embraced pretrial diversion as a way to reduce the burden of the criminal justice system on both budgets and people. In jurisdictions where it is adopted, diversion allows people accused of generally nonviolent crimes like traffic violations, bounced checks and shoplifting to stay out of the court system and keep their records clean, instead agreeing to pay a fine, take a class or complete other requirements.

Diversion has gradually become more common. In 1977, there were an estimated 200 diversion programs in the United States. By 2010, there were 298 such programs in 45 states, according to the Center for Prison Reform, a lobbying group. And as of 2017, according to the National Conference of State Legislators, 48 states and the District of Columbia offered some form of pretrial diversion.

The National Association of Pretrial Services Agencies, which promotes pretrial services reform, sets forth best practices for diversion programs, which include ensuring that a program's requirements relate to the "root cause" of the crime and are voluntary. The group also says diversion "should not be denied on the basis of inability to pay," and recommends creating a sliding scale of fees for people who have trouble paying. But there are no enforceable national standards for diversion, and programs can vary widely from jurisdiction to jurisdiction. Some are run by private, for-profit corporations; others, by prosecutors and judges. Some cater to drug offenders or veterans. Almost every diversion program requires a fee.

According to Fair and Just Prosecution, a nonprofit advocating for more progressive district attorneys, diversion programs are one of the core tenets of better prosecution; such programs "conserve resources, reduce reoffending, and diminish the collateral harms of criminal prosecution," as a recent report by the group put it. But despite diversion success stories across the country, the programs have also been trailed by criticism that they open the door for abuse—especially when, as in Louisiana, the decisions about whether and how to charge individuals for crimes or offer diversion are left to the sole discretion of prosecutors.

As the practice has become more common, reports have found that the conditions of diversion—such as mandated attendance at Alcoholics Anonymous meetings or weekly drug testing—can be onerous and that failure to comply can be costly. In Alabama, for example, where pretrial diversion has increased dramatically in recent years, people who have been admitted to diversion programs but are unable to make payments have been forced to plead guilty without trial and faced lengthy prison terms.

In places like Louisiana—where tax revenue is low, and criminal justice services are funded through fines and fees like those collected from diversion, as opposed to funding from the state—the incentive to milk diversion for cash increases. By creating their own diversion programs, prosecutors can exercise control over the funding without sharing the money they bring in with other county entities. In places where money is hard to come by, each part of the criminal justice system views fees and fines as funding up for grabs.

***

In recent years, even before Bruce Kelly started looking into the Rapides books, public defenders and court clerks in Louisiana had begun to notice that money from traffic tickets, the primary source of funding for public defenders in Louisiana, was going to prosecutors' offices at higher rates, according to Louisiana's state public defender, Jay Dixon. In many Louisiana parishes, the number of traffic tickets issued has dropped, while there has been an increase in traffic diversion, by which drivers pay the DA's office to avoid any record of a violation.

According to the Louisiana legislative auditor, an agency that tracks fiscal responsibility in the state, in 2014 the use of traffic diversion resulted in the loss of $1 million statewide that ordinarily would have gone to general court funds, including for public defenders. That same year, parish DA offices in Louisiana were getting 30 to 50 percent of their revenue from diversion fees, an increase from previous years, according to the legislative auditor. The auditor also found widespread irregularities in how prosecutors were recording profits and spending.

By 2018, these findings had prompted Louisiana Chief Justice Bernette Johnson—the first black Supreme Court chief justice in the state—to send a letter to all Louisiana prosecutors asking them to report their income from PTI to the research arm of the state Supreme Court. (Not every DA's office had participated in the legislative auditor's earlier study.) The Louisiana District Attorneys Association initially resisted the data collection, saying it would be too time-consuming and expensive. But Johnson, whose office declined to comment for this article beyond referring to her letter, shot back in an April 2018 speech: "Is it financially prudent and morally responsible to fund a co-equal branch of government on the backs of a few who are often the poorest and least fortunate members of our society?" In response, DA offices across the state have been filing information to the court.

Although they remain incomplete, these filings provide some insights into how Louisiana's DAs are using diversion, with plenty of variation across the state. Some charge thousands of dollars in fees; others allow participants to pay in installments over the course of two years. In St. Tammany Parish, north of New Orleans, a DWI dismissal costs $2,100 in total; in East Baton Rouge, a dismissal of the same charge costs $1,000. In some places, PTI isn't available at all. One part-time public defender in Rapides also told me that, in his experience, white defendants had an easier time getting diversion than black defendants. Some DA offices report relatively little income; DA offices at the upper end, like Terrell's, are making more than $2 million per year. (The DA in the state capital, Baton Rouge, which is almost twice the size of Rapides, makes about $1.3 million per year.)

Among critics of diversion in the state, particular attention has focused on a program called Local Agency Compensated Enforcement. Since the 1980s, LACE has allowed DAs and some municipal governments to pay off-duty deputies to conduct additional traffic enforcement, writing tickets that cost about $200 each, are payable direct to the DA's office and do not end up on the payee's record—nothing is ever filed in court. The stated purpose of the program is to enforce driving rules. But these same tickets, if adjudicated in court, would bring only $20 apiece to the DA's office, with the remaining $180 going to the criminal court fund. A LACE ticket allows the DA to capture the entire $200. Many DAs—including Terrell in Rapides—make most of their money from LACE, according to documents filed with the Louisiana Supreme Court.

According to a 2018 report by the Louisiana legislative auditor, District Attorney Gary Evans of DeSoto Parish in the northwestern part of the state, entered 3,629 drivers into pretrial diversion through LACE over the course of one year and caused other agencies in the parish to forfeit $1.07 million. The auditor also noted "deficiencies in record keeping, receipts, refunds issues and custody of payments received." Evans entered into an agreement to pay the parish public defender a cut of PTI revenue—$45 for each diverted ticket. When the scheme was questioned on appeal, a trial court held, and upper courts affirmed, that it was unconstitutional and a conflict of interest for prosecutors to pay public defenders.

Last year, the Southern Poverty Law Center filed a complaint about LACE with the Louisiana Ethics Administration Program, which investigates ethics complaints against government entities, alleging that prosecutors were violating their ethical duties by extracting money from people on purpose. In the complaint, one DA is in fact quoted as saying that district attorneys created the "industry" of diversion because "we just weren't making ... money." Dixon, who once received a LACE ticket himself, inspiring some local media coverage, agrees: "Paying folks extra to harass motorists is disgusting." A few parishes have since pulled out of the program.

Local news outlets have reported on other forms of corruption in Louisiana's diversion programs—from a DA in St. Tammany who allegedly awarded PTI on the basis of political ties to one in St. Charles who admitted to sexual contact with multiple women to whom he had offered diversion. In some parts of the state, including New Orleans, diversion programs have been implemented with better compliance and less profiteering.

Overall, while the final results of the state Supreme Court audit are not yet public, there is a growing sense among advocates, judges and defense attorneys that PTI programs in Louisiana are due for structure and limits. This comes on the heels of a number of justice reforms in the state in 2017—including efforts to reduce prison populations and shorten sentences—that have helped to move Louisiana from the country's most-incarcerated state to its second.

* * *

The lawsuits in Rapides Parish raised—but ultimately failed to resolve—the key question that will determine the future of prosecutor-led PTI in Louisiana: Should there be limits on how much a DA can make from diversion?

The local trial court judge who first took up the Rapides lawsuit ruled simply that the DA's office was permitted to collect and use PTI funds as it wished—even as he expressed hesitation, calling for the state Legislature to "investigate the question of what kind of fees are reasonable." By the time the case had reached an appellate court, both parties were suing each other over who was reasonably entitled to what money.

Last fall, I attended the appellate arguments at Louisiana's 3rd Circuit Court of Appeals, where both the police jury and Terrell's office presented their legal arguments. Most members of the police jury were there, along with Terrell and the lead attorney for the LDAA, E. Pete Adams (who drives a car with a vanity license plate "LDAA 1").

One member of the three-judge panel suggested that the entire lawsuit might be irrelevant because some reformers "are saying that pay-for-play is illegal overall," implying that prosecutor-led PTI programs like Terrell's might eventually become illegal. The judges all asked questions about alternatives to PTI that would have the same impact on participants without generating income for DAs. They seemed skeptical of the claim that Terrell could run "100 diversion programs" if he wanted to, as Adams had phrased it. Adams also argued that "thousands of lives are saved" by PTI, while Jimmy Faircloth, the lawyer representing the police jury, called it an "end-run around the court filing process."

When the arguments were over, the judges urged the parties to settle. "Consider how this looks to the public," one judge said, prognosticating that if no agreement were reached, the entire issue might be resolved by federal courts—which could decide to put an end PTI altogether, or at least fee-based versions. The 3rd Circuit said it would issue an opinion on the Rapides lawsuit two to three weeks after the oral argument, but none was issued before the two parties, after heeding the judges' words, resolved the case out of court in November.

Terrell and the police jury announced as part of the settlement that Terrell had agreed to a 10 percent cut in his personal salary, as well as salary cuts for all assistant district attorneys, keeping the office's operating expenses within the budget set by the police jury. He also agreed to adhere to new LDAA guidelines, released just before the case settled, advising DAs to limit diversion profits to "reasonable expenses." Kelly, over the phone, said he wondered "what 'reasonable' means" and seemed dubious the change would be effective. Adams told me via email that the guidelines were implemented in February and are still in effect. He did not comment on the Rapides case other than to say it was "settled and dismissed."

Faircloth told *Town Talk*, an Alexandria-based newspaper, that the collection of changes in Rapides "more fairly allocates the revenue and expenses of [the DA's] office." But Kelly told me he doesn't think the settlement was very productive—the DA isn't planning to give any money back to the police jury—and he is now concerned about the salaries and benefits of the prosecutor's employees. "I still gotta walk the hallways," he said.

Because there was no decision in the case, the issue of how much money PTI programs like Terrell's can bring in remains unsettled. The judges indicated that the state Legislature should be responsible for enacting PTI regulations; Kelly agrees. But no legislative fixes have emerged at the state level. Meanwhile, in 2019, Louisiana cut its annual state budget for public defenders by 83 percent.

Although the state Supreme Court's PTI audit is still ongoing, in April, the court issued a series of draft reports with suggested best practices for PTI accounting and ways to decrease the intake of fines and fees generally. One of the recommendations was to "cap the percentage of revenue that municipalities, towns and other locations can derive from traffic enforcement." The report also strongly suggested that law enforcement should not be linked to revenue.

Other states besides Louisiana are grappling with how to make their PTI programs fairer. Civil Rights Corps, an advocacy group focusing on reducing the impact of the criminal justice system on the poor, has brought a lawsuit against the district attorney of Maricopa County, Arizona, Bill Montgomery, alleging that his pretrial diversion for marijuana arrests requires people to pay $1,000 for treatment at a private facility from which Montgomery's office receives $650 per person. The group's complaint states that "between 2010 and 2016 MCAO collected nearly $15 million in revenue" from diversion. Montgomery called the claims "ill-informed and misguided."

Dixon, the Louisiana state public defender, is sympathetic to public defenders who have made deals with DAs to receive a portion of the PTI money, given how cash-strapped the criminal justice system is in Louisiana. And while he thinks too much money is "being bled from the system" to DAs, he says, "There's a pretrial diversion that's worthwhile."

Still, for some advocates, it's hard to shed the sense that a defendant offered diversion is "paying off" an arrest—to the benefit of a DA.

"The justice system serves everyone and protects everyone's public safety," Lisa Foster, co-director of the Fines and Fees Justice Center, a nonprofit advocacy group, told me. That, she says, should hold true for diversion, too.

Print Citations

CMS: Pishko, Jessica. "How a Criminal Justice Reform Became an Enrichment Scheme." In *The Reference Shelf: U.S. National Debate Topic: 2020–2021 Criminal Justice Reform,* edited by Micah L. Issitt, 179-186. Amenia, NY: Grey House Publishing, 2020.

MLA: Pishko, Jessica. "How a Criminal Justice Reform Became an Enrichment Scheme." *The Reference Shelf: U.S. National Debate Topic: 2020–2021 Criminal Justice Reform,* edited by Micah L. Issitt, Grey House Publishing, 2020, pp. 179-186.

APA: Pishko, J. (2020). How a criminal justice reform became an enrichment scheme. In Micah L. Issitt (Ed.), *The reference shelf: U.S. national debate topic: 2020–2021 criminal justice reform* (pp. 179-186). Amenia, NY: Grey House Publishing.

In California, Criminal Justice Reform Offers a Lesson for the Nation

By Tim Arango

The New York Times, January 21, 2019

LOS ANGELES—A police officer is shot dead in Whittier by a gang member. A mentally ill homeless man walks into a steakhouse in Ventura, Calif., and stabs a man to death in front of his family. In Bakersfield, a man angry over his divorce goes on a shooting rampage, killing his ex-wife and four others.

In the aftermath of these high-profile killings, some police officers, district attorneys and politicians were quick to use them as examples to show that criminal justice reform had let dangerous people onto the streets.

It turned out they were wrong. Not one of the crimes was directly linked to any of several new laws that seek to reduce incarceration and lower harsh penalties. But the cases show how muddled the debate over criminal justice has become, even in this liberal state.

Over the last decade, California has been at the forefront of the nation's efforts to reduce mass incarceration, in part because the state was forced by the courts to lower the population of severely overcrowded prisons. California, once a byword for get-tough-on-crime polices like its three-strikes law enacted in the 1990s, has let thousands of inmates out of prison or jail.

Overall crime rates, meanwhile, are at historic lows, with levels not seen since the 1960s. Yet some categories of crimes, like theft, have ticked up, feeding into a narrative by opponents of criminal justice reform that California's new measures have gone too far.

Now that President Trump has signed into law a federal criminal justice reform bill, California's experience, and the political fallout, is especially instructive. Experts are finally starting to study the effects on crime rates.

At the same time, powerful forces are lining up in an attempt to roll back some of the changes and, supporters of the new laws fear, return California to its get-tough-on-crime days.

Police unions have put up hundreds of thousands of dollars to support a ballot measure to expand the category of crimes that can be charged as felonies. And the grocery store chain Albertsons has also contributed to the effort, blaming the changes for a rise in shoplifting. Big bail companies have raised $3 million to overturn a recent California law that ends the cash bail system, which critics have long said unfairly targets the poor.

Jerry Brown, the former governor, left office recently with a $15 million campaign war chest, and has said some of that money can be used to defend his criminal justice legacy by trying to defeat the ballot measures.

The data on crime, and what it says about reforms, has been contested. Small upticks in some types of crime in some areas has muddied the picture. And Californians may well be confused about what to believe: One day, headlines say that crime is up; the next, that crime is down. For instance, violent crime rose in California in 2012 and between 2015 and 2017, allowing opponents of the laws to point to increases, even as scholars say arguments about criminal justice policies should not be based on short-term fluctuations—and that overall crime rates are declining.

Activists see parallels in the strategies of opponents of more lenient sentencing laws in California and the rhetoric on crime at the national level. The former attorney general, Jeff Sessions, warned early last year about a "staggering increase in homicides." Violent crime had ticked up in 2015 and 2016 after a long decline, but when F.B.I. statistics for 2017 were released—after Mr. Sessions's warning—they showed that violent crime had gone down again.

One of the most controversial changes in California was a law passed last year to end cash bail. Initially anticipated by liberal activists as a significant step to end the practice of holding poor defendants in pretrial detention because they could not afford bail, the final version of the law has been disavowed by many of its early supporters. That is because, activists say, the law gives judges more discretion to hold the accused before trial. The new system will also use algorithms to assess whether a defendant is a flight risk or might commit another crime—tools that activists say are biased against people of color.

Police unions have put up hundreds of thousands of dollars to support a ballot measure to expand the category of crimes that can be charged as felonies.

"It gives judges basically unlimited power without due process," said John Raphling, a senior researcher at Human Rights Watch in Los Angeles. The risk assessment tools that judges would use, he said, "embed racial bias."

The controversy over the bail law has essentially placed the bail industry and civil liberties advocates like the A.C.L.U. on the same side. But it is the bail industry that has backed a ballot measure to overturn the law, which has received enough signatures to go before California voters in 2020.

In pushing the measure, the industry has offered contradictory arguments, sometimes suggesting that eliminating cash bail would mean more criminals on the streets, and other times adopting the argument of the liberal activists that the new law could, in fact, end up locking up more people in a manner that would be unfair to poor African-Americans.

Jeff Clayton, the spokesman for a coalition of bail companies backing the ballot proposition, said the issue would be "focus grouped and polled" to figure out what the right message should be for advertisements in the run-up to the vote in 2020.

In one of the first academic studies on the effects of California's criminal justice reforms on crime rates, Bradley J. Bartos and Charis E. Kubrin, of the University of California at Irvine, found no links between Proposition 47—a ballot measure enacted in 2014 that reduced some drug crimes and thefts to misdemeanors—and violent crime. The study, published in the journal *Criminology and Public Policy*, found that larceny and auto thefts seemed to have increased moderately after the measure was enacted, but said other factors may have been to blame and that more study was needed.

"At the time I was hearing so many claims about what Prop 47 was doing to crime in the state," Ms. Kubrin said. "Prop 47 has nothing to do with violent crime."

Even so, her research was challenged by law enforcement groups. A statement released by the Los Angeles Association of Deputy District Attorneys attacked the study, saying that because crime had ticked up after Proposition 47 was enacted, the measure had "arguably failed."

Links between criminal justice policies and crime rates have long been tenuous. There are almost endless factors that can lead to crime, including poverty and drug addiction.

"The literature on how policing and levels of punishment relates to actual crime is so disputed," said Rob Smith, executive director of the Justice Collaborative.

Mr. Smith said that it was "important to understand that we are in a historic decline."

"So these year-to-year fluctuations don't really tell you much," he said.

While pointing to short-term increases in certain crimes in recent years, some—mainly law enforcement personnel and victims' rights advocates—have also been quick to seize on highly publicized crimes as evidence that California's policies have become too lenient.

In one example, John Cox, the Republican businessman who lost the race for governor, in several instances pointed to the death last year of Anthony Mele, a 35-year-old man who was killed in the steakhouse in Ventura by a homeless man.

Mr. Cox said he believed the system was too lenient and that "plea bargains" had allowed too many criminals onto the streets. "I think of Anthony Mele, a young man who was murdered in cold blood by a guy who was out," he said.

Richard Simon, the senior deputy district attorney in Ventura who is prosecuting the case and who believes California has become too liberal on criminal justice, said the suspect, Jamal Jackson, was not on the streets because of any recent changes.

Similarly, in the killing of the police officer in Whittier in 2017, law enforcement initially blamed criminal justice reform, saying the suspect would not have been on the streets had it not been for new sentencing guidelines. But the California Department of Corrections and Rehabilitation issued a statement saying the suspect was not released early as a result of justice reforms. And an investigation by the *Los Angeles Times* and the Marshall Project revealed that missteps by Los Angeles

County and probation officials—who were overseeing the suspect after his release from prison—had led to him being on the streets.

Another case that has galvanized opponents of the justice overhaul was a homicide last year in Fresno, in which a man was cited—but not arrested—for methamphetamine and then shortly after killed a young man in a robbery attempt. The mother of the victim and law enforcement officers have blamed the reforms, saying that under old laws the assailant would have been arrested and off the streets.

But activists and supporters of the new sentencing measures in California have pushed back. They note that no new law precludes an arrest for possessing drugs. And in the Fresno case, they say there were other circumstances, like the presence of guns in the hotel room where they found the suspect with meth hours before the killing, that could have justified an arrest.

Advocates worry that it is only a matter of time before a high-profile crime will be linked definitively to criminal justice reforms, giving opponents a Willie Horton-style example to stoke fear. They say that would hardly justify a return to a harsher system—that a free society should not lock up lots of people, at great cost, on the worry that one may commit a horrible crime.

"We all want to live in a society where you can walk from your house to work or the bus station or the subway and feel and be safe," said Mr. Smith of the Justice Collaborative. "And the reality is across California and across the country we are safer than almost at any time in history."

California's reform effort began in earnest in 2011, with a law that shifted many state prison inmates to county jails, and was followed by other measures approved by voters that reduced penalties for certain crimes and allowed for more inmates to be released early for good behavior. The high mark for California's prison population was 2006, with about 163,000 people incarcerated. Nowadays, there are about 115,000 people behind bars, according to the Public Policy Institute of California.

As California moves toward referendums in 2020 on sentencing laws and bail, scholars worry that opponents will be successful in stoking fear among the public about runaway crime.

"I really worry that people will make decisions based on fear rather than empirical data," Ms. Kubrin said.

Print Citations

CMS: Arango, Tim. "In California, Criminal Justice Reform Offers a Lesson for the Nation." In *The Reference Shelf: U.S. National Debate Topic: 2020–2021 Criminal Justice Reform,* edited by Micah L. Issitt, 187-190. Amenia, NY: Grey House Publishing, 2020.

MLA: Arango, Tim. "In California, Criminal Justice Reform Offers a Lesson for the Nation." *The Reference Shelf: U.S. National Debate Topic: 2020–2021 Criminal Justice Reform,* edited by Micah L. Issitt, Grey House Publishing, 2020, pp. 187-190.

APA: Arango, T. (2020). In California, criminal justice reform offers a lesson for the nation. In Micah L. Issitt (Ed.), *The reference shelf: U.S. national debate topic: 2020–2021 criminal justice reform* (pp. 187-190). Amenia, NY: Grey House Publishing.

Bibliography

Balko, Radley. "There's Overwhelming Evidence That the Criminal-Justice System Is Racist: Here's the Proof." *Washington Post*. Sep 18, 2018. Retrieved from https://www.washingtonpost.com/news/opinions/wp/2018/09/18/theres-overwhelming-evidence-that-the-criminal-justice-system-is-racist-heres-the-proof/.

Barnes, Harry Elmer. "Historical Origin of the Prison System in America." *Journal of Criminal Law and Criminology* 12, no. 1 (1921).

Bauer, Shane. "The True History of America's Private Prison Industry." *Time*. Sep 25, 2018. Retrieved from https://time.com/5405158/the-true-history-of-americas-private-prison-industry/.

Beccaria, Cesare. *An Essay on Crimes and Punishments*. 1764. Online Library of Liberty. Retrieved from http://oll-resources.s3.amazonaws.com/titles/2193/Beccaria_1476_EBk_v6.0.pdf.

Casiano, Louis. "These States Recently Enacted Bail-Reform Laws." *Fox News*. Feb 22, 2020. Retrieved from https://www.foxnews.com/politics/these-states-recently-enacted-bail-reform-laws.

Dailey, Jane Elizabeth. *The Age of Jim Crow: A Norton Casebook in History*. New York: W. W. Norton & Company, 2009.

Dickens, Charles. "Philadelphia, and its Solitary Prison." 1842. *The Victorian Web*. Retrieved from http://www.victorianweb.org/authors/dickens/pva/pva344.html.

Eisen, Lauren-Brooke. "Criminal Justice Reform at the State Level." *Brennan Center*. Jan 2, 2020. Retrieved from https://www.brennancenter.org/our-work/research-reports/criminal-justice-reform-state-level.

Elliot, Mary. "Four Hundred Years after Enslaved Africans Were First Brought to Virginia, Most Americans Still Don't Know the Full Story of Slavery." *New York Times Magazine*. Aug 19, 2019. Retrieved from https://www.nytimes.com/interactive/2019/08/19/magazine/history-slavery-smithsonian.html.

"The Entman-Rojecki Index of Race and the Media." *University of Chicago*. 1996. Retrieved from https://www.press.uchicago.edu/Misc/Chicago/210758.html.

"Federal Sentencing Reform." *ABA*. American Bar Association. 2019. Retrieved from https://www.americanbar.org/advocacy/governmental_legislative_work/priorities_policy/criminal_justice_system_improvements/federalsentencingreform/.

"Forensic Science Reform." *CJPP*. Criminal Justice Policy Program. Harvard Law School. Retrieved from http://cjpp.law.harvard.edu/forensics.

Gonchar, Michael. "What Should Be the Purpose of Prison?" *New York Times*. Feb 27, 2015. Retrieved from https://learning.blogs.nytimes.com/2015/02/27/what-should-be-the-purpose-of-prison/.

Gorman, Steve. "California Bans Private Prisons and Immigration Detention Centers." *Reuters*. Oct 11, 2019. Retrieved from https://www.reuters.com/article/us-california-prisons/california-bans-private-prisons-and-immigration-detention-centers-idUSKBN1WQ2Q9.

Grawert, Amex, and Tim Lau. "How the FIRST STEP Act Became Law—and What Happens Next." Brennan Center for Justice. Jan 4, 2019. Retrieved from https://www.brennancenter.org/our-work/analysis-opinion/how-first-step-act-became-law-and-what-happens-next.

"Influencing Forensic Science for a Decade: Remembering the 2009 NAS Report." *CSAFE*. Feb 19, 2019. Retrieved from https://forensicstats.org/blog/2019/02/19/influencing-forensic-science-for-a-decade-remembering-the-2009-nas-report/.

"Jim Crow Laws." *American History*. Smithsonian Institution. Retrieved from https://americanhistory.si.edu/brown/history/1-segregated/jim-crow.html.

Krehbiel, Randy. "'Retroactivity' Criminal Justice Bill That Reclassifies Felonies Clears Oklahoma House." *Tulsa World*. May 17, 2019. Retrieved from https://www.tulsaworld.com/news/retroactivity-criminal-justice-bill-that-reclassifies-felonies-clears-oklahoma-house/article_a3770284-445a-57ae-b879-18709206e346.html.

Lopez, German. "Mass incarceration in America, Explained in 22 maps and charts." *Vox*. Oct 11, 2016. Retrieved from https://www.vox.com/2015/7/13/8913297/mass-incarceration-maps-charts.

Martin, Nicole. "The Major Concerns around Facial Recognition Technology." *Forbes*. Sep 25, 2019. Retrieved from https://www.forbes.com/sites/nicolemartin1/2019/09/25/the-major-concerns-around-facial-recognition-technology/#446cc4044fe3.

"Mass Incarceration." *ACLU*. American Civil Liberties Union. 2019. Retrieved from https://www.aclu.org/issues/smart-justice/mass-incarceration.

Molla, Rani. "Law Enforcement Is Now Buying Cellphone Location Data from Marketers." *Vox*. Recode. Feb 7, 2020. Retrieved from https://www.vox.com/recode/2020/2/7/21127911/ice-border-cellphone-data-tracking-department-homeland-security-immigration.

Oliver, Mary Beth. "African American Men as 'Criminal and Dangerous': Implications of Media Portrayals of Crime on the Criminalization of American Men." *Journal of African American Studies* 7, no. 2 (September 2003): 3–18.

Oliver, Willard M., and James F. Hilgenberg. *A History of Crime and Criminal Justice in America*. New York: Pearson, 2006.

Oppel, Richard A. Jr. "Sentencing Shift Gives New Leverage to Prosecutors." *New York Times*. Sep 25, 2011. Retrieved from https://www.nytimes.com/2011/09/26/us/tough-sentences-help-prosecutors-push-for-plea-bargains.html.

Platt, Tony. "The Perils of Criminal Justice Reform." *History News Network*. George Washington University. Mar 31, 2019. Retrieved from https://historynewsnetwork.org/article/171611.

"Poll Shows Americans Overwhelmingly Support Prison, Sentencing Reforms." *Senate Judiciary Committee*. Aug 23, 2018. Retrieved from https://www.judiciary.

senate.gov/press/rep/releases/poll-shows-americans-overwhelmingly-support-prison-sentencing-reforms.

Pray, Roger T. "How Did Our Prisons Get That Way?" *American Heritage* 38, no. 5 (1987).

"Rep. Takano Introduces the Justice in Forensic Algorithms Act to Protect Defendants' Due Process Rights in the Criminal Justice System." *Takano*. Sep 17, 2019. Retrieved from https://takano.house.gov/newsroom/press-releases/rep-takano-introduces-the-justice-in-forensic-algorithms-act-to-protect-defendants-due-process-rights-in-the-criminal-justice-system.

Sah, Sunita, Casadevall, Arturo, Bell, Suzanne S., Gates, James Jr., Albright, Thomas D., and M. Bonner Denton. "We Must Strengthen the 'Science' in Forensic Science." *Scientific American*. May 8, 2017. Retrieved from https://blogs.scientificamerican.com/observations/we-must-strengthen-the-science-in-forensic-science/.

Simonite, Timothy. "The Best Algorithms Struggle to Recognize Black Faces Equally." *Wired*. Condé Nast. Jul 22, 2019. Retrieved from https://www.wired.com/story/best-algorithms-struggle-recognize-black-faces-equally/.

Statt, Nick. "Microsoft to End Investments in Facial Recognition Firms after Anyvision Controversy." *The Verge*. Mar 27, 2020. Retrieved from https://www.theverge.com/2020/3/27/21197577/microsoft-facial-recognition-investing-divest-anyvision-controversy.

Valentino-DeVries, Jennifer. "Tracking Phones, Google Is a Dragnet for the Police." *New York Times*. April 13, 2019. Retrieved from https://www.nytimes.com/interactive/2019/04/13/us/google-location-tracking-police.html.

Wagner, Peter. "Are Private Prisons Driving Mass Incarceration?" *Prison Policy Initiative*. Oct 7, 2015. Retrieved from https://www.prisonpolicy.org/blog/2015/10/07/private_prisons_parasite/.

Widra, Emily. "Incarceration Shortens Life Expectancy." *Prison Policy Initiative*. Jun 26, 2017. Retrieved from https://www.prisonpolicy.org/blog/2017/06/26/life_expectancy/.

Ye Hee Hee, Michelle. "Does the United States Really Have 5 Percent of the World's Population and One Quarter of the World's Prisoners?" *Washington Post*. Retrieved from https://www.washingtonpost.com/news/fact-checker/wp/2015/04/30/does-the-united-states-really-have-five-percent-of-worlds-population-and-one-quarter-of-the-worlds-prisoners/.

Ye Hee Lee, Michelle. "Yes, U.S. Locks People Up at a Higher Rate Than Any Other Country." *The Washington Post*. Jul 7, 2015. Retrieved from https://www.washingtonpost.com/news/fact-checker/wp/2015/07/07/yes-u-s-locks-people-up-at-a-higher-rate-than-any-other-country/.

Websites

American Society of Criminology (ASC)
www.asc41.com

The American Society of Criminology is an international professional organization that provides resources and research on a number of criminal justice issues and provides community and support for professionals working in the field. The organization provides access to research from members working in a variety of subfield, including forensics, etiology, crime prevention, treatment, and criminal law. The ASC also publishes the peer-reviewed journals, *Criminology, the Criminologist, and Criminology and Public Policy*.

The Innocence Project
www.innocenceproject.org

The Innocence Project is a nonprofit legal advocacy organization that aims to help individuals who have been wrongly incarcerated. Innocence Project reports and investigations have increased public interest in forensic science reform and DNA testing and the Innocence Project has participated in cases resulting in high profile exonerations. Reports published by the Innocence Project. The Innocence Project is one of the most prominent organizations in the Innocence Network as professional association of legal, educational, research, and journalistic organizations that collaborate to eliminate and address cases of wrongful arrest and/or conviction.

The Marshall Project
www.themarshallproject.org

The Marshall Project is a nonprofit advocacy and journalism organization focusing on promoting criminal justice reform. The organization was started in 2013 by *New York Times* editor Bill Keller and Neil Barsky. The Marshall Project works with media agencies to provide data on a number of criminal justice issues including mass incarceration, forensics reform, and advocacy for investigations into sentencing. In 2016, the Marshall Project and ProPublica won a Pulitzer Prize for a series on failures within the criminal justice system to effectively manage cases involving rape.

Nolan Center for Justice
www.conservativejusticereform.org

The Nolan Center for Justice is a conservative criminal justice advocacy group and part of the American Conservative Union Foundation. The organization tends to lobby for economic criminal justice reforms that can reduce tax expenditures. Representatives of the organization produce op-ed articles, provide media interviews, and lobby politicians on behalf of conservative reform proposals.

Sentencing Project
www.sentencingproject.org.

The Sentencing Project is a research and advocacy organization located in Washington, D.C. The organization's chief goal is to influence policies that reduce incarceration rates and to study and address racial disparities in U.S. criminal justice. The Sentencing Project was established in the 1980s and has produced reports cited in the establishment of both state and federal criminal justice reforms. In addition to funding and supporting research, the Sentencing Project provides resources for public defense attorneys. The Sentencing Project website provides free access to past research, press releases, and reviews of current research.

United States Bureau of Justice Statistics (BJS)
www.bjs.gov

The Bureau of Justice Statistics is a federal agency established in 1979 and under the supervision of the U.S. Department of Justice. The organization collects and publishes reports on a variety of different statistical estimates relevant to U.S. criminal justice. The BJS is authorized to collect data from both state law enforcement and criminal justice agencies and from the federal government. Statistics gathered by the BJS are available through the web and in print and also publishes analyses of data from the field.

Vera Institute of Justice
www.vera.org

The Vera Institute of Justice is a nonprofit research and lobbying organization founded in New York in the 1960s. The Vera Institute focuses on mass incarceration, racial bias in policing and the courts, and law enforcement public relations. The Vera Institute organized a Commission on Safety and Abuse in Americas Prisons to study violence and abuse within correctional institutions. The Vera Institute provides public access to research and reports through the organization's website.

Index